OXFORD WORLD'S CLASSICS

PROPERTIUS

The Poems

Translated with Notes by
GUY LEE

With an Introduction by
OLIVER LYNE

OXFORD
UNIVERSITY PRESS

OXFORD
UNIVERSITY PRESS

Great Clarendon Street, Oxford OX2 6DP

Oxford University Press is a department of the University of Oxford.
It furthers the University's objective of excellence in research, scholarship,
and education by publishing worldwide in

Oxford New York

Auckland Bangkok Buenos Aires Cape Town Chennai
Dar es Salaam Delhi Hong Kong Istanbul Karachi Kolkata
Kuala Lumpur Madrid Melbourne Mexico City Mumbai Nairobi
São Paulo Shanghai Singapore Taipei Tokyo Toronto

with an associated company in Berlin

Oxford is a registered trade mark of Oxford University Press
in the UK and in certain other countries

Published in the United States
by Oxford University Press Inc., New York

Translation and Notes © Guy Lee 1994
Introduction © R. O. A. M. Lyne 1994

First published by the Clarendon Press 1994
First published as a World's Classics paperback 1996
Reissued as an Oxford World's Classics paperback 1999
Reissued 2009

British Library Cataloguing in Publication Data

Data available

Library of Congress Cataloging in Publication Data
Propertius, Sextus. [Elegia. English. 1994]
The poems/Propertius; translated with notes by Guy Lee;
with an introd. by Oliver Lyne.
Includes bibliographical references.
1. Propertius, Sextus—Translations into English. 2. Elegiac
poetry, Latin—Translations into English. 3. Love poetry, Latin—
Translations into English. 4. Man–woman relationships—Rome—
Poetry. I. Lee, Guy. II. Title.
PA6645.E51.44 1994 874'01—dc20 93–42190

ISBN 978–0–19–955592–5

1

Printed in Great Britain by
Clays Ltd, St Ives plc

TRANSLATOR'S NOTE

IN preparing the present translation of Propertius I have chiefly used the text and commentary of my friend Mr W. A. Camps, to whom I owe a debt of gratitude for the help he has given me over the years in discussion and correspondence on Propertian problems. As his text is based by permission of the Delegates of the Oxford University Press on the Oxford text of E. A. Barber (2nd edn., 1960), it has seemed best to record in an Appendix, for the information of those who are interested in such things, my differences from that Oxford text (now in its eighth impression, 1987); the evidence for the Latin reading quoted will usually be found in Barber's *apparatus criticus* or, failing that, in Camps's commentary.

Some idea of my indebtedness to other scholars and translators can be gained from the Brief Bibliography, which, however, with the exception of Enk and Luck omits a number of important names writing in languages other than English. To Dr Oliver Lyne in particular I owe special thanks for his kindness in providing this book with an Introduction; also to Professor Wendell Clausen for reading and commenting most helpfully on the translation of Book I.

As regards the translation, though in verse, it is meant to be faithful and unadorned, an attempt at a version which would enable Propertius to be read and studied in English as the Bible has been read and studied for centuries, a contribution, one might perhaps be allowed to dream, towards some future Authorized Version of the Latin poets.

A. G. L.
St John's College
Cambridge
October 1992

CONTENTS

INTRODUCTION

I. *Background and career*

1. Cynthia ... momentarily

There is a tempting and romantic thesis: the most important factor in Propertius' background, career, and indeed politics is Cynthia, the woman who supposedly dominated much of his life. It may be far from untrue. But I shall proceed cautiously, merely registering 'Cynthia''s vital and dominating existence at the outset.

2. Equestrian Class, financial independence, patronage

You, says the figure Horus, 'were yourself reduced to hard-up Lares. | Though many were the steers that ploughed your country estate | The ruthless rod annexed your landed wealth' (iv. 1. 127–30). In these words, Propertius, born about 50 BC, contrives to tell us that his family lost property during the confiscations of 41 BC.[1] But unlike, say, Horace, Propertius was not thereby reduced to penury. Far from it. His family was equestrian in his own time— very possibly senatorial in the next generation—and there is no sign that the poet was ever burdened by the need to earn a living. His spirit was naturally independent and irreverent, but it was buttressed by the confidence that money and class tend to bring.

Unburdened by the need to earn a living, he had of course no need to seek the sort of patron who would provide him with financial support. Here we may see a contrast. In the *Eclogues* we find Virgil addressing patrons actual and potential. By 39 or 38 BC Virgil is under the economic protection of Augustus' minister Maecenas. Similarly Horace, only a year or so later; and Horace dedicates *Satires, Epodes*, and *Odes* I–III, and Virgil dedicates *Georgics*, to the great imperial patron. But Propertius addresses his

---

[1] Information on the historical background is included in my chapter 'Augustan Poetry and Society' in *The Oxford History of the Roman World* (Oxford University Press paperback 1991).

first book, published about 29, to Volcacius Tullus, nephew of the proconsul of Asia. And, like Catullus' introductory poem to Cornelius Nepos, his poems to Tullus are those of one friend to another, written on terms of equality. They are not the poems of patronized to patron. The Volcacii were of similar social standing to the Propertii.

Propertius did not address a patron in his first book. He does not solicit an economic patron ever. Nevertheless we find our independent equestrian dedicating his second book of Elegies to none other than the great Maecenas. I say 'dedicating', but the dedication is not markedly deferential. The introduction of the great man's name (ii. 1. 17) is preceded by the sensuous and funny lines on Cynthia as Propertius' Muse (see below, Section III.3). It is followed by a lengthy refusal to do what Maecenas has asked him to do, namely write an epic on Augustus, a poem that the princeps desired and, historically, had every reason to expect. Nor does the lengthy refusal lack barbs (when glancing at what he would have written about, had he written the epic, Propertius includes episodes in Augustus' earlier career that Augustus would certainly have preferred forgotten or rephrased). We sense the persisting independence. But why bother to acknowledge Maecenas at all? It must be because he is enjoying some of the advantages of belonging to the great man's entourage of poets. Book I had brought him to public notice. Maecenas invites him to join the inner circle in some capacity, so we infer. Propertius accepts, in some capacity. Why?

Propertius did not need Maecenas' money, but Maecenas had other things to offer: in particular the salon society. In the Rome of Propertius' time, the public recitation of a literary work was an important stage of publication. It was the occasion at which a poet might acquire or increase his popularity. The house of the fabulously rich Maecenas offered the most glamorous venues for recitations in the capital. Propertius had much to gain by proffering the minimum obeisance necessary to gain admission.

And Maecenas? If he entertained ambitions that Propertius might write the epic that Augustus so dearly wanted, he must have been swiftly disabused. But there were other ways of building the image of the regime besides epicizing its emperor, and Maecenas might have thought that Propertius could be induced to pursue one of these. And, anyway, the provocative poet of Book I was perhaps safer within the fold than without. There was another consideration.

Propertius was an entertaining, and, on his day, extremely good poet. Maecenas was not only a minister of Augustus. He was a lover of literature and culture for its own sake. He could also— as we can tell from Horace—take a joke.

The relationship between Propertius and Maecenas endured until the late 20s BC. It was a good time. It was the period modern historians call the 'First Augustan Period', when the *princeps* was feeling his way towards monarchy, and was less inclined to stamp his will upon people. It was also the period in which the cultured and diplomatic Maecenas was there to mediate for the poets, ex- plaining and excusing their writings to a perhaps puzzled *princeps* —and to support those who needed support (Horace, Virgil) without attaching too many strings.

II. *Propertius' Political Poetry*

1. Political poetry: before and during the patronage of Maecenas

In his first book, Propertius is most keen to establish himself as a love poet, and I shall discuss this in the next section. His love poetry itself has implications for politics to a quite large degree (cf. Section III.2). But I shall confine my attentions in Book I to the last two poems, for these in the context of politics merit our most immediate attention.

The final poem is the type of poem the ancients called a 'signet ring' (*sphragis*): its supposed function was to identify the poet and his provenance. Now Propertius in fact came from Assisi, as he tells us with more directness in iv. 1. 125. With elaborate indirectness he tells us this in i. 22. I paraphrase: 'If you know Perusia (the modern Perugia) and of the calamitous civil war that occurred there, the place where I lost a relative, well, I come from *near* there.' In 41 BC Perusia had been besieged by Augustus, the then Octavian, in what was an opening shot in the struggle between himself and Marcus Antonius. The city had been captured by him, and treated with ruthless brutality. When we consider the way Propertius phrases himself in i. 22, it is clear that he is a great deal more concerned to tell us about Perusia, from which he did not come, and to identify himself with its sufferings, than he is to tell us about

Assisi from which he did in fact come. The *sphragis* has been distorted to polemical ends.

The fact—and pointedness—of his identification with the sufferings of Perusia is reinforced by the collocation of poem i. 22 with i. 21. The latter, written in the tradition of a grave epigram, contains the words of a dead soldier who had opposed Octavian at Perusia. It is impossible to resist the inference that this man and the dead Propertian relative of i. 22 are one and the same. Note perhaps especially how the remains of both bodies are described as being wretchedly and similarly neglected in the chaotic aftermath of the battle. Propertius therefore identifies not just with the sufferings of Perusia, but with the sufferings of the defeated of Perusia: with Octavian's enemies. He is exploiting the 'signet-ring' poem to make (I would say) not just a polemically human and humane point, but a political one too. In the early 20s, the early years of the reign of Augustus, it was not tactful to recall the savager actions of Augustus in his earlier guise as Octavian. It was more than untactful to do so and simultaneously identify with his enemies. Our poet has independence and bite.

As I said above, Propertius is to some extent within Maecenas' circle of poets by the beginning of Book II. And Maecenas *was* Augustus' minister as well as a man of culture. The influence of this connection is evident, even in Propertius' poetry. But while it is not infrequent to find 'Augustan' material in Propertius' Books II and III, it is unusual to find it without shades of irony, levels of ambiguity—or sheer cheek. In ii. 1 he paid lip service to political-literary requirements. In iii. 11 he constructs a subtly ambiguous political poem. Here Cleopatra and her ambitions are duly castigated: 'The harlot queen forsooth of incestuous Canopus . . .' (iii. 11. 39 ff.). But the theme of the poem is announced as 'Why be surprised that a woman manages my life, | Leading my manhood captive as her slave . . .?' (iii. 11. 1–2), i.e. the theme of Propertius' domination by a powerful woman, Cynthia. Cleopatra's appearance in the poem is structurally justified as a parallel to the power of Cynthia. Unspoken but undeniably present is therefore Marcus Antonius, dominated by Cleopatra as Propertius was dominated by Cynthia. Antonius' domination by Cleopatra was of course shocking. Shocking, too, as Propertius has often enough stressed (e.g. i. 6. 25–6), was Propertius' domination by Cynthia. On the other hand it was his chosen and cherished lot (i. 4, i. 6, etc.; see below,

Section III.2)—and the dominating, cruel Cynthia is also the adored mythical divinity (i. 3.1 ff., ii. 2.5 ff.). Cleopatra denounced in a poem in which her analogue is Cynthia is not unambiguously denounced, and if Propertius mutely compares himself to Augustus' glamorous enemy this is a double-edged game he has played more explicitly before: ii. 16. 35 ff. Does the comparison make Propertius wickedly but glamorously bad? Or Antonius shockingly, romantically, and blissfully pitiable?

Other poems offer an undermined patriotism. For those listening to Propertius recite in Maecenas' palatial house on the Esquiline, these must have been amusing days if you were prepared to be amused. For example, iii. 4: Propertius will turn out to applaud Augustus' impending triumph, but languorously 'resting on a dear girl's bosom' (iii. 4. 15). Nor should it escape the notice that iii. 4. 1, 'Caesar the God plans war . . .,' has a chirpy and subversive antistrophe in iii. 5. 1, 'Love is the God of peace . . .' Another poem that amusingly engages great men and great issues is iii. 9. Here Propertius refuses the epic on Augustus (again), and combines and explains his refusal with apparent praise of Maecenas. Lines 21 ff. laud Maecenas for his lack of ambition, and it is this example, says Propertius, that encourages his own 'modesty' in literature: 'But it's your rule of life that I accept, Maecenas . . . When you might in Roman office move imperial axes . . . You hold back, humbly restrict yourself to modest shadow . . .' Now it is true that Maecenas eschewed public and official office. But this was not through lack of ambition. Men of shrewd sense saw that real power, interesting power, lay with Augustus' trusted personal advisers. And Augustus himself shrewdly preferred to trust those who opted not to rise above the equestrian order to a public career and to senatorial office. Maecenas was one of these trusted inner advisers—equestrian, yes, but unambitious in the real Augustan world, no. Maecenas of course knew this, and he knew that Propertius knew it; and, a man of wit as well as political acuity, he will (I am sure) have relished the poet's deft, presumptuous evasion.

In other poems Propertius feels free to be openly defiant in his political stance, even in Maecenas' entourage. Class, money, and courage could still talk at this stage of Augustus' reign. II. 7 celebrates the failure of marriage legislation that would have put some sort of an obstacle between himself and Cynthia (see below Section III.1):

> 'And yet Caesar is great.' Yes, Caesar is great in war,
>   But conquered nations mean nothing in love.
> I'd sooner let this head be parted from my shoulders
>   Than lose love's torches at a bride's behest . . .
> Why should I breed sons for our country's Triumphs?
> From blood of mine shall come no soldier.

(ii. 7. 5 ff.) That's telling it straight. Likewise ii. 15. 41 ff.:

> If all were keen to engage in such a life
>   And lie back, charging limbs with wine,
> There'd be no cruel steel or men-of-war—no bones
>   Of ours would welter in Actium's waves,
> Nor Rome, beset so often by her own successes,
>   Grow tired of loosening her hair in grief.

That is telling it extraordinarily straight. Propertius talks patently of the civil war that Actium historically was. But this was not the normal way to describe the great national victory over the barbaric Eastern forces of Cleopatra, which, in the propaganda of the early part of the regime, Actium was supposed to be. Reciting this poem and ii. 7 on the Esquiline, Propertius must have caused more than mere amusement, some considerable *frisson*.

2. *Political poetry: the post-Maecenas period*

The period during which Propertius was on the free periphery of Maecenas' enlightened literary circle lasted until the late 20s (the periods of Books II and III). Then, most scholars believe, Maecenas fell from imperial favour. The poets whom he had economically protected—Horace, Virgil—came under the direct umbrella of Augustus. Those like Propertius who had profited from his society found it prudent to abandon it, or at least not to acknowledge it.

But poets had to cope not just with the eclipse of a luxurious and tolerant patron. The whole political climate was changing. Historians identify a 'Second Augustan Period', beginning about 20 BC, in which the *princeps*, frustrated by failures, became less inhibited in the exercise and demonstration of power. The poets therefore not only had no elegant mediator between themselves and the *princeps*; they had the proximity of an emperor whose displeasure was easier to arouse and whose power was more intrusive. The results of this are most apparent in Horace's later work.

They are visible in Propertius IV too. To show this I backtrack momentarily.

Since the days of his entry to Maecenas' circle, Propertius had aligned himself with the aesthetics of the Alexandrian poet Callimachus. Scholars of cynical persuasion do not believe that Propertius was in actuality much influenced by Callimachus in Books II and III. They believe that his professed allegiance was largely due to the convenient fact that Callimacheans did not write epics—and to the fact that Virgil (in *Eclogue* VI) had already shown that Callimachean authority could be gracefully deployed in the service of declining the unwelcome task of writing an epic for a Roman general. In the entourage of Maecenas Propertius had been exposed to the pressure for an epic (see above). *Ergo*, the cynical among us say, he assumed the mantle of Callimachus—but without much visible sign of its affecting his poetry.

The situation is different in Book IV. Here the influence of Callimachus, direct or indirect, is at last visible in his poetry. The informing principle of Callimachus' most famous book, his *Aetia*, had been origins, 'causes': with wit, narrative skill, and pedantry, the Alexandrian poet expounded the stories behind Greek rituals and institutions. In the new political climate 'Rome's Callimachus' (iv. 1. 64) thought it prudent not just negatively to exploit Callimachean authority (no epics) but to perform a passing pastiche of his professed model, and to construct poems around Callimachus' informing principle, 'causes'. More than that, some of the poems which he constructed in this way had patriotic potential: the moral tale of Tarpeia, for example (iv. 4), or the origin of the great new Temple of Apollo on the Palatine, diplomatically but unhistorically seen by Propertius as a thank-offering for Apollo's support to Augustus at Actium (iv. 6).

But the alert will not miss signs of the old irreverence. It is arguable, for example, how suited the Callimachean rococo manner is to a great Roman battle. Lines iv. 6. 25–30 hit off the Callimachean manner brilliantly, including the sort of glancing parenthesis on a quite irrelevant topic that Callimachus favoured. But does this style ('Nereus at last had curved the lines into twin crescents . . . Phoebus . . . Posted himself on Augustus' poop') match the serious Romanness of the occasion, the Battle of Actium? A good writer fits form to content, a bad or malicious writer contrives incongruity. In this poem too Propertius plays a card he had played back in iii.

11. 39 ff. He mercilessly belittles and castigates the despicable Cleopatra. This is fine propaganda of course, given that Cleopatra was Rome's mortal enemy. On the other hand such belittling risks belittling the victory achieved over such a despicable foe, a mere woman. Thus iv. 6. 63 ff.: '*She* makes for Nile, a fleeing skiff's dishonoured cargo . . . Thank heaven! A fine Triumph one woman would have made | On streets where once Jugurtha was paraded!' Contrast the desperate efforts of Horace *both* to castigate Cleopatra *and* to build her up into a worthy foe in *Odes* i. 3.37.

The alert will also find pleasure in discovering that the motive for Tarpeia's treachery was love, not (as was traditional) greed: Propertius writes his moral tale but he mixes it with his own and his literary coterie's taste. The alert and the literate will find extreme pleasure in iv. 9. This tells the 'cause' of women's exclusion from Hercules' rites at the Ara Maxima. It is a very funny poem, casting Hercules in a number of inglorious lights. There is on the face of it nothing politically dubious about this. Augustus had made no comparisons between himself and Hercules; Hercules had no public ideological significance as, say, Apollo had. On the other hand, to *readers*, readers of poetry, Hercules did have such significance. Horace in *Odes* iii. 14 had compared Augustus, returning heroically from Spain, to Hercules arriving in Italy from Spain after defeating the monster Geryon. Then came Virgil. After Hercules had arrived in Italy, his next adventure was at the site of the future Rome: Cacus stole cattle from him that he had taken as booty from Geryon; and Hercules killed him for his pains. Virgil tells us this story in *Aeneid* VIII, picking up as it were where Horace left off, picking up too Horace's idea of figuring Hercules as the mythical paradigm of Augustus; but Virgil's is a probing and honest portrayal of Hercules, a probing and disturbing picture of Augustus' paradigm. And then came Propertius. Hercules' next problem, after despatching Cacus, was an immense thirst, which the maiden servants of the Bona Dea refused to assuage: hence their exclusion from Hercules' rites. This tale Propertius tells in iv. 9. with humorous gusto, with puns on 'thirst', and with a general huge indulgence of fun at the expense of Hercules: i.e. at the expense of Augustus' paradigm, *if* you have read and interpreted your Horace and Virgil correctly. You did not have to be up in literature to appreciate the irreverence of ii. 7 etc. To appreciate the irreverence of iv. 9 you do: you have to be alive to stylistic nuance and to contemporary poetical strategies. To that extent—confining his insolence to this sort of market—Propertius has adapted to the different political climate.

III. *Propertian Love Poetry*

1. Cynthia

Who is Cynthia? One way to answer this, and an important way, is to say: she is the successor of Catullus' Lesbia. Catullus had virtually created a genre of literature by writing his intense cycle of poems to and about the compelling and dominant mistress he calls Lesbia—most probably Clodia, wife of the nobleman Q. Metellus Celer, consul in 60 BC. After Catullus we find that art is stimulated by art, and life is stimulated by art, and poet after poet finds himself compelled to write cycles of intense poems about dominating mistresses: Cornelius Gallus and Cytheris, Propertius and Cynthia, Tibullus and Delia (and Nemesis), and others. I say that it is not only art but life that is stimulated by art, and that perhaps needs a little unpacking. I do not doubt that a historical Propertian Cynthia existed. But Propertius would have been a poor servant of fashion if he had not felt himself bound to love her at least as much and as agonizingly as Catullus loved Lesbia in his epoch-making poems —just as he would have been a poor poet if he had not had an eye on presenting his love affair in a way that did not in some way cap and supersede the Catullan collection. Historically founded, 'Cynthia' must inevitably be an embellished literary construct too —as to an extent Lesbia will of course have been, as to an extent any figure in 'autobiological' literature is. We will never disentangle what is historical reality and what is embellishment in 'Cynthia'— any more than we will disentangle reality from embellishment in the 'I'-construct 'Propertius' who figures in Propertius' poems. I do little more than utter truisms about 'autobiographical' poetry. But because of the revolutionary and captivating nature of Catullan poetry, embellishment and literary pose is perhaps more evident in Catullus' 'autobiographical' successors than it is in some other 'autobiographical' poetry.

It is worth noting however that, for whatever reason, we get a firmer—I do not say 'truer'—picture of Cynthia than the discreet

xviii   *Introduction*

Catullus offers of Lesbia. Physically: 'Red-gold hair, long hands, big build—she moves like | Juno' (ii. 2. 5f.); she has a fair complexion (so prized among the Mediterranean Romans), 'well-groomed hair rippling' over her 'smooth neck', star-like eyes . . . (ii. 3.9 ff.). As a love-maker, she is at once tease and tigress (ii. 15). And there is more on her physique and physical prowess, as the reader will find. Propertius shows the romantic's comprehensible disinclination to go into physical details, but he lacks Catullus' extreme delicacy, which, in the case of Lesbia—but not in the case of other girls—excludes virtually all physical reference at all. Culturally: Cynthia is a great dancer and lyre-player (ii. 3.17ff., i. 2. 28), poetess (i. 2. 27), graceful conversationalist (i. 2. 2). Again I could cite more references and information. On the other hand, some of these may well be rhetorically determined by the 'Propertius' of the moment to persuade the 'Cynthia' of the moment. Psychologically: broad aspects of her personality and the effect that her personality had on Propertius belong in the next subsection; other aspects are too detailed or too subtle to submit to the crude summary of an introduction.

One thing we should like to know is irritatingly difficult to pin down: the social status Cynthia is supposed to occupy. Poem ii. 7 seems to exult in the failure of legislation that would have pressurized Propertius into marrying, presumably by the penal taxation of bachelors. But why could he not marry Cynthia? An obvious answer to this would be that Cynthia was married already—perhaps quite a grand lady, like 'Lesbia'. Another explanation offers itself: she was a freedwoman, and the proposed legislation forbade marriage of free Romans to freedwomen. There are objections to both these explanations. The objection to the latter is that the law that was later passed (18 BC) specifically allowed marriage of free and freed, so keen was Augustus to get reluctant Roman men into the married state. The objection to the former is that the dancing, singing, sexually liberated Cynthia sounds more like a freedwoman professional lover than a Roman lady—until one remembers the Sempronia immortalized by Sallust or the Clodia that Cicero exposes with less delicacy than Catullus. A definitive answer is probably impossible, if only because of the blurring of social barriers in later Republican Rome. Thus, some married Roman women were so scornful of tradition that they lived and loved like 'courtesans' (Clodia, Sempronia), while freedwomen

'courtesans' achieved sufficient elegance and won enough respect
to be accepted in polite society (e.g. Gallus' Cytheris, the freed-
woman of Volumnius Eutrapelus: see Cicero, *Letters to his Friends*
ix. 26). In these circumstances it can be impossible to tell the
difference. With Cynthia, we shall have to conclude thus: she is to
be imagined as belonging by right, or electing to join, a class of
sexually emancipated women who were utterly desirable to Roman
men of the upper class. Unlike the flute-girls and other 'entertainers'
who lurk behind the graceful furniture of Horatian convivial poetry,
their favours could not crudely be bought: they could say No, No,
and No again, until their lovers went mad. But like those 'enter-
tainers', but for different and differing reasons, it was impossible
to marry them.

2. *Propertius and Cynthia: Propertian love poetry: declarations and stances*

'Cynthia first . . . caught wretched me | Smitten before by no desires
. . .' 'Love pressed my head, | Until he taught me hatred of chaste
girls . . . and living aimlessly.' '. . . mania.' 'Seek remedies for a
heart diseased. | Bravely will I suffer knife and cautery [a reference
to servile torture as well as surgery], | Given liberty to speak as
anger bids.' 'I warn you shun this evil.' These are all quotations
from the first poem of the first book. It does not sound much fun:
defeat, immorality, irrationality, madness, disease, slavery, evil.
And yet this is Propertius' *first* poem, the poem in which he
introduces the woman and the love that will engross a book of love
poetry (in fact more than one book, but we do not know that yet).
It is a strange way to start. Propertius' evocation of love sounds
like the sort of condemnation of hopelessly passionate love that we
find in authors as diverse as Euripides and Lucretius. Or to put it
another way: the tone of his opening poem would more suit the
expression of a man striving to quit love than the programmatic
poem of someone presumably about to embark upon it. And it has
indeed strong echoes of Catullus poem 76, the poem in which
Catullus was, apparently, trying to quit love. The language of the
devoted Catullus, of Catullus in love, even despairingly, was always
other: romantic and idealistic. Not until 76 does he sound such
notes of condemnation. But Propertius *starts* with them.

    It is apposite here to recall some remarks which I made above.

Propertius would have been a poor servant of fashion if he had not felt himself bound to love Cynthia at least as much and as agonizingly as Catullus loved Lesbia, and he would have been a poor poet if had not had an eye on presenting his love affair in a way that did not in some way cap and supersede the Catullan collection. Poem i. 1 is strategically pitched. Propertius' love is as torturing as Catullus' was when he was trying to give it up, but this is where Propertius comes in. Where will it all end? The reader is enticed into the book, for clearly this evil and diseased love affair will take off. Propertius may ask his friends to 'Seek remedies for a heart diseased', but one gets the firm impression they would get short shrift if they actually tried to do so.

This—the novel programmatic poem—is Stage One of Propertius' strategy of supersession. Stage Two we may name upping the stakes and emblazonment of the implicit.

It will have been noticed that one of Propertius' descriptions of his love in i. 1 conveyed *slavery*. Only glancingly, on one occasion, did Catullus imply servitude to Lesbia (68. 136). His characteristic vision of their love was one of equality, friendship. True, the Roman concept of friendship entailed lofty and reciprocal obligations, and the offer of this by a gentleman to his lover was in Catullus' time something quite revolutionary. But Propertius, following the lead of Cornelius Gallus, trumps this. He offers not equality but inferiority, gross inferiority: he is, indeed he will prove willingly to be, Cynthia's slave: compare i. 4. 1–4, where the Latin words behind 'mistress' and 'bondage' are explicit about such slavery; or i. 5, a poem which tries to explain to a potential rival the terrifying nature of slavery to the dominating figure of Cynthia. Propertius, obedient to love's fashion and literature's interest as well as to reality, loves Cynthia more agonizingly than Catullus loved Lesbia, and Cynthia is more awesome than ever Lesbia was.

And Propertius has his eye on *emblazoning* the shocking aspects of his love more prominently and provokingly than Catullus did. Take the question of love and life. If a young equestrian wished to adopt a public career—as would be expected of him—a conventional stage was to serve in the chosen entourage of a provincial governor. Contacts and money were made thereby. Hilarious poems of Catullus (10, 28, cf. too 45) testify to Catullus' depressing endeavour in this department. Therefore, we infer, he gave up all thought of a public career; thereafter, we infer, literature and love were his sole preoccupations (for the latter cf. e.g. poem 109). But in Catullus we have to make the inference; Propertius engineers poems that emblazon his position. Poem i. 6 is particularly important in this respect. It purports to be a response to an invitation by Volcacius Tullus to join the entourage of his proconsular uncle. Answering it, Propertius can advertise what is only implicit in Catullus: love is my life. Or as he provocatively puts it, love is my career: 'By birth I am ill-equipped for glory or for arms; | Fate drafted me for this campaigning' (29–30). The Latin word for 'campaigning' (*militia*, literally 'soldiering') allows him a neat dissociative pun. A word that covers 'military' service in the proconsul's entourage, it also revives an old erotic metaphor, the 'soldiering' of love, love as battle. Love is my campaigning, says Propertius, making explicit in a word his dissociation from the normal path of equestrian life. He makes explicit his dissociation from another obvious equestrian pursuit in i. 14: business and money-making. This is Catullus made explicit. These are Catullan attitudes packaged to provoke.

3. Propertius and Cynthia: romanticism

I quote a definition of 'romantic' and 'romanticism': 'an attitude, character, or decision which reveals a willingness for irrational . . . sacrifice in exchange for some individual, visionary goal'. Propertius the willing slave is clearly a romantic by this definition, victim we might say of the Romantic Agony. His poetry is not always so tortured, his romanticism not always so perverse. Indeed humour, far from absent from the poems already discussed, can come right to the fore. Delightfully, too, he shows himself highly aware of his own irrational romanticism.

One of Propertius' typical resources is mythology. And his typical use of it is to adumbrate the visionary goal: the Cynthia who might be, the Cynthia who should be, the love that will be, the love that wasn't. Myth suits such a function, since the sort of myth Propertius selects is pretty, it is an attractive and moving story, but it *isn't true*—not to the unromantic Roman burgher, it isn't. Consider the opening lines of i. 3. Here Propertius narrates a romantic vision and mood that he conceived one night. Coming to Cynthia's house in the early hours, his capacity for romanticism enhanced by wine, he found her asleep. And oh how mythic she appeared! 'As the girl from Knossos [Ariadne], while Theseus' keel receded, | Lay limp on a deserted beach . . .', as Andromeda, 'as a Maenad . . .' Swoons on grassy Apidanus, | So Cynthia seemed to me to breathe soft peace . . .' You cannot conceive and picture more romantically than that: the limp, sleeping Cynthia 'who should be'. But the narrating poet shows himself gloriously self-aware. Humour comes to a head when Propertius explodes his visionary romanticism. For Cynthia wakes up — 'So! (and she dug an elbow into the couch)', line 34 — and it's not 'the girl from Knossos' but a whining and much aggrieved woman from contemporary Rome. The poem has taken us through the experience of the romancing lover, and through his rude enlightenment, with beauty, grace, and wit.

Consider too the opening of ii. 1: again delightful wit, unagonized irrational romanticism. Propertius tells us that he can dispense with Apollo and any normal poetic inspiration. Cynthia is his Muse, 'My only inspiration is a girl.' (4). This conceit is then unpacked with humorous literalness. Every move she makes is a poem. 'Suppose she steps out glittering in silks from Cos, | Her Coan gown speaks a whole volume' (5–6). 'Or if she closes eyelids exigent for sleep | I have a thousand new ideas for poems' (11–12). Then wit, and sensuality, dominate: 'Or if, stripped of her dress, she wrestles with me naked, | Why then we pile up lengthy *Iliads*.' *Iliads* of literature and *Iliads* of sex. Mythology is used to adumbrate the visionary, impossible joy of sex with Cynthia at ii. 14. 1 ff., with exuberance and humour.

4. . . . *and the sadness*

Lest I suggest Propertius is all romantic pose, provocation, and humour, consider these lines (ii. 6. 41–2): 'No wife, no girl-friend ever shall lead me astray; | Always you'll be girl-friend and always wife to me.' This is said after a poem that radiates Propertius' knowledge of Cynthia's infidelity, and, whatever hints of humour one may choose to find in the poem, bespeaks moving romantic sacrifice. And myth is called upon for romantic purposes, this time to adumbrate impossible grief, in ii. 8:

> I'm being robbed of the girl for so long dear to me
>   And you, my friend, forbid me to shed tears? (1–2)

> After his sweetheart was abducted lonely Achilles
>   Let his weapons lie idly in his hut.

He saw the Achaeans cut down in flight along the shore,
  The Doric camp ablaze with Hector's torches;
He saw Patroclus' mutilated body sprawled
  In the dust, his hair matted with blood;
All this he bore for beautiful Briseis' sake;
  So cruel the pain when love is wrenched away.
But after late amends restored the captive to him
  He dragged brave Hector behind Thessalian steeds.
As I am far inferior both in birth and battle,
  No wonder love can triumph over me! (29–40)

Propertius' explicit statement of inferiority scarcely conceals the mythic status to which he seeks to promote his grief. And successfully: these are deeply moving lines. Deeply moving lines composed on account of one who, Propertius tells us, 'was iron', who never said 'I love you' (12). Such emotion may seem misplaced, it may seem to the Roman burgher an absurd sacrifice, but it is in its own way visionary.

A CHRONOLOGY

25   Aelius Gallus, Cornelius' successor as Prefect of Egypt, invades Arabia. ?Propertius II.

23   Death of Marcellus, nephew and son-in-law of Augustus, in his nineteenth year. ?Horace, *Odes* I–III. ?Ovid, *Amores* (1st edn.). In this or the next year Varro Murena and Fannius Caepio conspire against Augustus and are executed.

21   ?Propertius III.

20   Augustus forces a settlement with Parthia and recovers the standards lost by Crassus at Carrhae in 53.

19   Death of Virgil. His unrevised *Aeneid* published by literary executors. ?Horace, *Epistles* I.

18   ?Death of Tibullus and publication of Tibullus II.

17   Celebration of the centennial Secular Games at Rome. Horace, *Carmen Saeculare*. Marcus Lollius defeated by German raiding tribes in this or the next year.

16   Propertius' funeral elegy for Cornelia, sister of the Consul of the year, Cornelius Scipio (iv. 11).

15   Drusus and Tiberius, Augustus' stepsons, defeat the Raeti and other Alpine tribes. ?Propertius IV.

13   ?Horace, *Odes* IV and *Epistles* II.

1   ?Ovid, *Remedia Amoris*—line 764 implies that Propertius is dead.

TRANSLATION

NARRATIVE ORDER?

* Repetition of names not
  inconsistant with sequence
* Gaps in pairs introduce periods of time

BOOK I

INTRO

subject of poem

*P is desperate
cannot make any
headway with C*

I

Love's martyr

Cynthia first, with her eyes, caught wretched me
  Smitten before by no desires;
Then, lowering my stare of steady arrogance,
  With feet imposed Love pressed my head,
Until he taught me hatred of chaste girls—   5
  The villain—and living aimlessly.
And now for a whole year this mania has not left me, *time frame*
  Though I am forced to suffer adverse Gods.

Milanion by facing every hardship, Tullus,
  Conquered the cruelty of Atalanta.   10
Sometimes, distraught, he roamed the glens of Parthenius
  And was gone to watch the long-haired beasts.
Stunned by that blow from Hylaeus' club he even
  Groaned in anguish to Arcadian crags.
So he was able to master his fleet-footed girl;   15
  Such power in love have prayers and kindnesses.
For me, though, Love is slow, can think of no devices,
  And forgets to go his legendary way.

But you who know the trick of drawing down the moon
  And the task of atonement on magic altars,   20
Here is your chance; come, change my mistress' thinking
  And make her face paler than mine.
Then I could believe you have the power to move
  Rivers and stars with Colchian sorcery.

link to Medea

And you, friends, who (too late) call back the fallen,   25
  Seek remedies for a heart diseased.
Bravely will I suffer knife and cautery,
  Given liberty to speak as anger bids.

introduces main themes.

Bear me through farthest nations, bear me over the waves
　　Where no woman will know my road.   30

Stay home, all you to whom God nods with easy ear,
　　And be paired in love forever true.
On me our Venus levies nights of bitterness,
　　And empty Love is ever present.
I warn you, shun this evil. Let each man's darling hold him   35
　　Nor quit when love has grown familiar.
But if to warnings anyone should turn slow ears,
　　Alas, how bitterly he'll rue my words!

2

Natural beauty

Why choose, my life, to step out with styled hair
　　And move sheer curves in Coan costume?
Or why to drench your tresses in Orontes' myrrh
　　And sell yourself with foreign gifts
And lose the charm of Nature for bought elegance,   5
　　Not letting limbs shine with their own attractions?
This doctoring of your looks is pointless, believe me;
　　Love, being naked, does not love beauticians.

See what colours beautiful land sends up,
　　How ivies in the wild thrive better,   10
Arbutus grows more beautifully in lonely glens
　　And water knows by nature where to run.
Beaches appeal, with native pebbles painted,
　　And artlessly the birds sing sweeter.

Not in such gear Leucippus' Phoebe and her sister   15
　　Hilaïra inflamed Castor and Pollux
And on her father's shores Evenus' daughter once
　　Set eager Idas and Apollo at odds;
And Hippodamía, carried off on foreign wheels,
　　Used no false white to win a Phrygian husband.   20
But they had looks beholden to no jewels,
　　Fresh as Apelles' use of colour.

They were not out to pick up lovers wholesale;
   Chastity, for them, was beauty enough.

Now I'm not afraid you hold me cheaper than those others,   25
   But a girl who pleases one man is smart enough—
Especially as Phoebus gladly grants you his poetry
   And Callíope her Aonian lyre,
And your delightful talk discloses unique grace—
   All things that Venus and Minerva approve.   30
For these, while I'm alive, you'll always be most dear—
   So long as you've no taste for wretched finery.

3

Late for an appointment

As the girl from Knossos, while Theseus' keel receded,
   Lay limp on a deserted beach,
And as Cephéan Andromeda in first sleep rested,
   From hard rocks freed at last,
And as a Maenad, no less tired by the ceaseless dance,   5
   Swoons on grassy Apídanus,
So Cynthia seemed to me to breathe soft peace,
   Leaning her head on relaxed hands,
When I was dragging footsteps drunken with much
   Bacchus
   And the boys shook torches in the small hours.   10

Not yet bereft of all my senses I prepared
   To approach her, gently, pressing the couch.
But, though a prey to double passion, under orders
   (From Love on this flank, Bacchus on that, both ruthless Gods)
To edge an arm beneath her, reconnoitring,   15
   And kiss, with hand at work, and stand to arms,
Still I dared not disturb my lady's peace,
   Fearing the fierce abuse I knew so well; = unrequited love.
But there I stuck, staring intent, like Argus
   At Io's unfamiliar horns.   20

And now I loosed the garland from my forehead
    And placed it, Cynthia, on your temples,
Or pleased myself by re-arranging your stray hair,
    Or to cupped hands gave stolen fruit;
no use when asleep But all my gifts were lavished on ungrateful sleep,   25
    Gifts rolled from my pocket often as I leant.

Whenever, rarely moving, you drew a sigh,
    I froze in superstitious dread = fear of waking her
That dreams were bringing you strange fears
    And some man forced you to be his—   30
Until the moon, passing the window opposite,
    The busy moon with lingering light
Opened those calm closed eyes with weightless beams.
    'So!' (and she dug an elbow into the couch)
'At last, humiliation brings you back to our bed,   35
    Thrown out from another woman's door!
Where have you wasted the long hours of my night,
    Limp, alas, now the stars are set?

Villain, O how I wish you could endure such nights
    As you always inflict on wretched me!   40
Sometimes I cheated sleep with crimson thread
    Or a tired tune on Orpheus' lyre;
Or I whispered complaints to my forsaken self
    At unmarried love's long absences—
Until I dropped off, stroked by Slumber's welcome wings,   45
    That thought, above all, made me weep.'

4

Cynthia's dangerous attractions

tells Bassus to leave him to Cynthia

Why press me, Bassus, by your praise of all those girls
    To change my mind and leave my mistress?
Why not let me spend whatever life is left me
    In the familiar bondage?

Praise as you may the beauty of Spartan Hermíone   5
    And Nycteus' daughter Antíope

And all the women born in Time's beautiful days,
   Cynthia leaves them nameless.
Much less would a harsh critic mark her down as inferior
   When compared with minor figures.   10

But her beauty's the smallest part of my obsession, Bassus.
   Greater things there are that make it sweet to die: *suicide refference*
Well-bred complexion, grace of many accomplishments,
   And joys over which I'd rather draw a veil.
So the more you strive to destroy our love, the more   15
   We frustrate you with our mutual trust.

You'll suffer for it. She'll get to know of your wild words
   And you'll have made no inarticulate foe.
Cynthia won't trust us together after this, and won't
   Invite you. She'll remember your offence. *= adultry*   20
In her wrath she'll slander you to all the other girls;
   No door, alas, will welcome you. *= reputation*

No shrine will be ignored by her lamenting,
   No sacred stone soever or wherever.
No loss is a more serious blow to Cynthia   25
   Than when her charms are robbed of love—
Specially of mine. I pray that it remain so always
   And I find nothing to reproach her for.

4 & 5 strong link

5

Warning to a rival, a philanderer

tells Gallus to leave Cynthia
Cynthia to him

   Jealous, high time you disciplined that tiresome tongue
      And let us run our present course in double harness.
   Is it your mad desire to suffer my obsession?
      Unhappy man, you rush towards your ruin—
   To blunder perilously over hidden fires   5
      And drink all Thessaly's poisons.

   She'll prove no flighty girl in the encounter;
      You'll find her anger is no joke.

Even if she's not resistant to your prayers,
   She'll still bring you troubles—by the thousand.   10
You'll sleep no more. Her image will not leave you.
   Her moods make proud men puppets.

Ah, many's the time you'll run to my door humiliated,
   Your brave boasts sunk to sobs.
On tearful whining trembling dread will supervene   15
   And fear leave its ugly mark on your face.
When you complain, the words you look for will escape you;
   Poor wretch, you won't know who or where you are.

Then you'll be forced to learn subservience to our mistress
   And what it means to go home rejected.   20
You'll cease to express amazement at my pallor
   Or wonder why I'm a mere skeleton.
As lover noble birth will not assist you;
   Love recognizes no ancestral masks.

And if you give the smallest hint of misbehaviour,   25
   Your great name will become an instant scandal.
I shall not then have power, when asked, to offer comfort,
   As I can find no cure for my own trouble.
But paired in misery and shared love we'll be forced
   To weep on one another's shoulder.   30

So make no question, Gallus, of my Cynthia's power;
   When invoked, she comes—with vengeance.

6

An invitation to serve abroad declined

It's not that I'm scared to get to know the Adriatic
   Or sail with you the salt Aegean, Tullus—
With you I'd climb Rhipaean peaks, or march
   Far south beyond the home of Memnon—
But I'm verbally estopped by a girl embracing me,   5
   Who often lends her grave pleas cogent colour.

All night long she protests her passion, and when I leave her
  Charges the Gods with non-existence,
Alleging she's no longer mine, with menaces
  Of injured girl-friend to ungrateful man.   10
Even for an hour I can't endure this prosecution;
  Ah, perish all cold-hearted lovers!

Would it be worth my while to visit learned Athens
  And view the ancient wealth of Asia,
If Cynthia demonstrates at the ship's launching,   15
  Scratching my face with her wild censorship,
And, if the wind's against, claiming a debt of kisses
  On grounds of cruelty by a faithless man?

You must strive to surpass your uncle's well-earned axes
  And bring back law to forgetful allies.   20
Never has your youth taken time off for love,
  But served the fatherland in arms.
Never on you may that Boy bring a lover's hardships
  Or the auspices my tears have taken.

Let me, whom Fortune wills among the fallen,   25
  Lay down my life in extreme misconduct.
Many the willing casualties in love's long service,
  Among whom let me too be buried.
By birth I am ill-equipped for glory or for arms;
  Fate drafted me for this campaigning.   30

So, where effete Ionia extends, or where
  Pactólus waters Lydian fields,
Whether you cover land on foot or sea by oar,
  Participant in welcome discipline,
Should any hour then bring you memories of me,   35
  Know that I owe my life to a cruel star.

Lo says he will not travel & does

7

To an epic poet in praise of love poetry

[handwritten: AB format]
[handwritten: epic poet]

Ponticus, while you are telling of Cadmus' Thebes
    And of grim warfare between brothers
And rivalling (bless me!) the primacy of Homer
    Provided Fate is tender to your verse,
We, as comes natural, agitate our love
    And seek ideas to move a hard mistress,
Forced rather to be slave of suffering than of wit
    And to complain of youth's hard times.

[handwritten right margin: trying to soften Cynthias heart] 5

Thus I grind out my life's measure, this is my fame,
    For this I wish my verses to be named.   10
Let them praise me, Ponticus, because I only pleased
    A cultured girl—and suffered her abuse.
Hereafter may neglected lovers daily read me, finding
    Help in the knowledge of our troubles.

[handwritten right margin: fame ~ reputation]

[handwritten: if he falls in love epic will be no use]

Should even you be hit by the Boy's inerrant bow   15
    (Which may the Gods in our heaven forbid!),
Far from your epic camp, poor wretch, and the Seven Captains,
    You'll weep, while they lie dumb—in dust eternal.
You'll long in vain to write the verse of tenderness, *[handwritten: elegy]*
    But late love will refuse you inspiration.   20

Then you will marvel at me as no minor poet,
    And give me first place among Roman wits,
And young men at my grave be moved to murmur
    'Great poet of our passion, down at last.'
So take care in your pride not to despise my verse: 25
    Belated love can charge high interest.

[handwritten: the more love is delayed the more painful it often is]

8A

Cynthia plans to go abroad (with a rich lover)

Are you out of your mind? Does thought of me not give you pause?
  Do I mean less to you than Illyria's ice?
And do you really think so well of whoever he is
  That you'd sail without me in the worst weather?
Surely you can't brave the roar of the raging sea   5
  And a hard berth amidships?
Or press with those frail feet persistent frosts
  And face blizzards, Cynthia?

O that the season of winter storms were twice as long
  And lagging Pleiades kept sailors idle,   10
That your stern-rope never were loosed from the Tyrrhene shore
  Nor an ill wind blew away my prayers!

And yet when the wave does carry your ship from harbour
  Let me never see such winds subside
As leave me stranded on an empty shore   15
  Shaking my fist and calling you cruel.

But however badly you treat me, traitress,
  May Galatea smile on your voyage,
And after prosperous oarage past the Ceraunians
  Óricos greet you with level calm.   20

For never, my life, shall other women tempt me
  To end my just complaining at your door,
Nor shall I tire of interrogating busy sailors:
  'Tell me what port interns my girl?'
And I'll say 'Though she land on Autáric or Hylléan coasts,   25
  Her future will be mine.'

8B

She changes her mind

It's here she'll be. She has sworn to stay. Ill-wishers can go hang!
   We've won. She has given in to my entreaties.
Eager envy can drop its glad illusions:
   Our Cynthia returns to her old ways.   30

She calls me *dear* and Rome *most dear* because of me,
   Would 'find no kingdom sweet without me',
Prefers to rest with me, though in a narrow bed,
   And be mine, at whatever cost,
Than dowered with Hippodamía's ancient kingdom   35
   Or the wealth that Elis' horses won.

To all his great gifts and even greater promises,
   Not being greedy, she prefers my pocket.
I could not move her with gold or mother of pearl,
   But only with devoted verse.   40

So the Muse exists and Apollo makes haste to help the lover;
   In that faith I love, for peerless Cynthia's mine.
Today I walk in heaven, among the stars.
   Come day, come night, she's mine.
No rival can rob *me* of my true love;   45
   That glory shall my grey hairs know.

9

A sequel to i. 7

I told you so

Cynic, I told you love would come
   And you'd lose free speech.
Look, you've fallen—a woman's submissive suppliant—
   Slave of some girl bought yesterday!

In love Chaonia's doves can't beat me at divining   5
    Which young men are which girl's conquest.
I've earned my expertise by tears and suffering:
    Would I were heart-whole and a layman!

Much good it does you now, poor wretch, to mouth your epic
    And weep Amphíon's lyre-built walls.   =Thebes   10
In love a line of Mimnermus is more help than Homer.   = contrast
    Civilized love needs soft music.   contrasting images
Please go and stow away those gloomy cantos
    And sing what every girl would like to hear.

It's not as if she refused to see you. Why, at present   15
    You're like a madman in midstream demanding water.
You're not even pale as yet. The true fire hasn't touched you—
    Just the first spark of future trouble.

Then you'll sooner face Armenian tigresses,
    Sooner be bound in Hell to Ixíon's wheel   20
Than in your marrow feel so often the Boy's bow
    And have no power to say her anger nay.
Love never offers anyone an easy flight
    Without at other times depressing him.

Don't be deceived because she's willing, Ponticus;   as in 7   25
    When a girl's yours her sting goes deeper.   being addressed.
Your eyes once caught, Love won't allow you to withdraw them
    Or lie awake for someone else's sake.
He does not show until his hand touches the bone.
    Run, whoever you are, from his temptations.   30
Stocks and stones are powerless to resist them,
    Much less your poor lightweight soul.

So for goodness sake confess your error now. In love
    It's often a relief to name one's ruin.

make narrative sense in the order we find them

IO

A sequel to i. 5

O the delicious peace, after witnessing first love
    As an accomplice of your tears!
O the delicious pleasure in remembering that night,
    To be asked for—O how often!—in my prayers,
When I watched you, Gallus, dying in a girl's embrace   5
    And breathing intermittent words!
Though sleep hung heavy on my drooping eyelids
    And the riding moon blushed in mid-sky,
I could not absent myself from your love-play,
    So passionate that dialogue.   10

But since you had the courage to confide in me,
    Accept my tribute to shared joy.
Not only have I learnt to keep your passion secret,
    I offer something greater, friend, than loyalty:
I have the power to reconcile estranged lovers   15
    And to open a mistress' reluctant door.
I have the power to heal another's new-found troubles;
    My words contain strong medicine.
Cynthia has taught me what to seek and what to shun
    On each occasion; Love has helped.   20

Shun the desire to fight with a moody girl,
    And proud speech, and long silence.
Do not, when she wants a thing, refuse ungraciously,
    Nor let her kind words fall unheeded.
She comes, when slighted, in bad temper, and when wronged   25
    Forgets to drop her rightful threats.
But the more humble you are and deferential to love,
    The oftener you'll enjoy success.
He who forgoes freedom and the uncommitted heart
    Can find abiding bliss with one girl.   30

11 ✳ New chapter ✳ TRAVEL.

Cynthia on holiday at Baiae

setting

While you're on holiday in Baiae, Cynthia,
   Where the causeway lies along Hercules' shore,
And marvel how sea-water from near famed Misenum
   Was channelled lately to Thesprotus' realm,
Does thought of me occur—to bring night memories?   5
   Is there room for me on love's margin?
Or has some enemy, Cynthia, play-acting passion
   Removed you from my poetry?

I had far rather a little dinghy powered by paddles
   Detained you on the Lucrine Lake,   10
Or water yielding easily to alternate arms
   Imprisoned you in Teuthras' ripples,
Than you be free to hear another man's sweet whispers,
   Relaxed on a beach that tells no tales.

A girl without protection is apt to fall,   15
   Play false, and forget mutual vows—
Not that I doubt your proven reputation,
   But there love's threat is ever-present.
So please forgive me if my writings cause you
   Any distress. Fear must take the blame.   20

Would I protect more anxiously my own dear mother?
   Without you what would my life be worth?
You, Cynthia, only you are home to me and parents,
   You all my times of happiness.
Whether on meeting friends I am gloomy or delighted,   25
   In every mood I should say 'Blame Cynthia!'

But you must quickly leave degenerate Baiae;
   Those beaches bring divorce to many,
Beaches for long the enemy of decent girls.
   A curse on Baiae's waters, love's disgrace!

absent love

12

The poet deserted

Know-all Rome, why not stop falsely accusing me
    Of idleness because she keeps me here?
As many miles divide her from my bed as Hýpanis
    Is far from Venetian Erídanus.
It is not me her embraces feed with familiar love,   5
    Nor in my ear does *Cynthia* sound sweet.

I was favoured once. In those days no one had the luck
    Of loving with like faithfulness.
We were envied. So, does God abase me? Or some herb
    Picked on Prométhean heights divide us?   10

I am not what I was, for travel changes a girl.
    So great a love so quickly gone!
Now I must learn to know long nights alone
    And be a weariness to my own ears.

Happy the man who could weep in his girl's presence   15
    (Love can enjoy the sprinkling of tears)
Or who, when scorned, could redirect his ardour
    (There is also joy in bondage transferred).
My fate is neither to love another nor break with *her*:
    Cynthia was first and Cynthia shall be last.   20

13

Further to i. 10

As usual, Gallus, you'll take pleasure in my plight—
    That I am love-bereft, at lonely leisure.
But I refuse to imitate your treacherous tongue:
    Never may girl wish, Gallus, to trick *you*.

While growing famous for female deception   5
　　And coolly looking for short-term love,
You've fallen for someone and turn pale with ill-timed passion—
　　The first slippery step to ruin.
She'll be the punishment for those despised unfortunates,
　　The One to avenge the wrongs of many.   10
She'll put a stop to your promiscuous affairs;
　　You'll cease to enjoy the search for novelty.

It was not gossip taught me this, nor augury;
　　I've seen. Can you deny my evidence?
Gallus, I've seen you swooning away, with neck held tight,   15
　　And weeping long under close arrest,
Eager to lay down your life on longed-for lips—
　　The rest my friendly modesty conceals.

I could not separate your mutual embrace,
　　So wild the passion between you both.   20
With love less easy, in the guise of river-god,
　　Neptune embraced Salmóneus' daughter.
With love less ardent Hercules experienced heavenly
　　Hebe, first joy after Oeta's pyre.

On that one day all lovers were outrun,   25
　　So fierce the fire she kindled in you.
Nor has she let your previous arrogance return.
　　There's no escape. Passion will drive you on.
No wonder, when she's worthy of Jove, second to Leda,
　　Greater than Leda's girls, one against three,   30
More seductive than all the heroines of old Argos.
　　Her words could win the love of Jove.

But as you're doomed this time to die of love, enjoy it.
　　No other door was good enough for you.
You've had a strange lapse. May it bring you luck,   35
　　And she be the one for all your wishes.

14

Love and money

Though you lounge luxuriously by the waves of Tiber
    Drinking Lesbian wine from Mentor's work
And gazing, now at swift lighters running past,
    Now at slow barges hauled by ropes,
And though each landscaped grove stretches up as tall   5
    As the trees that crowd on Caucasus,
Still such things can't be matched against my love:
    Love has no respect for money.

Whenever she prolongs with me the wished-for night
    Or spends all day in easy love,   10
Then beneath my roof Pactólus' freshets flow
    And Red Sea pearls are gathered;
Then my joys guarantee me king of kings—
    And may they last until I die.
Who can enjoy his wealth with Love against him?   15
    No prizes for me if Venus frowns.

She can break the staying-power of heroes,
    Bring pain to the hardest heart.
She's not afraid to trespass on the onyx threshold
    And mount the crimson couch, Tullus,   20
And keep a wretched young man tossing on his bed;
    No comfort then in coloured silken covers.
But granted her gracious presence, I'll not hesitate
    To scorn a kingdom or Alcinous' gifts.

P abandones the atempt to divert her from other men

15

Cynthia slow to visit him in his illness

Many the hurts I've often feared from your light conduct,
    But never, Cynthia, this betrayal.
Look at me, Fortune's victim, in grave danger,
    But you're not frightened, though you've come at last.
And you can use your hands to re-do yesterday's hairstyle,   5
    And spend an hour on your make-up,
Can even flash a string of Eastern pearls
    As if in honour of a new lover.

Unlike Calypso, who on the Ithacan's departure
    Wept beside the lonely sea;   10
For many days in mourning, hair unkempt,
    She sat complaining to the cruel salt waves,
And though she'd never see him more, felt sorry for him,
    Remembering their long happiness: 14
Nor like Hypsípyle—when winds swept Jason off,   17
    Distraught, immobile in her empty bower,   18
Hypsípyle thereafter felt no other love,   19
    Pining only for her Haemonian guest.   20
Evadne, proud to burn on her poor husband's pyre,   21
    Died a paragon of Argive purity.   22
Alphesiboea to avenge a husband killed her brothers,   15
    Breaking blood's precious bond for love.   16
Could none of these inspire you to amend your ways   23
    That you too might become a legend?   24

Say nothing, Cynthia, now to recall your perjury;   25
    Beware of arousing forgetful Gods.
Alas, too reckless you would suffer at my peril,
    Should any harm befall you.
Rivers will cease to flow into the sea,
    Seasons of the year run in reverse,   30
Before my heart's concern for you could alter.
    Be what you will, I should never leave you.

You must not hold so cheap those eyes of yours
    Which pass off treason as my truth.
You swore by them that if you told a lie   35
    They'd drop out into your hands,
And can you raise them now to the great Sun-God
    Without one tremor of guilt?
Who forced you to turn pale so variously
    And those reluctant eyes to weep?   40
For them I'm dying now, and warning fellow lovers
    'O it's unsafe to trust sweet words!'

P is alone at night a
Cynthia is with another

16

A house-door complains

'Long ago I've stood wide open for great Triumphs,
    A door famed for Tarpeian chastity,
Whose threshold, wet with prisoners' suppliant tears,
    Gilded chariots celebrated.
Now I must often groan, disfigured by nocturnal   5
    Drunken brawls and thumped by vulgar fists.
And all the time disgraceful garlands hang upon me,
    And torches, exclusion's token, lie around.

I cannot guard my mistress from unsavoury nights,
    My noble self being subject to graffiti.   10
Nor does she stop to think of reputation, living
    More loosely than even our time's permissiveness.
What's more, I'm forced to weep and wail in sympathy
    With a suppliant's long nights of watching.
He never gives my doorposts any peace, singing   15
    Over and over this whining serenade:

"Door, crueller by far than even your mistress' self,
    Why with hard panels closed to me and silent?
Why are you never unbarred to admit my love
    Or moved to deliver clandestine pleas?   20
Will never an end be vouchsafed to my pain, and must
    I sleep in disgrace on this lukewarm threshold?

poets complaints directly to the door & indirectly to Cynthia

Midnights and full moons and breezes that dawn frost chills
   Feel sorry for me lying here.
You only, never pitying human pain,   25
   Answer me back with silent hinges.

If only my feeble voice could enter through that crack
   And find a way to strike my mistress' ear!
Be she more cusséd than Sicanian rock,
   Harder be she than iron and steel,   30
Yet surely she could not remain dry-eyed
   And would heave a sigh in reluctant tears.
But now she lies in the lucky arms of another man,
   While I waste words on the midnight wind.

You, door, my only, you my greatest cause of pain,   35
   Are never taken with my gifts.
My tongue has never shocked you with immodest words
   Uttered when drunk in angry jest,
That you should let me whine on here until I'm hoarse,
   Keeping tormented vigil in the street.   40
No, I have often spun you a song in modern verse
   And, kneeling, pressed kisses on your steps.
You traitor, many a time I've turned in homage toward you
   And secretly paid the vows I owed."

With this and much else typical of wretched lovers   45
   He tries to drown the birds' dawn chorus.
So now, for a lady's faults and a lover's endless weeping,
   I'm the lasting butt of malicious gossip.'

17 & 18 Propertius is alone & away from Cynthia

In a storm at <u>sea</u>

And serve me right for having run away from her
   That I'm now haranguing lonely halcyons,
Nor will Cassiópe see my keel safe harboured   ** he travels eastwards*
   And all my vows are wasted on thankless sand!

Why, Cynthia, in your absence the waves take your part!   5
   Look how the gale howls cruel threats!
Is there no chance of the storm abating?
   Will that patch of sand cover my corpse?
Change cruel reproaches for the better, and take night
   And treacherous shoals as punishment enough.   10
Will you, dry-eyed, be able to ask about my fate
   And never hold my bones to your breast?

Ah perish whoever first constructed hull and sail
   And voyaged the unwilling deep!
Was it not lighter work to weather a mistress' moods   15
   (However heartless, she was peerless still)
Than thus to gaze on a shoreline flanked by unknown forest
   And pray hard for the Tyndarids?

There, if some fate had entombed my sorrow
   And the last stone stood over buried love,   20
She would have offered her dear hair at my funeral
   And laid the bones gently on rose petals.
She would have cried my name over the final dust
   That earth might be weightless upon me.

But you, the deep-sea daughters of shapely Doris,   25
   In happy dance unfurl white sails:
If ever Love, in transit, touched your waves,
   Grant a fellow-sufferer safe landing.

18

In a lonely place

Yes, this lonely place will hush up my complaining;
   The grove is Zephyrus' empty property.
Here one can safely voice unspoken sorrows,
   If solitary rocks can keep a secret.

To what shall I first trace, my Cynthia, your disdain?   5
   Where, Cynthia, do I begin to weep?

I who was lately numbered among the lucky lovers
    Must now incur a black mark in your love.
Where is my guilt? What (slander) changes you toward me?
    That I've taken a new girl to make you jealous? 10
So come you back to me, light as you are: no other
    Woman's pretty feet have crossed my threshold.
This suffering of mine may owe you many a hurt,
    Yet I could never feel such savage anger
As justified your being mad at me and made 15
    Your bright eyes dull with flooding tears.

Or do you count my change of colour a paltry symptom?
    Does no devotion cry out from my face?
If trees can know love, they shall be witnesses—
    Beech and pine that's friend to Arcadia's God. 20
Ah, in their tender shade how often my words echo
    And written on their bark is *Cynthia*. = on bark on tree

Or is it that your cruelty breeds in me resentment,
    Only divulged to your silent door?
I am used to bear timidly all your decrees, 25
    Not to lamenting shrilly at what you do,
And in return am given sacred springs, cold cliffs,
    Hard resting on rough paths;
And every tale of woe I have to utter
    Must be told in solitude to shrill birds. 30

Yet, be as you will, the woods for me shall echo *Cynthia*
    And the lonely rocks repeat your name.

19

It is not death he fears

1 & 19 are opposites

It's not that I'm scared, my Cynthia, of the Underworld death
    Or mind fate's debt to the final pyre,
But the fear that when dead I may lose your love
    Is worse than the funeral itself.
Not so lightly has the Boy clung to our eyes 5
    That with love forgotten my dust could rest.

morbid mood but he is at peace with her.

There, in the unseen world, Phylácides the hero
  Could not forget his lovely wife,
But eager to clutch delight with disappointed hands
  Came as a ghost to his old home Thessaly.   10
There, whatever I am, I shall ever be called your shadow;
  Great love can cross even the shores of fate.

END?

There let them come in troops, the beautiful heroines
  Picked by Argives from the spoils of Troy,
No beauty of theirs for me could match yours, Cynthia—   15
  Indeed (may Mother Earth in justice grant it)
Though fate remand you to a long old age,
  Yet to my tears will your bones be dear.

If only the living you could feel this for my ashes,
  Then death, wherever, for me would have no sting.   20
Ah Cynthia, how I fear that love's iniquity
  Scorning the tomb may drag you from my dust
And force you, though loth, to dry the falling tears;
  A faithful girl can be bent by constant threats.

So while we may let us delight in loving; } *Good end*   25
  No love is ever long enough.

20-22 = no connection with Cynthia or hetrosexual love at all

20 - 22

Hercules and Hylas: a warning

Ansceston

For lasting love's sake, Gallus, we give you this advice
  (Let it not slip a heedless mind):
'Often bad luck befalls the lover unaware'—
  Cruel Ascanius could have told the Minyae.

adresto Gallus

You have a flame most like Theiódamas' son Hylas,   5
  No less in looks, no different in name.
Whether you pass by Anio's shady-wooded stream
  Or dip your feet in its ripples
Or promenade the beach along the Giants' Coast *seaside*
  Or anywhere a stream gives wayward welcome,   10

beach resort

Protect him always from Nymphs' greedy ravages
   (Ausonian Dryads are no less amorous)
Lest you be haunting rugged mountains, Gallus,
   And icy rocks and untried pools—
What Hercules' wretched wandering suffered on foreign shores   15
   And wept by wild Ascanius.

For long ago, they say, from docks at Pagasa
   Argo set sail for distant Phasis,
And gliding on, Athamantis' waves already passed,
   Found mooring at the Mysian rocks.   20
Here the band of heroes, halting on calm shore,
   Cover soft sand with gathered leaves.
Meanwhile the unconquered youth's attendant went ahead
   To fetch rare water from a special spring.

Myth

Pursuing him two brothers, breed of Aquilo,   25
   Above him Zetes and above him Cálaïs
Hovered with dangling hands to steal kisses and give
   Upward kisses in alternate flight.
He, bending down, protects himself beneath their wing-tips
   And with a branch drives off the airborne ambush.   30
So Pandionian Orithyia's brood departed:
   Ah grief! Hylas was going, going to the Hamadryads.

Here, beneath Arganthus' peak, was the spring Pege,
   A damp home dear to Thynian Nymphs,
Above which hung, indebted to no tending,   35
   Dewy fruit on forsaken trees,
And round them, in a water-meadow, lilies grew
   Tall and white among crimson poppies,
Which now he nips off childishly with tender nail,
   Preferring flowers to the task before him,   40
And now leans over the pretty waves unwarily,
   Prolonging truancy with flattering reflexions.

At last he dips his hands, ready to draw from the stream,
   Leaning on right shoulder as he filled up,
When, fired by its whiteness, the Dryad maids in admiration   45
   Left their customary dances

Theocratis 13 Subject, Structure theocrates 11.

※ LINKS TO CATTULUS ※ PARALELL

68 = his brother who dies in Troy], going eastwards
share a poem with love

And lightly drew him down head first in yielding water;
　　At his body's rape then Hylas gave a cry.
Far off repeatedly Alcides answers, but
　　From the distant spring the breeze returns the name.　　50

※ By this advised, O Gallus, you will guard your love,
　　For I've seen you trust fair Hylas to the Nymphs.

21 & 22 linked

A dead kinsman of the poet speaks

Adresses someone he knows

'You who hurry to avoid a kindred fate,
　　Wounded soldier from the Etruscan lines,
Why at my groan do you roll those bulging eyes?
　　※ I am your closest fellow-campaigner.

leads to speculation.

So may your parents celebrate your safe return;　　5
　　Let your sister learn what happened from your tears:
That I, Gallus, rescued from the midst of Caesar's swords,
　　Failed to escape from hands unknown;　　DEATH
And of all the scattered bones she finds on Etruscan hills,
　　Let her know that these are mine.'　　10

mysterious but highly specific circumstances

22

The poet's birthplace and his loss

SPHRAGIS
"this is mine stamp"
1st poem

You ask my rank and birth and my Penates, Tullus,
　　In the name of our enduring friendship.
If the Perusine graves of our fatherland are known to you,
　　The dead of Italy's troubled times
When Rome's dissension drove her citizens to ruin,　　5
　　(But specially to me, Etruscan dust, the grief:
It was you allowed my kinsman's limbs to lie outcast,　　same as 21.
　　It was you refused his poor bones burial)
Umbria, next adjoining on the plain below,　　= ?
　　A fertile land, deep-breasted, bore me.　　10

Fighting at Perusia 4140 (look a decade after)

remove characters from world of LOVE & connect them harshly
with historical events (familiar to reader, politically sensitive)

BOOK II

I

He is fated to write love poetry

You ask me how it is I write so often of love
    And how my verses come soft on the tongue.
These no Apollo, no Calliope sings to me;
    My only inspiration is a girl.
Suppose she steps out glittering in silks from Cos,   5
    Her Coan gown speaks a whole volume.
Suppose I spot an errant ringlet on her brow,
    Praise of the lock makes her walk taller.
Suppose her ivory fingers strike a tune on the lyre,
    I marvel at her hand's deft pressure.   10
Or if she closes eyelids exigent for sleep
    I have a thousand new ideas for poems.
Or if, stripped of her dress, she wrestles with me naked,
    Why then we pile up lengthy *Iliads*.
Whatever she may do, whatever she can say,   15
    A saga's born, a big one, out of nothing.

But if the Fates, Maecenas, had given me the power
    To lead heroic troops to war,
I would not sing of Titans and Ossa on Olympus
    Piled for Pelion to make a sky-road,   20
Or ancient Thebes or Pergama of Homeric fame
    Or the joining of two seas at Xerxes' order,
Or Remus' first realm or the pride of lofty Carthage,
    The Cimbrian menace and Marius' good deeds:
No, I'd record your Caesar's wars and works, and you   25
    Would be the second theme to mighty Caesar.

For when I sang of Mutina or Rome's graveyard Philippi
    Or the war at sea with Sicilian refugees
And the overthrow of the hearths of the old Etruscan race
    And the captured shores of Ptolemaic Pharos   30

Or of Egypt when the Nile was dragged into the city
    And limped along, his seven channels captive,
Or of gold fetters clinking on the necks of kings
    And Actian prows sailing the Sacred Way,
My Muse would always weave yourself into these exploits,   35
    A headman true alike in peace and war.
On earth Achilles and in Hades Theseus witness,
    One to Menoetius' son, the other to Ixion's.

* * * * *

But those Phlegréan broils of Jove and Enceladus
    Thunder not from Callimachus' narrow breast,   40
Nor have I the heart to trace back Caesar's name
    In rugged verse to Phrygian ancestors.
The sailor talks of squalls, the ploughman of his oxen;
    The soldier counts his wounds, the shepherd sheep:
But we engage in battles on a narrow bed.   45
    We should all rub along in our own way.

It's glorious to die for love, and glorious to be granted
    One to enjoy. O may none but I enjoy my love!
She's quick, as I recall, to criticize light girls
    And faults the *Iliad* because of Helen.   50
Even if I had to touch stepmother Phaedra's potions,
    Potions unable to harm her stepson,
Even if I had to perish by Circe's poisons, or
    The Colchic cauldron boiled me on Iolcan fires,
As there's one only woman robbed me of my senses   55
    It's out of *her* house I'll be carried feet first.

Medicine can heal all merely human ailments;
    Love alone hates the pathologist.
Machaon healed the crippled leg of Philoctetes,
    Chiron Phillyrides the eyes of Phoenix.   60
The Epidaurian God with Cretan herbs restored
    Dead Andrógeon to his father's hearth.
The Mysian youth when wounded by Achilles' spear
    Found that the selfsame spear could cure him.
But were there a man could rid me of this vice of mine   65
    He'd be the man to hand Tantalus fruit,
The man to fill the large vat from those virgin urns,

Lifting the liquid load from tender necks,
To liberate Prometheus' arms from the Caucasian
    Crag and drive the vulture from his heart. 70

Therefore whenever Fate calls in my loan of life
    And I am shrunk to a name in modest marble,
Maecenas, you the hope and envy of our youth,
    In life and death my rightful pride,
If you should chance to take the road that flanks my tomb 75
    Halt your British gig with its engraved yoke
And over my dumb ashes shed a tear and say
    'A heartless girl was this poor fellow's fate.'

2

A description of Cynthia

I spoke my mind, planning to live and sleep single,
    But after the armistice Love double-crossed me.
How is it such human beauty lingers here on earth?
    I can forgive Jove's early lapses.

Red-gold hair, long hands, big build—she moves like 5
    Juno, fit sibling for Jove himself,
Like Pallas pacing by Dulichian altars,
    Breasts covered by the snake-haired Gorgon;
Or like Ischómache, the Lapith heroine,
    Sweet spoil for Centaurs at their wine, 10
Or virgin Brimo who lay with Mercury, we learn,
    By the waters of Boebéis.

Make way now, Goddesses whom once a shepherd saw
    Stripping on Ida's peak!
O may old age refuse to mar her beauty 15
    Though she live for the Sibyl's centuries!

3

She is irresistible

'Despite your boast that now no girl could hurt you
   You're stuck. Your pride has had a fall.
Poor wretch, you've hardly managed one month's relaxation
   And a second volume of your shame is promised.'
Yes, I tried to learn if fish could live on dry sand   5
   And wild boar in mid-ocean,
Or if I could spend sleepless nights in serious study:
   Love can be deferred but never dropped.

It's not so much the face, fair as it is, that caught me
   (Lilies are no whiter than my mistress;   10
Picture Maeotian snow vying with Spain's vermilion,
   And rose petals floating on pure milk;)
Nor the well-groomed hair rippling over that smooth neck,
   Nor the eyes, those twin flares, my stars,
Nor when she shimmers in Arabian silk   15
   (No, as a lover I'm hard to please),
But that she dances beautifully when Iacchus is served,
   Like Ariadne leading a troop of Maenads,
And that with Aeolian plectrum she tries out tunes,
   Her skill a match for Aganippe's lyre,   20
And that she sets her own against classic Corinna's writings
   And thinks Corinna's not up to her own.

When you were born, my life, in those first days did not
   Radiant Love wish you luck with a sneeze?
Those heavenly gifts, the Gods bestowed them on you;   25
   You must not think your mother gave them.
No, no, such gifts are not of human origin;
   Ten lunar months could not produce them.
You have been born unique, the glory of Roman girls—
   Helen's beauty returns in you to the world.   32
Nor will you always visit mortal beds with us;
   You'll be first Roman girl to lie with Jove.   30

Small wonder then that she has set our youth aflame.
    Troy had better have fallen for her.
I marvelled once that a girl could cause so great a war   35
    At Pergama between Europe and Asia.
Now I think Paris wise, and Menelaus too—
    The one for asking, the second for refusing.
Fitting it was that Achilles die for such a face,
    And Priam find it just cause of war.   40
Should any painter seek fame greater than the old masters'
    Let him take my mistress as his model.
Then if he shows her in the West or the Orient
    He'll set the Orient and the West ablaze.
This be my limit, here let me stay—or if a fiercer   45
    Love attack me, let me die!

Just as a bull will fight at first against the plough,
    Then used to the yoke go gentle to the field,
So wild young men in love at first play up
    But when tamed endure both fair and foul.   50
The seer Melampus bore the shame of manacles,
    Found guilty of stealing Iphiclus' cattle;
It was not greed but lovely Pero made him do it,
    A future bride in Amythaon's house.

4

Girls torment their lovers; boys are kind

First you are bound to complain of your mistress' many offences,
    Often to ask for something, often to be refused,
And often to bite your undeserving nails
    And to tap your foot in angry suspense.
I plastered unguents on my hair and sauntered   5
    Pompously along—to no avail.

No herbs can help you here, no midnight sorceress,
    No simples mixed by Perimedë.
We can observe no cause and no visible wound
    But where such troubles come from is a mystery.   10

This patient needs no doctors and no restful bed;
  It's not the season or the air that harms him.
He's up, and suddenly friends marvel at a corpse!
  So unpredictable what they call 'love'.
What fortune-teller has not lied at my expense?   15
  What hag not weighed my dreams a dozen times?

I wish all enemies of mine could love a girl
  And any friend enjoy a boy.
Calmly downstream you glide in a safe rowing-boat.
  What wave off so small a shore can harm you?   20
A single word will often alter a boy's mood
  But a girl will hardly come round though you bleed.

5

A warning to Cynthia

Is this fair, Cynthia? You're the talk of Rome?
  Your life's a public scandal?
Have I deserved such treatment? Traitor, I'll make you pay.
  I too can sail off, Cynthia,
And among so many fickle yet find one   5
  Who wants my verse to give her fame,
Who will not trample on me callously, but make you
  Jealous. Too late you'll weep, my long belovèd.

Now, while anger's fresh, now is the time to part:
  When the pain's over, love returns.   10
Carpathian waves are not so various in north winds
  Nor black clouds shift in fitful southern gales
So easily as angry lovers change at a word:
  Then, while you may, shake off the unjust yoke.
You'll find it painful—yes, for the first night.   15
  Love's pains are light if you accept them.

But, life of mine, by the sweet rights of Lady Juno,
  Don't harm yourself with your own arrogance.
Not only bulls with curling horns attack the foe,

But even sheep when hurt fight back. 20
I would not rip the dress from off your perjured body
   Nor in my anger break down your locked door,
Nor would I dare to disarrange your braided hair
   Or cruelly manhandle you.
Some peasant can engage in such disgraceful brawls, 25
   Whose head's uncrowned by the ivy garland.
No, I shall write what long as you live you'll never live down:
   'Cynthia's fair-faced, Cynthia's false.'
Believe me, Cynthia, though you scorn the buzz of Fame,
   You'll blanch at this one line. 30

6

Jealousy and pornographic pictures

Less crowded was the house of Ephyréan Lais
   Before whose door all Greece lay down;
Not such a multitude besieged Menander's Thais,
   With whom Erichthon's folk had fun,
And Phryne, able to rebuild the ruins of Thebes, 5
   Was blessed with wealth by fewer lovers.
Besides, you often pass off strangers as your kin
   When there's no lack of relatives to kiss you.

Young men, their portraits, mention of their names, and even
   A babe in arms can cause me hurt, 10
So too your mother if she kisses you too much,
   Your sister, any girl-friend sleeping with you.
Everything hurts me. I feel threatened (forgive my fears)
   And suspect a man under every dress.

In the past, we're told, such faults would lead to fighting. 15
   One sees they caused the casualties at Troy.
The self-same madness drove Centaurs to smash embossed
   Wine-cups on Piríthoüs' head.
But why cite Greek examples? It was you, Romulus,
   The she-wolf's nursling, sanctioned felony. 20
You licensed that unpunished rape of Sabine girls,

And now in Rome Love sticks at nothing.
Lucky Admetus' wife, lucky Ulysses' bed,
   And every woman who loves her man's home.
Temples to Chastity, what good are they to girls   25
   If any bride can be anybody's?   26
But with good reason cobwebs canopy her shrine   35
   And weeds overwhelm neglected Gods.   36

The hand that painted the first pornographic pictures   27
   And put disgraceful sights in chaste homes
Thereby depraved the innocent eyes of free-born girls
   And made them share its own corruption.   30
Ah, let them groan in darkness whose crude art profaned
   The mysteries mute ecstasy concealed.
In old days ceilings were not garnished with such figures,
   Walls not frescoed with obscenities.   34

So what guard could I set and what door lock on you   37
   That foot of foe could never overstep?
Strict watch on an unwilling woman is no good;
   She who's ashamed to sin is safe enough, Cynthia.   40
No wife, no girl-friend ever shall lead me astray;
   Always you'll be girl-friend and always wife to me.

7

A proposed law withdrawn

Cynthia, how pleased you were when that law was withdrawn
   Whose issue some time since caused both of us to weep
Long, lest it part us—though to separate two lovers
   Not even Jove has power against their will.
'And yet Caesar is great.' Yes, Caesar is great in war,   5
   But conquered nations mean nothing in love.

I'd sooner let this head be parted from my shoulders
   Than lose love's torches at a bride's behest
Or as a bridegroom pass your closed door, looking back
   At my betrayal with tear-filled eyes.   10

Ah, to what slumbers would my wedding-flute then play you,
    Flute mournfuller than funeral trumpet!
Why should I breed sons for our country's Triumphs?
    From blood of mine shall come no soldier.

But were I truly serving, with the colours of my mistress,   15
    Castor's horse would not step high enough for me.
For it is from her my glory earned so great a name,
    Glory that has spread to frozen Borysthenes.
Cynthia, I love you only, may you love only me;
    Such love is worth even more than fatherhood.   20

8

He contemplates suicide and murder

I'm being robbed of the girl for so long dear to me
    And you, my friend, forbid me to shed tears?
No enmities but those of love are rancorous;
    Try murdering me, I'll be a gentler foe.
How can I bear to see her in another's arms?   5
    Once known as mine shall she be called his now?
Everything changes. Certainly loves change.
    You win or lose as love's wheel turns.
The great have often fallen—great captains and great kings;
    Thebes was a power once and Troy a city.   10
How many presents I gave! What poems I composed!
    But she was iron—she never said 'I love you'.

Was I really fool enough over so many years
    To put up, selfish girl, with you and yours?
Have you ever thought of me as free, or will you always   15
    Hurl at my head arrogant words?

Well, Propertius, will you die like this in your first youth?
    Die then. Let her revel in your ruin.
Let her torment my spirit, persecute my shade,
    Jump on my pyre and trample on my bones.   20
At Antigone's tomb did not Boeotian Haemon

Fall dead, wounded by his own sword,
And mix his bones with those of the poor girl
    Without whom he would not go home to Thebes?

But you shall not escape; you have to die with me.   25
    The blood of both shall drip from this same blade.
Though such a death for me will be dishonourable,
    I'll die dishonoured to make sure you die.

After his sweetheart was abducted lonely Achilles
    Let his weapons lie idle in his hut.   30
He saw the Achaeans cut down in flight along the shore,
    The Doric camp ablaze with Hector's torches;
He saw Patroclus' mutilated body sprawled
    In the dust, his hair matted with blood;
All this he bore for beautiful Briseis' sake;   35
    So cruel the pain when love is wrenched away.
But after late amends restored the captive to him
    He dragged brave Hector behind Thessalian steeds.
As I am far inferior both in birth and battle,
    No wonder love can triumph over me!   40

9

He prays to die of love and curses his rival

What *he* is *I*'ve been—often. But perhaps within the hour
    She'll drop him too for another dearer.

For twice ten years Penelope could live secure,
    Deserving of so many suitors;
She could postpone re-marriage by Minerva's guile,   5
    Unravelling at night the day's weaving;
And though expecting never again to see Ulysses
    She stayed true—grew old waiting for him.
Briseis too, embracing lifeless Achilles,
    Tore her fair cheeks with frenzied fingers.   10
A prisoner in mourning, she washed her blood-stained lord
    Beside the sandy pools of Simois,

Threw dust on her hair and lifted in her little hands
   The huge bones of great Achilles.
For Peleus was not there, nor your blue-eyed mother,   15
   Nor Deidamia the widowed Scyrian.
Then Greece was therefore blessed with true brides;
   Then honour prospered, even in war.

But you could not lie idle for a single night,
   Faithless, nor be alone for a single day!   20
No, you two drank your wine amid much laughter
   And maybe slander against me.
This is the man who left you once, and still you want him.
   I wish you joy of your infatuation.
Was it for this I made those vows for your recovery   25
   When the waters of Styx had gone over your head,
And we, your friends, were standing round the bed in tears?
   Who was he then, and where, you traitor?
Suppose I were a soldier in far-off India
   Or my ship were becalmed at sea?   30

But it's easy for you to lie and scheme. Such work
   Is the one thing women always learn.
The Syrtes are not shifted by the fickle breeze
   Nor do leaves shiver in the stormy south wind
So fast as an angry woman breaks her word,   35
   Whether for weighty or petty reason.
Now, as you have made your mind up, I'll give in.
   Boy Cupids, please choose sharper darts.
Compete to shoot and take away this life of mine!
   My blood will be a fine prize for you.   40
Stars are my witness and the frosts of early morning
   And the front door slily opened to wretched me:
Nothing in life for me was more precious than you,
   Nor will be now, despite your enmity.
No other mistress shall set body on my bed;   45
   I'll be alone, since I cannot be yours.

But how I wish, if I have faithfully lived out my years,
   That man could turn to stone while making love.
The Theban princes, with their mother as spectator,

Did not die for a throne beneath cruel weapons sooner   50
Than I, if I could fight, with my girl as spectator,
Would welcome death in return for your death.

10

It's time to sing of Caesar

But it's time to circle Helicon with other dances;
Time now to give Haemonian horse the field.
I am eager now to mention squadrons strong in battle
And to tell of my leader's Roman campaigns.
If strength be lacking, surely ambition will be praised;   5
The intention in great matters is enough.
Let first youth sing of Venus, last of civil strife.
As my girl is written up, I'll sing of wars.
I wish now to proceed more gravely, eyebrows raised;
My Muse teaches me now a different cithara.   10

Mount upward, spirit. Clothe yourselves in strength, my songs.
Pierides, one now needs a big mouth.
Euphrates now refuses to guard the Parthian rider's
Rear and regrets detaining Crassus.
Even India bows her neck, Augustus, to your Triumph   15
And unexplored Arabia quakes before you.
Whatever land retreats to the edges of the world,
Later defeated let it feel your hand.
This is the line I'll follow, becoming through your lines
A great poet. Fate keep that day for me.   20

As, when one cannot reach the head of a great statue,
One lays a garland at its feet,
So we today, powerless to mount the chariot of praise,
Bring cheap incense, the poor man's offering.
As yet my songs are ignorant of Ascra's fountain;   25
Love has just dipped them in Permessus' stream.

II

A threat to Cynthia

Others can write about you, or you can stay unknown:
    To praise you is to sow barren ground.
You and all those gifts, believe you me, one couch
    Shall carry off at last on death's black day,
And passers-by will disregard your bones, not saying   5
    'These ashes once were a clever girl'.

12

Love's picture interpreted

Whoever he was who painted Love as a child
    Don't you think he had marvellous hands?
First he saw that lovers live senselessly
    And that light passions lose great goods.

Nor was he mistaken in adding flighty wings   5
    And making him a God who flies from human hearts;
For we are tossed about on alternating waves
    And the breeze, for us, keeps changing direction.

Rightly too is Love's hand armed with barbed arrows
    And a Cretan quiver hangs down from each shoulder: 10
For he strikes while we're off guard, before we see the foe,
    And after that wound no one is well.

For me his darts are there and the childish form is there
    But certainly he has lost his wings,
Because, alas, he never flies off from my heart   15
    But makes me bleed in his continual warfare,

Do you really enjoy living in marrow drained dry?
    For goodness' sake transfer your warfare elsewhere.

You had better attack the heart-whole with your poison.
  You are flogging not me but my feeble shadow.   20

If you destroy it, who will write this kind of verse—
  This light Muse of mine does you great honour—
And sing of the head and fingers and black eyes of a girl
  And the delicate movement of her feet, in sandals?

13

The poet's ambition. He orders his funeral

Fewer Achaemenid arrows defend Susa
  Than Cupid has shot darts into my heart.
He forbade me to deride Muses so slender
  And told me to dwell thus in Ascra's grove,
Not that Pierian oaks should follow my words   5
  Or that I draw beasts from Ismarus' vale,
But rather that my verse should dumbfound Cynthia:
  I'd then be an artist more famous than Argive Linus.

I am no mere admirer of distinguished looks
  Or of a woman's pedigree;   10
I'd like to read my work in the lap of a clever girl
  And have it approved by faultless ears.
Should I succeed, farewell to society's babble;
  A mistress's verdict acquits me.
And if only she listens kindly as my friend,   15
  Then I can bear the enmity of Jove.

Whenever therefore death shall close my eyelids
  Let this be the order of my funeral:
No long cortège bearing ancestral images,
  No trumpet vainly bewailing my fate,   20
No couch with ivory fittings to carry me,
  Spread for my death with cloth of gold,
No line of incense-bearing platters, but the small-scale
  Rites of a plebeian funeral.
Procession enough for me if I have three slim volumes   25
  To bring as my best gift to Persephone.

But you must follow, tearing your naked breasts,
    Tirelessly calling my name,
Pressing the last kisses on my frozen lips
    And pouring Syrian unguent from full onyx.   30
Then when the heat below has turned me into ashes
    Let a small clay pot receive my spirit,
And above it plant a bay-tree on the narrow grave
    To shade the site of my burnt-out pyre,
And write there these two lines: 'Who now lies horrid dust   35
    Was once the slave of but one love.'
And this my tomb will grow to be as famous
    As the Phthian hero's bloody sepulchre.
You also, when white-haired you come to die, remember
    To come this way to the recording stone.   40
Meanwhile beware of slighting us the buried;
    Dust is conscious and can sense the truth.

If only one of the Sisters Three had decreed
    That I lay down my life in the cradle!
Why prolong breath for so uncertain an hour?   45
    Three generations passed before Nestor was ashes;
But had the doom of his long-lived old age been shortened
    By a soldier in the Trojan lines,
He had not seen the burial of Antilochus
    Or said 'O death, why come for me so late?'   50

Still you will weep at times for the friend whom you have lost;
    Always love is due to one's man who has passed away.
Witness a goddess, when the wild boar gored Adonis
    Hunting on the Idalian height;
He lay there, lovely, in the marshes, and you came   55
    To him, Venus, with streaming hair.
But, Cynthia, you will call back my dumb spirit in vain;
    My bits of bones will have nothing to say.

14

His triumph and the secret

Atrides' pride in his Dardanian triumph
    When Laomedon's great empire fell,
Ulysses' joy at the end of his wanderings
    When he touched Dulichia's dear shore,
Electra's when she saw her brother Orestes living   5
    While she was weeping over his false bones,
Ariadne's when she knew Theseus was safe, led back
    By flaxen thread from his Daedalian quest—
These joys were less keen than my rapture this past night;
    Another such will make me immortal.   10

Yet while I stooped and cringed in supplication
    I rated cheaper than a dried-up puddle.
But now she thwarts me no more with her stuck-up moods
    Nor sits there unmoved while I weep.
O if I'd only known it earlier, the secret!   15
    Now medicine comes when I'm a corpse.
Before my feet a path shone bright, but I was blind.
    In mad love no one can see straight.
This I have found works best: lovers must learn disdain;
    Then she'll consent today, though last night it was No.   20

Others could knock in vain, declare themselves her slaves;
    It was my lap that held her heedless head.
To me this victory means more than Parthia conquered,
    Than booty, captive kings, triumphal chariot.
Cythera's Queen, I'll hang great gifts up in your porch,   25
    Adding this couplet in my name:
'These prizes, Goddess, at your shrine Propertius offers,
    The lover with the night-long welcome.'

Yours now to decide, light of my life, if my laden ship
    Comes safe to shore or grounds upon a sandbank.   30
But if through any fault of mine you change towards me
    May I lie dead before your door.

15

A night of love

O lucky me! O dazzling night! And O you darling
   Bed beatified by my blisses!
What talk we had by lamplight!
   What battles in the dark!
Breasts naked, she would wrestle with me— then   5
   Stall by covering up.
She mouthed open my drowsy eyelids, saying
   'Time to get up, doormat.'
How various our embraces! How long
   My kisses lingered on your lips!   10

But moving blind spoils love-making;
   In love it's the eyes that lead.
Paris fell for Helen naked
   As she left Menelaus' bed.
Endymion naked caught Diana's eye   15
   And lay with the naked Goddess.

If you insist on going to bed clothed
   I shall use force and tear your dress.
Indeed, if anger pushes me beyond the limit,
   You'll have bruised arms to show your mother.   20
No drooping breasts as yet prevent you playing;
   Leave that worry to embarrassed mothers.
Let us sate our eyes with love while Fate allows.
   The long night comes and the day of no return.

If you would only bind us in this close embrace   25
   With a bond that time could never break!
Take doves paired off in love as model—
   Male and female a perfect match.
One's wrong to look for limits to love's madness;
   True love knows no bounds.   30

Earth will sooner frustrate farmers by breeding false,
    The Sun-God sooner drive black steeds,
Rivers call their waters back to source
    And fish dehydrate in dry ocean
Than I could shift my passion elsewhere;   35
    I'm hers alive, hers dead.
Should she grant me such nights now and then,
    A year will be a lifetime.
But granted many I'll be immortalized;
    One night can deify everyman.   40

If all were keen to engage in such a life
    And lie back, charging limbs with wine,
There'd be no cruel steel or men-of-war—no bones
    Of ours would welter in Actium's waves,
Nor Rome, beset so often by her own successes,   45
    Grow tired of loosening her hair in grief.
For this at least posterity can justly praise us:
    Our battles have not grieved the Gods.

Only don't *you*, while daylight lasts, forgo life's fruit;
    All your kisses are still too few.   50
For just as petals drop from fading garlands
    To float haphazard in wine-bowls,
So for us lovers who now walk so tall
    Tomorrow may bring the fated close.

16

The Praetor returns from Illyricum

The Praetor is lately back from Illyricum, Cynthia—
    For you a big prize, for me big trouble.
Why couldn't he have drowned beneath Ceraunian cliffs?
    Ah, Neptune, what gifts I'd have given you!
Now there are parties and lavish dinners—but not for me;   5
    Night-long the door stands open—but not to me.
So, if you're sensible, don't miss the proffered harvest
    And shear the stupid brute skin-close.

Then when he's poor and has no more to give
    Tell him to sail to fresh Illyrias.   10

Cynthia's not one to follow rank or care for honours;
    She always weighs up a lover's purse.
O Venus, help me now in my distress—
    Let non-stop lusting rupture him.
It seems that anyone with gifts can purchase love.   15
    Jove, my girl is ruined by shameful gain.
She sends me into Oceanus to look for pearls
    And bids me bring presents back from Tyre.

If only there were no rich men in Rome, and even
    Our leader lived in a reed hut!   20
No girl-friend then would ever sell herself for gifts
    But grow old with one lover.
Nor would you ever sleep apart for seven nights—
    Fair arms embracing so foul a man,
Not, you well know, through fault of mine, but because   25
    Beauty and frailty are commonly fast friends.

A barbarian marks time at the double, loins aquiver,
    And suddenly has the luck to rule my kingdom.
Look at the anguish Eriphyla found through gifts,
    At the torture that burnt the bride Creüsa!   30

Will no ill treatment serve to staunch my tears?
    Or is my passion tied to your faults?
It's many a long day since I enjoyed the theatre,
    The Campus Martius, or even my food.
'You should be ashamed!' Yes, certainly— but, as they say,   35
    Disreputable love is deaf.
Witness the leader who lately filled Actian seas
    With the empty clamour of doomed troops.
Base love commanded him to put his fleet about
    And run away to the world's end.   40
Caesar's worth and Caesar's glory, though, is this:
    His conquering hand buries the sword.

But all those gifts to you of clothes and emeralds
    And yellow olivine,

Let me see a whirlwind sweep them off into the void, 45
    Turning some to dust and some to water!
Jove does not always laugh at lovers' perjuries
    And calmly turn a deaf ear to their prayers.
You've seen the thunder rumbling round the sky
    And lightning leaping down from the ether: 50
That's not the Pleiads' doing or watery Orion's
    Nor does the lightning's fury fall for nothing.
At such times God is apt to punish perjured girls,
    For he also has wept and been deceived.
Therefore don't rate Sidonian purple so high 55
    That you're terrified when storm-clouds gather.

17

Cheated and locked out

Breaking a date, cheating a lover with promises—
    This way you'll stain your hands with blood. 2
Traitress, I'm tempted to hurl myself from hard rock 13
    Or lay my hands on pounded poison. 14

Such is my song of woe as often as I'm left 3
    To bide a bitter night racked in the double bed.
You may pity Tantalus' fate in the stream 5
    That teases his dry-throated thirst.
You may marvel at Sisyphus' endurance
    As he rolls his awkward load uphill.
But in this world there's no life harder than a lover's,
    None a wise man would wish for less. 10

Not long ago admiring envy called me lucky,
    But now I'm hardly admitted once a fortnight— 12
Not even allowed to lie in the road by dry moonlight 15
    Or speak through a crack in the door. 16
But in spite of this I'll take care not to change my mistress;
    One day she'll see how true I've been and weep.

18A

Better not complain

Continual complaints make many hated
  But women are disarmed by a silent man.
Always deny it if you've seen something;
  Always deny it if you've been hurt.

18B

Contrast Aurora's love for Tithonus

What if my time of life were glossed with white-haired years   5
  And weary wrinkles gashed my cheeks?
Aurora never spurned the old age of Tithonus
  Or let him sleep alone in their eastern home.

Her duty done, she'd often hug and fondle him
  Before she unyoked and rubbed down her horses,   10
And when on India's verge she slept with arms around him
  She'd grumble that the day returned again too soon.
Mounting her car she'd call the Gods unfair
  And pay the world reluctant duty.
The life of old Tithonus gave her more delight   15
  Than Memnon's loss gave sorrow.

To sleep with an old man did not shame such a girl
  Or to lavish kisses on white hair.
But you hate me while I'm still young, traitress, though soon
  You'll be a bent old woman yourself.   20

Why don't I worry less? It's often Cupid's way
  First to be good to one and then unkind.

18C

Hair-dyeing iniquitous

Are you now mad enough to copy woaded Britons
    And fool around with exotic hair-dye?
Every feature is right as Nature made it;   25
    Belgic dye on a Roman head looks wrong.

In Hades woe betide the foolish girl
    Who cheats by doctoring her hair!
Stop it, for my sake. You can look lovely as you are.
    For me you're lovely enough if you come often.   30
If so-and-so were to dye her hair unheard-of blue
    Does that make blue good form?

Since you have no brother and no son, only
    Let me be your son and brother.
Let your own couch keep guard upon your honour   35
    And don't sit around with too ornate a hair-do.
Give me no cause to credit gossip about you;
    Scandal leaps over land and sea.

19

Cynthia in the country

Although you're leaving Rome against my wishes, Cynthia,
    I'm glad you'll be in rural isolation.
Clean fields will harbour no youthful seducer
    To tempt your virtue with sweet words.
There'll be no brawling underneath your window,   5
    No shouting of your name to spoil your sleep.

You'll be alone with nothing to see but lonely hills,
    Cattle, and small farms, Cynthia.
No public shows there to seduce you, or

Temples that so often excuse your sins. 10
Nothing to watch but oxen ploughing
    And vines being shorn by skilled sickles.
Once in a while at some rough shrine you'll offer incense
    When a kid is killed at the rustic altar;
And afterwards bare-legged you'll copy country dances 15
    Provided no strange men are present.

Myself, I'll take up hunting. I'm keen now to perform
    Diana's rites and break my vows to Venus.
I'll learn to net wild beasts, to dedicate their horns
    On pinetrees and control the eager hounds. 20
Not that I'd dare to take on huge lions
    Or get to hasty grips with wild boar.
Daring, for me, would be to net innocuous hares
    Or fix birds with extending lime-rod,
Where with his sacred woods Clitumnus overlays 25
    The lovely stream and washes cattle white.

Whenever you are tempted, life of mine, remember
    That a few Morning-Stars will lead me to you.
But neither lonely woods nor wandering streams that pour
    Down moss-grown screes can stop me while I'm here 30
From fearing that your fame will be on every tongue;
    To hurt the absent is a human weakness.

20

Ever faithful

Why weep more sore than kidnapped Briseis? Why weep
    More bitterly than captive Andromache?
Why tire the Gods with these wild tales of my deceit?
    Why charge me thus with broken faith?
Not so with nightly lamentation does the sombre 5
    Attic bird clamour in Cecrops' leaves,
Nor Niobe, whose pride brought twice six to the grave,
    So rain down tears from troubled Sipylos.

Suppose my arms fast bound in brazen bonds
    And you in Danaë's house a captive,   10
For you, my life, I'd even burst those brazen fetters
    And leap into Danaë's iron-clad house.

All tales of you are told to my deaf ears.
    Never you doubt that I'm in earnest.
By mother's bones I swear to you, and father's bones,   15
    (If I lie, alas, may their ashes punish me)
Yours I shall remain, my life, till the final dark;
    One faith, one day, shall carry us both off.

And if neither your name nor your beauty could hold me,
    Your gentle discipline would do it.   20
Now the full moon completes her seventh orbit
    Since you and I have been street-corner talk.
Meanwhile not seldom has your door been kind to me,
    Your bed not seldom welcoming.

Nor have I purchased any night with costly gifts;   25
    For what I have been all thanks to your goodwill.
Though many wanted you, you only wanted me.
    Can I forget your kindness—ever?
That day, you Tragic Furies, persecute me,
    And Aeacus, judge of the dead, condemn me—   30
Yes, sentence me to wander among Títyos' vultures
    And roll the stone of Sisyphus.

No need to honour me with letters of entreaty;
    From first to last you'll find me faithful.
This is my prescriptive title: the only lover   35
    Not to start blindly or lightly end.

21

Panthus a liar

Ah, for the lies you've read about me on Panthus' page
    May Venus pay him back with equal hate!
But now you find me a truer prophet than Dodona:
    Your lover-boy has taken a wife.

So many wasted nights! How shaming! Look, he flaunts 5
  His freedom, while you, the dupe, sleep single.

Together they talk about you, His Arrogance maintaining
  He'd often been with you against his will.
I'm damned if all he wanted wasn't to boast about you;
  That way, as husband, he gets kudos. 10
So Jason once deceived his Colchian protectress;
  Out she went when Creüsa caught him.
So too was Calypso cheated by the young Dulichian—
  She saw her lover sail away.

Let girls who lend an ear, alas, too easily, 15
  Learn from desertion to be cautious.
Even she, though,—can you beat it?—has long looked for another;
  After your first folly you should take more care.
But as for me, in every place and all the time,
  In sickness and in health, I'm with you still. 20

22A

'One girl is not enough'

You know how many girls I fell for yesterday;
  You know what trouble comes my way, Demóphoön.
My feet can traverse no piazza unrewarded.
  Oh, public shows—they're given to ruin me,
Whenever a dancer parts pale arms in invitation 5
  Or a flute-girl plays a tuneful medley.
And all the while my eyes are seeking to be wounded
  By a pretty girl in the audience with bare breast
Or wandering curls adrift on a smooth forehead,
  Clasped at the crown by an Indian gem. 10
But if she turned me down with an unfriendly stare
  Cold sweat would break out on my brow.

You ask, Demophoon, why I am so susceptible,
  But love can never answer the question *Why?*
Why do some folk slash themselves with sacred knives 15

Or whip themselves to mad Phrygian music?
To everyone at birth Nature allots a failing;
   Mine happens to be love, forever love.
Even if the fate of singer Thamyras befell me,
   I'd never be blind, my envious friend, to a pretty girl.   20

But if you think me undersized and skinny-limbed,
   You're mistaken; Venus' worship never tires one.
Investigate—you'll find that girls have often enjoyed
   My whole attentions all night long.
Jove for Alcmena's sake caused the Twin Bears to rest   25
   And heaven was two whole nights without its king.
But back he came as fresh as ever to his lightnings;
   Love never exhausts its own strength.
Think of Achilles when he left Briseis' arms—
   Did Phrygians stop running from his spear?   30
Or when fierce Hector rose from Andromache's bed
   Didn't Mycenae's ships fear battle?
Those heroes could demolish barriers and fleets;
   In my field I'm fierce Hector and Achilles.

See how the sky is served in turn by sun and moon.   35
   Likewise for me one girl is not enough.
One can embrace and cuddle me whenever
   The other has no room for me.
Or if one should lose her temper with my servant
   She can know there's another longing to be mine.   40
Two cables moor a vessel more securely;
   Twins cause a mother less anxiety.

22B

Love's sharpest hurt

Either say No if you're cruel, or, if you're not cruel, come.
   Why do you treat words too with contempt?
This is the sharpest hurt of all for any lover,   45
   When his hopes must accept her sudden backword.
How many sighs toss him from side to side of the bed

While he cannot admit that she will not come
And wearies his boy with questions, harping on what he has heard,
    Bidding him question the doom he dreads!   50

23

Call-girls are best

To me who would even avoid the unlettered public's paths
    Water fetched from a public cistern now tastes sweet.
Does any free man give another's slave a bribe
    To take a prior message to his mistress,
Or ask repeatedly 'What portico today   5
    Shelters her?' or 'In what park does she parade?',
Then, when you've undergone Hercules' famous labours,
    To have her write 'Is there a gift for me?'
For the privilege of seeing the face of her glum keeper
    And hiding, when caught out, in a filthy hovel?   10
At what cost once in a whole year your night comes round!
    Ah, death to the men who like locked doors!

By contrast, she who walks out free with cloak thrown back,
    Fenced by no fear of keepers is the one I fancy—
Whose muddy slippers wear away the Via Sacra   15
    And whom one can accost directly.
She'll never keep you waiting or talk you into giving
    What a tight-fisted father would deplore.
She'll not say 'Quick! I'm scared. Please get up now. Worse luck,
    My man's due back today from the country.'   20
Give me the girls Euphrates and Orontes send;
    No virtuous love-intrigues for me!
As every lover now must lose his liberty,
    Every would-be lover's a willing slave.

24A

He defends that choice

'Fine talk from you, when you're notorious for a book
　　And your *Cynthia*'s read throughout the Forum!'
These words would raise the sweat on any free man's brow;
　　The choice for him is decency or clandestine love.
Had Cynthia breathed upon *me* comparable favour,　　　　5
　　I wouldn't now be called the arch-debauchee
Or be so grossly slandered everywhere in Rome—
　　Despite my passion the pseudonym would have deceived.
So it's no wonder that I'm looking for cheap girls:
　　They cause less scandal. Surely a sound reason?　　　　10

　　　　　*　*　*　*　*

Sometimes she wants a fan made of proud peacock's feathers
　　And a cool crystal ball to hold in her hands
And sometimes wants me to bid for ivory dice
　　Or some flashy gift from the Via Sacra.
Oh I'm hanged if I grudge the expense, but now I'm ashamed　　15
　　To be the butt of a deceitful mistress!

24B

'There's nothing I'll not suffer'

　　Was this the special reason you gave me to be glad?
　　　　So lovely aren't you ashamed to be so light?
　　One or two nights of love are hardly over
　　　　And I am called a burden to your bed.　　　　20
　　Yesterday you praised me and read my poems:
　　　　That love of yours, can it take wing so soon?

　　Let him compete with me in wit and artistry,
　　　　Learn above all to make love in one house.
　　If it should please you, let him fight Lernéan hydras　　　　25
　　　　And fetch you apples from the Hesperian dragon;

Let him drink poison gladly, and after shipwreck brine;
    Let him never refuse to suffer for your sake:
(Would that you'd try *me* out, dear life, in all these labours!)
    You'll find a common coward in that loud-mouth,   30
Whose present boastfulness has puffed him into favour,
    Though next year you'll be separated.
But I shall not be changed in the Sibyl's thousand years,
    Not by Alcides' labours, not by the black day.

You'll say as you lay mine to rest 'Are these bones yours,   35
    Propertius? Alas, you were faithful to me.
Faithful you were, alas, though not ennobled by
    Ancestral birth and though not very rich.'
There's nothing I'll not suffer. Insults never change me.
    I reckon bearing a beauty is no burden.   40
For that face, I believe, have fallen not a few,
    But many, I believe, have not kept faith.
Theseus for a brief space fancied the Minoan,
    And Demóphoön Phyllis—both evil guests.
Medea has long been known to you from Jason's ship   45
    And how the man she saved abandoned her.

Heartless is she who fakes a specious love for many,
    And the girl who dresses up for more than one.
Never have dealings with the rich or nobly born;
    Scarce one will gather up your bones on the last day.   50
I shall be he, but sooner, I pray, let it be you
    Who loosen hair and beat bare breasts for me.

25

'One woman's trouble enough'

Unique, most lovely trouble, born to make me suffer,
    (For my fate excludes the words *Come often!*),
That beauty shall be made world-famous by my books—
    Your pardon, Calvus—by your leave, Catullus.

Old soldiers, handing in their weapons, sleep alone;   5
   Aged oxen refuse to pull the plough;
Derelict ships rest on the empty beach,
   And battered shields hang idle in temples:
But age will never dispossess me of your love,
   Though I become a Tithonus or a Nestor.   10

Had I not better be the slave of some harsh tyrant
   And moan in cruel Perillus' bull?
Not better be turned to stone by the Gorgon's glare
   Or even devoured by Prometheus' vultures?

No, I'll stand firm. Steel blades are worn away   15
   By rust, and flint by dripping water,
But love's not worn away by an accusing mistress;
   Love stays and puts up with her unjust threats.
When scorned he asks again. Though wronged he takes the blame,
   And back he comes, if on reluctant feet.   20

As for you who pride yourself on Love's fulfilment,
   Poor fool, no woman is un-light for long.
Does anyone pay vows while storms are raging,
   When ships are often wrecked in harbour?
Or claim the prize before the race is run   25
   And his wheel has rounded the seventh turn?
Love's following wind can play deceptive games;
   The longer delayed, the greater the fall.

Meanwhile, however much she loves you, still
   Keep your joy locked in a silent breast.   30
For in love it is a man's own boastful words
   That somehow always harm him.
Although she invites you often, remember to go rarely;
   What causes envy seldom lasts long.

Yet if the days approved by girls of old existed   35
   I'd be what you are now; the times defeat me.
Still, these bad days will never change my character;
   Each man must choose the way that suits him.

But you who recommend attentions to many loves,
 What pain you force your eyes to suffer!   40
You see a pretty girl with fair skin and fair hair,
 You see a brunette—both colours attract.
You see some girl of Grecian build walk by,
 You see our girls—both shapes enchant.
One wears plebeian dress, another scarlet—   45
 Either way you're badly wounded.
Since *one* can bring your eyelids sleepless nights enough,
 One woman's trouble enough for any man.

26A

A dream of Cynthia shipwrecked

I saw you in a dream, my life, shipwrecked,
 Heaving weak hands through Ionian foam
And confessing all the lies you ever told me,
 Your sea-drenched hair weighing you down,
Like Helle tossing on the purple waves,   5
 Who rode the golden sheep's soft chine.

How scared I was lest the sea should bear your name
 And sailors gliding through your waters mourn you!
What then I vowed to Neptune, to Castor and his twin,
 And to the deified Leucóthoë!   10
But hardly lifting fingertips above the swell
 And almost gone you kept calling my name.

Had Glaucus caught sight of your eyes, you'd now
 Be an Ionian Sea-Nymph
And envious Nereids would criticize you,   15
 Nesaea fair, blue-eyed Cymóthoë.

But then I saw a dolphin speed to your support—
 The same, I fancy, as carried Arion's lyre;
And I was going to fling myself from the cliff-top
 When sheer fright shattered the vision for me.   20

26B

Devotion and a voyage together

Now let them marvel that so beautiful a girl's
　　My slave and I've a potent name in Rome.
Even to earn the gifts of Croesus and Cambyses
　　She'd never say 'Rise, poet, from my bed'.
For when she reads my work she says she hates the rich;　　25
　　No girl so reverences poetry.
In love devotion counts for much, and faithfulness;
　　A man can give many presents and not be true.

　　　　　*　　*　　*　　*　　*

Or if my girl should plan a voyage I'll follow her
　　And the same breeze will drive a faithful pair.　　30
We'll sleep on the same beach with the same tree for shelter
　　And often drink of the same water;
And the same plank can bring together two lovers,
　　Whether my quarters are fore or aft.

I'll put up with everything, though savage Eurus blows　　35
　　And freezing Auster fills the sails at random,
With all the winds that persecuted poor Ulysses
　　And the thousand Greek ships off the Euboean shore,
And those that moved two shores when a dove was sent
　　To guide the Argo on unknown seas.　　40
Only let her never be absent from my eyes
　　And Jove himself can blast our ship.
At least we shall be tossed together naked on one beach;
　　The waves can take *me* if only earth covers *you*.

But Neptune is not cruel to love as great as ours;　　45
　　Neptune in love is his brother's equal.
Witness Amymóne the water-carrier clinched
　　In the fields, and the fen of Lerna trident-smitten.
The God in that embrace fulfilled his prayer, while her
　　Golden pitcher poured God-given water.　　50

Even Orithyia, forced by Boreas, never called him
    Cruel. This God can tame land and deep sea.
Believe me, Scylla will be kind to us, and gaping
    Charybdis with her ceaseless ebb and flow.
The very stars will be occulted by no darkness;   55
    Orion will shine bright, and bright the Kid.

But if I must lay down my life upon your body
    This exodus will do me no dishonour.

27

'Only the lover knows when he will die'

And do you mortals seek to know the funeral's
    Uncertain hour and the manner of death's coming?
Do you seek in cloudless skies Phoenician inventions—
    Stars favourable to man and stars malefic?

But if we march to Parthia or sail to Britain,   5
    Sea or land, the hazards of the way are hidden.
Again, we weep when our heads are exposed to civil strife,
    When Mars sets doubtful hands at odds.
Besides, you fear your house may burn or tumble down,
    That black potions may pass your lips.   10

Only the lover knows when he will die and by what
    Death, nor does he dread weapons or Boreas' blasts.
Even if he sit as oarsman under Stygian reeds,
    Watching the infernal ferry's gloomy sails,
If only the breath of a cry from his girl should call him back,   15
    He will return by the route no law allows.

28A

Cynthia's illness

Jove, at long last have pity on a girl in sickness;
    You will be blamed if one so lovely dies.   2
Juno your wife will surely pardon you for caring;   33
    A dying girl can break even Juno's heart.   34
The time has come when sultry air is sweltering
    And earth parched by the Dogstar's drought.   3

And yet heat-wave and sky are not so much to blame   5
    As repeated failure to honour the Gods.
This is the ruin, has long been the ruin, of wretched girls;
    Their vows are swept away by wind and wave.
Does Venus resent comparison with her? That Goddess
    Envies all who are beautiful as she.   10
Or did you neglect the temple of Pelasgian Juno,
    Or dared you find fault with Pallas' eyes?
You beauties never learn to discipline your speech;
    Beauty and a guilty tongue brought this upon you.

And yet for you whose life is plagued by many perils   15
    Will come at day's end a gentler hour.
Io, her head deformed, had lowed in her first years;
    The heifer that drank Nile water is now a Goddess.
Ino too in her first life wandered the world;
    Poor sailors pray to her as Leucothea.   20
Andromeda was pledged as a sea-monster's prey;
    She became Perseus' famous bride.
Callisto as a bear had roamed Arcadian fields;
    Her star directs benighted sails.

But if so be that Fate should hasten your repose,   25
    Bliss will be the fate of your entombment.
You will tell Semele of beauty's peril and she
    Will listen, taught as a girl by her own pain.
You among all the Maeonian heroines shall have
    First place, with none dissenting.   30

But now in your weakness bear with Fate as best you may;
   God and the drastic day can turn.

28B

The magic fails but Dis relents

Stilled is the magic wheel that whirred to incantation,   35
   Charred lies the laurel on a burnt-out hearth,
The moon refuses yet again to fall from heaven,
   And the night-bird screeches a fatal warning.
One ship of doom shall ferry both our loves
   Under blue sails on the lake below.   40

Take pity, I beseech you, if not on one, on two!
   I live if she lives; if she goes I go.
For which request I pledge myself to a sacred verse:
   'Thanks to great Jove', I'll write, 'my girl is saved',
And she herself will sit in worship at your feet   45
   And, sitting, will describe her long ordeal.

Let this your mercy last, Persephone, and you,
   Persephone's consort, be no crueller.
With those below are so many thousands of lovely women;
   Grant, if you may, one beauty to the world above.   50
With you is Íope, with you flaxen-haired Tyro,
   With you Europa and unchaste Pasíphaë,
And all the beauties born to old Troy and Achaea
   And Thebes and aged Priam's ruined realm;
And every Roman lady to be reckoned with   55
   Is gone; the greedy fire has had them all.
Beauty is not forever and no one's luck will last.
   Further or nearer one's own death is waiting.

But since you have been saved, my light, from grave danger,
   Pay Diana dances, her due gift;   60
Pay also vigils to the Goddess once a heifer,
   And give ten votive nights to me.

29A

Arrested by Amorini

Yesterday night, my light, when I was roving drunk
    And had no servants to lead me along,
A crowd of little boys met me (I do not know
    How many—fear stopped me counting them).
I saw that some were carrying little torches, others   5
    Arrows, and a few had cords to tie me up.
But they were naked. Said a naughtier one of them
    'Arrest this man. You know him well by now.
This was the one the angry woman hired us for.'
    And as he spoke a noose was round my neck.   10
Then one said 'Push him into the middle', and another
    'He thinks we're not Gods. He must die!
She's been expecting you for hours on end, but you,
    Ungrateful lout, seek someone else's door.
When she's untied the Sidon snood she wears at night   15
    And opened wide her drowsy eyes,
Fragrance will waft around you, not of Arabian grass
    But made by the hands of Love himself.
Now free him, brothers. Now he promises true love,
    And look, we've now come to the house as ordered'   20
And with this, putting on my cloak again, they said to me
    'Go now and learn to stay at home of nights.'

29B

An early morning visit

It was early morning. I wanted to see if she slept alone.
    Yes, Cynthia was alone in bed.
I stood entranced—had never seen her more beautiful,   25
    Not even when in crimson tunic
She was going off to tell her dreams to chaste Vesta
    For fear of harm to herself or me:

She looked like that, I thought, freshly released from sleep.
   Ah, how powerful sheer beauty is! 30
'What's this?', she said, 'The dawn patrol on mistresses?
   Do you think my morals are like yours?
I'm not so fickle. One tried man's enough for me.
   You perhaps—or someone truer.
You'll find no marks or indentations in the bed, 35
   No signs that two have tumbled here.
Look, there's no bodily exhalation,
   Not one breath of adulterous guilt.'
She spoke and fending off my kiss with her right hand
   Leapt into bedroom slippers and away. 40
So I, the would-be guardian of true love, was foiled.
   Since then I've never had a happy night.

30A

No escape from Love

Ah, mindless, where do you run? There's no running away.
   Though you run to the Tánais Love will still follow.
Not if you ride the air on the back of Pegasus,
   Not if the wings of Perseus speed your feet
Or if breezes cleft by winged sandals sweep you along 5
   Will Mercury's highway help you at all.

Always Love presses, presses on the lover's head
   And settles heavily on the neck once free.
As guard he keeps a strict watch and will never let you
   Lift your eyes from the ground once they are caught. 10
But if you should offend he is a forgiving God,
   If only he sees prompt repentance.

30B

But loving is no crime

Insensitive old men can criticize these parties;
    Let us, my life, just rub along as planned.
Their ears can be burdened with antiquated rules;   15
    This is the place for the clever pipe to sound,
Which, wrongly cast out, floated down Meander's flood
    When puffing uglified the cheeks of Pallas.

Now am I wrong to refuse to sail the Phrygian waves
    And seek the shores of the Hyrcanian sea   20
To spatter our shared Household Gods with mutual slaughter
    And win the family Lares dreadful spoils?
Should I be ashamed to live content with one girl-friend?
    If this is an offence the offence is Love's.
Let no one blame *me*.—Cynthia, please to share with me   25
    A dewy grotto on moss-clad heights.
There you shall see the Sisters Nine haunting the rocks
    And singing the sweet thefts of old-world Jove,
How he was burnt by Semele, how wild for Io,
    And how he flew to Troy disguised as a bird.   30

But if there's no one who can beat the Winged One's weapons,
    Why am I alone guilty of a crime all share?
Nor can you shock the modest faces of those Maidens;
    Their chorus knows what it is to love,
If it is true that one, embraced by handsome Oeagrus,   35
    Lay with him once on Bistonian cliffs.

Here when they set you in the forefront of the dance
    And Bacchus in the midst with clever thyrsus,
Then shall I suffer the holy ivy to wreathe my head,
    For without you my wit is powerless.   40

31

The opening of Palatine Apollo's portico

You ask why I have kept you waiting? Phoebus' golden
  Portico was opened by great Caesar,
Ranged to spectacular effect on Punic pillars,
  Between which stands old Danaus' female throng.
I saw there, truly, a Phoebus finer than himself,   5
  In marble, mouthing song to a mute lyre;
And round an altar stood his cattle, Myron's work,
  Four lifelike images of oxen.
Then in the midst arose a temple of bright marble
  Dearer to Phoebus than his native Ortygia.   10
Above its pediment stood the Sun-God's chariot
  And its noble doors were Libyan ivory;
One leaf bewailed the Gauls hurled from Parnassus' height,
  The other the dead of the daughter of Tantalus.
Beyond, between his mother and sister, the God himself   15
  As Pythian in long robe is making music.

32

'I'm not disturbed by peccadilloes'

Oh Cynthia, why Praeneste's dubious sortilege,   3
  Why seek Aeaean Telégonus's walls?
Why go by chaise so often to Herculéan Tibur   5
  And to Lanuvium on the Appian Way?
If only you would saunter here when you have leisure,
  Cynthia! But the crowd makes me distrust you,
When they see you running, under vow, with kindled torch
  To Nemi, bearing light for the Trivian Goddess.   10
Whoever sees you falls; so he who has not seen you   1
  Will not desire you. Eyes are the guilty parties.   2

So you disdain the pillared shade of Pompey's Porch,　　　11
　　Famed for its Attalid tapestries,
The close-grown avenue of equally matched plane-trees,
　　The streams that fall from sleeping Maron
And from the Nymphs who lightly plash around their basin　　15
　　When Triton suddenly spouts water?

You are wrong. Your journeying indicates a love-affair.
　　It's not Rome but my gaze you madly avoid.
You gain nothing by planning futile plots against me,
　　Laying foolish traps for an old hand.　　20
It matters less to me, but the loss of your good name,
　　Alas, will cost you dear, as you deserve.
My ears have lately been assailed by an ugly tale
　　About you, and all Rome has heard it.

But there's no call for you to heed unfriendly gossip;　　25
　　Scandal's the price that beauty always pays.
Your name has not been lost by proof of poisoning;
　　Phoebus will testify your hands are clean.
And if you *have* spent one or two long nights in dalliance
　　I'm not disturbed by peccadilloes.　　30

Tyndaris exchanged her country for an outside love
　　And was brought home alive, without decree.
Venus herself, we hear, seduced by lustful Mars,
　　Remained no less respectable in heaven.
Though Ida tells how a Goddess loved the shepherd Paris　　35
　　And lay with him among the flocks,
A crowd of her Hamadryad sisters were spectators
　　And the old Sileni and the Father of the Dance himself;
With them Oenone gathered fruit in the glens of Ida,
　　Catching it in cupped hands as it fell.　　40

Among this teeming lechery does anyone inquire
　　'Why's she so rich? Who's given it? From what source?'?
O Rome, too lucky in this modern age
　　If one girl acts unfashionably!
Before her there was Lesbia, safely doing the same.　　45
　　Surely an imitator is less blameworthy?

The man who seeks old Tatiuses and uncouth Sabines
    Has only lately set foot in our city.

You'll have a better chance of drying ocean waves
    And plucking down the stars by hand   50
Than of persuading our girls not to go astray—
    That was the rule in Saturn's reign.
But when Deucalion's flood submerged the globe,
    And ever since Deucalion's flood,
Tell me, could anyone keep his bed chaste,   55
    Or any Goddess live with one God only?

Great Minos' wife, they say, was long ago seduced
    By the beauty of a wild white bull.
Danaë too, though shut in by a wall of brass,
    Couldn't be chaste and say No to great Jove.   60
So, if you've done the same as Grecian girls and Latin,
    My verdict is *Long life to you—and freedom*!

33A

The cult of Isis

Now once again comes round the ritual I detest:
    Now Cynthia pays ten nights of obligation.
And how I wish them lost, those rites the Inachid
    Has sent from the warm Nile to Ausonian wives!
The Goddess who so often sunders ardent lovers,   5
    Has she, however named, always been cruel?

Certainly, Io, you of all Jove's secret loves,
    Felt what it means to go down many roads,
When Juno ordered you, a girl, to carry horns
    And lose words in the bellowing of a beast.   10
Ah, how often you hurt your mouth on oak-leaves
    And chewed arbutus cud in the byre!

Because Jove took away your country features,
    Is that why you've become so proud a Goddess?

Is Egypt with her swarthy nurslings not enough?   15
  Why have you travelled the long road to Rome?

What help is it to you that girls should sleep alone?
  Trust me, you'll soon have horns again.
Or else we shall expel your cruelty from our city,
  For Nile has not been popular with Tiber.   20

But you who have been too gratified by my distress,
  When free of those nights let's go the course three times.

33B

Cynthia at a party

You do not listen, letting me waste words. Though now
  Icarus' oxen wheel their slow stars round,
Heedless you drink. Can't midnight change your mind?   25
  Aren't you tired yet of throwing dice?

Ah, curse whoever it was found the undiluted grape
  And with its nectar first debased good water!
Icarus, rightly murdered by Cecropian farmers,
  You know how bitter is the smell of vine-shoots!   30
O Centaur Eurýtion, wine was your destruction too;
  Yours also, Polyphemus—Ismarian wine!
Beauty is destroyed by wine, by wine is youth debased;
  Wine makes a girl not recognize her man.

Alas, Lyaeus does not alter her at all.   35
  Drink on. You're lovely. Wine does you no harm,
When the garland slipping down trails forward into your cup
  And you read my poems in a low-keyed voice.
Then soak the board more lavishly with spilt Falernian
  And let gilt goblets foam more lushly.   40

Passion is always warmer towards absent lovers;   43
  Availability cheapens men-in-waiting.   44
Still, no girl likes retiring to a lonely bed;   41
  At Love's insistence you all miss something else.   42

34

To Lynceus on love and poetry

Why should anyone now trust his mistress' beauty
　　To Love? That's how I nearly lost my girl.
In love—I speak from knowledge—no one can be trusted;
　　A pretty woman is fair game for most.
This God denatures blood-relations, divides friends,　　　5
　　And calls associates to bitter warfare.
As Menelaus' guest there came an adulterer,
　　And didn't the Colchian follow a strange man?

Lynceus, you cheat, how could you touch my charge?
　　Did not your hands then falter?　　　10
What if she had not been so loyal and true-hearted?
　　Could you have lived with such dishonour?

You can try to stab my heart or poison it,
　　But whatever you do hands off my mistress;
You can share my soul, you can share my body;　　　15
　　Friend, I entitle you to all my goods:
But from my bed, and only from my bed, I ban you;
　　I could not tolerate Jove as a rival.
Alone I'm even jealous of nothing, of my shadow—
　　A fool to keep trembling with foolish fear.　　　20

Yet there is one excuse which earns your crime my pardon;
　　Your words ran wild with too much wine.
But your ascetic frown will never deceive me;
　　All know by now how good a thing is love.

My Lynceus too has fallen madly in love at last;　　　25
　　I'm glad that you of all men turn to our Gods.
What use now is your wisdom from Socratic books
　　Or the power to explain the ways of things?
What use the poems of Aratus' couch?
　　Against love's might your old bard fails.　　　30

Your Muse had better copy long-memoried Philetas
    And the dreams of unfulsome Callimachus.

You mayn't retell the tale of Aetolian Achelóus,
    How brokenly he flowed in his great love;
How too the deceptive water of Meander wanders   35
    The Phrygian plain, disguising its own flow;
And how Adrastus' winning horse Arion spoke
    At the tragic funeral of Archémorus.
The fate of Amphiaráus' chariot will not help you,
    Or the fall of Cápaneus that pleased great Jove.   40

Then cease compounding words for the Aeschylean cothurnus,
    Cease, and relax your limbs in supple dances.
Begin now to enclose your lines on a narrow lathe,
    Harsh poet, and make a poem of your passion.
You'll not go safer than Antímachus or Homer: 45
    A right girl scorns the mighty Gods.

But the bull will not surrender to the heavy plough
    Until his horns are caught by the lasso,
Nor on your own will you endure the harshness of love,
    But first your spirit must be broken by us.   50

No woman wants to learn about cosmology
    Nor why the moon wanes for her brother's horses,
Nor whether part of us survives the Stygian waves
    Nor whether a purpose aims the thunderbolt.
Consider me, the heir to a modest patrimony,   55
    With no ancestral Triumphs in past wars,
How I am king among the many girls at parties,
    Thanks to the wit that you belittle in me!

I'm glad to wilt, laid out in yesterday's garland,
    Shot to the bone by an inerrant God.   60
Phoebus' protection of the Actian shore, and Caesar's
    Brave fleet—Virgil's glad to tell of these.
He now calls up the arms of Trojan Aenéas
    And the walls he built on the Lavinian shore.
Make way, you Roman writers, and you Greek, make way!   65
    A greater than the *Iliad* is born.

You sing, beneath the pinewoods of shadowy Galaesus,
   Thyrsis and Daphnis with practised reed-pipe,
And how girls can be led astray by ten apples
   And the gift of a kid still pushing the udder.   70
Lucky the man who buys his love cheaply with fruit,
   Though even Tityrus sings to a thankless girl!
And lucky Corydon, trying to pick up untouched
   Alexis, favourite of his farmer master!
Although he rests for weariness of his oaten pipe,   75
   He is praised among the easy Hamadryads.
You sing the maxims of the old Ascréan poet,
   What field will green the grain, what slope the grape,
Making such music upon learned tortoiseshell
   As the Cynthian plays with finger pressure.   80

Yet not ungratefully will this reach any reader,
   Be he a tiro in love or be he adept.
And here the tuneful Swan proved no less spirited,
   Though less loud, than the Goose's untaught song.
Varro too played at this when Jason was made perfect,   85
   Varro, his own Leucadia's great flame.
Writings of mischievous Catullus too sang this—
   Made Lesbia more famous even than Helen.
Learned Calvus' page also confessed to this
   When he sang the fate of poor Quintilia.   90
And lately Gallus, dead for beautiful Lycoris,
   Bathed how many wounds in the stream below!
Cynthia (why not?) shall live, praised in Propertius' verse,
   If Fame agrees to add me to that list.

BOOK III

I

The poet's Greek masters and his achievement

Shade of Callimachus and sacrifices of Coan Philetas,
    Pray grant *me* admission to your grove.
I enter first as priest of a pure fountainhead
    To offer Italian mysteries in Greek dances.
Say in what grotto did you both refine your song?   5
    On what foot entering? What water drinking?
Ah, farewell whoever holds Phoebus back in armour!
    Verse should move with finish from fine pumice;
For which Fame lifts me high above the ground, the Muse
    Born of me triumphs with garlanded steeds,   10
And with me in the chariot little Cupids ride,
    A crowd of writers following my wheels.

Why vainly loose your reins competing against me?
    It's no broad road that runs to the Muses.
Many will add your praises to their *Annals*, Rome,   15
    Singing of Bactra as the Empire's future bound.
But my page has brought down this work from the Sisters' mount
    By a new-found path for peacetime reading.
Vouchsafe your poet, Pegasids, a soft garland;
    No heavy wreath will suit my head.   20

Yet what the envious crowd withholds from me in life
    Honour will pay me after death at double interest.
Everything after death is magnified by age:
    A name beyond the grave sounds greater in the mouth.
Else who would know of citadels battered by a Wooden Horse,   25
    Of rivers fighting an Haemonian hero,
Idéan Símoïs and Jove's offspring Scamander,
    Of wheels on the plain disfiguring Hector thrice?
Deíphobus, Hélenus, Polýdamas, and Paris,

That craven warrior, their own land would hardly know.   30
Small mention now there'd be of Ilium and Troy
   Twice captured by the might of Oeta's God.
Great Homer too, remembrancer of Troy's downfall,
   Has found his work grow with posterity.

Rome shall applaud me also among her later grandsons;   35
   Myself, I predict that day beyond the pyre.
It is decreed, the Lycian God approving my prayer,
   That no dishonoured tombstone mark my bones.

2

The power and immortality of poetry

Let us return meanwhile to our song's familiar round—
   To touch and delight a girl with its music.

Orpheus, they say, bewitched wild animals and held
   Back rushing rivers with his Thracian lyre.
Cithaeron's rocks, hustled to Thebes by music's art,   5
   Of their own accord combined to bond a wall.
Yes, and below wild Etna Galatéa turned
   Her spray-drenched steeds towards Polyphemus' songs.
What wonder, by the grace of Bacchus and Apollo,
   If girls in plenty worship my words?   10

Though my house is not supported on Taenarian columns
   And has no ivory room with gilded beams,
Nor do my fruit-trees match the orchards of Phaeacia
   Nor artificial grot drip Marcian water,
Still the Muses befriend me, my songs are dear to readers   15
   And Callíope unwearied by my dances.
Lucky the girl who is celebrated in my book;
   Each song will be a reminder of her beauty.

Neither the expense of Pyramids reared to the stars
   Nor Jove's Eléan home copying heaven   20
Nor rich good fortune of the Mausoleum

Escape the extreme necessity of death.
Or flame or rain will dispossess their honour, or
    They'll fall by thrust of years and their own weight.
But age will not destroy the name achieved by talent;   25
    Talent's glory stands—immortal.

3

The poet's dream and his mission

I had seen myself reclining in Helicon's soft shade
    Where runs the rill named for Bellérophon's horse,
And managing to mouth your kings and your kings' deeds,
    Alba, (such hard work for my powers)
And I had just applied my lips to the great spring   5
    Whence thirsty father Ennius once drank
And sang of Curian brothers, Horatian javelins,
    Aemilian trophies borne on royal barges,
Fabius' invincible inaction, Cannae's
    Luckless field, Gods moved by duteous vows,   10
The Lares driving Hannibal in flight from Rome
    And Jupiter saved by cackling geese,
When Phoebus eyeing me from the Castalian tree and leaning
    On his gilded lyre near a cave spoke thus:

'Idiot, what right have you to such a stream? And who   15
    Told you to turn your hand to epic?
There's not a hope of fame, Propertius, for you here;
    Your little wheels must groove soft meadows.
Let your slim volume be displayed on bedside tables
    And read by lonely girls waiting for their lovers.   20
Why has your page diverged from its appointed round?
    You must not overload the rowboat of your wit.
With one oar feather water, with the other sand,
    And you'll be safe. Most flounder in mid-ocean.'
So saying with ivory quill he points me to a seat   25
    To which on mossy ground a new path led.

Here was a grotto green embellished with mosaics
    And from its tufa vault hung tambourines
The Muses' *orgia*, Father Silenus' effigy
    In clay, and your reed pipes, Tegéan Pan;   30
And Lady Venus' birds, my crowd of trouble, doves
    Dip red beaks in the Gorgonéan pool.
The several Maidens, allocated their nine duties,
    Busy tender hands with special gifts.
This one picks ivy for a thyrsus; this one fits tunes   35
    To strings; that one plaits roses with both hands.

One Goddess of their number touched me (from her face
    I judge it was Calliopéa) saying:
'Content yourself to be conveyed by snow-white swans
    And ride no neighing charger into battle.   40
Not yours to blow the raucous laudatory trumpet
    Or sully the Aonian grove with Mars;
Or tell on what field Marian eagles fought
    And Rome repelled Teutonic power,
Or how the barbarous Rhine ran red with Swabian blood,   45
    Rolling maimed bodies down his grieving tide.
You'll sing of lovers garlanded at an alien door
    And drunken signs of nocturnal escapes,
So those who wish to steal a march on strict husbands
    May learn from you to charm girls from internment.'   50
Thus far Calliope. Then, drawing from the fountain,
    She wet my lips with water of Philetas.

4

Caesar plans war with Parthia

Caesar the God plans war with wealthy India,
    To furrow with his fleet pearl-bearing seas.
Big booty for his men. The world's end offers Triumphs.
    Tigris and Euphrates will flow under his rule.
Belatedly Ausonian rods will gain a province;   5
    Parthian trophies will get used to Latium's Jove.
Go speedily, spread sail, you prows proven in war!

Armed cavalry, lead on—your usual duty!
The signs, I foretell, are lucky. Wipe out Crassus' defeat.
   Go and stand up for Roman history!   10

O Father Mars and Holy Vesta's fateful flame,
   Let come, I pray, before my death the day
When I see Caesar's axles heavy-laden with spoil
   And his horses often halt at the mob's cheers,
And resting on a dear girl's bosom I start to watch   15
   And from their labels read the captured towns,
The flying horse's missiles, the trousered soldier's bows,
   And captive leaders sitting under their armour.

Venus, save your offspring. Let this visible stock
   Descended from Aeneas live for ever.   20
The spoil be theirs whose hardships have deserved it;
   I'll be content to applaud on the Sacred Way.

5

The poet worships peace. His future plans

Love is the God of peace; we lovers venerate peace:
   Enough for me tough battles with my mistress.
But then neither does my heart crave hated gold
   Nor my thirst drink from precious jewels
Nor do a thousand yokes plough fat Campania for me   5
   Nor do I buy bronzes from the ruins of poor Corinth.

O luckless the primal clay modelled by Prometheus!
   With too little care he worked on the heart.
Arranging the body he overlooked the mind in his plan.
   He should have straightened out the emotions first of all.   10
As it is, wind tosses us far out to sea. We look
   For enemies and multiply armaments.

You will carry no wealth to Acheron's waves, but travel
   Naked, poor fool, on the raft below.
Victor and vanquished will mix on equal terms as ghosts;   15

Captive Jugurtha sits beside consul Marius.
Lydian Croesus pairs off with Dulichian Irus.
   Death that comes in the course of nature is best.

I am glad in first youth to have cultivated Helicon
   And joined hands in the Muses' dances.   20
I am also glad to fetter my thoughts with much Lyaeus
   And always to wear spring roses on my head.

But when the heavy years have interrupted Venus
   And white old age has speckled my black hair,
Then be it my delight to learn the ways of Nature,   25
   What God controls this household of the world,
How rising moons appear, how wane, whence every month
   With horns conjoined return to full,
How winds prevail on the salt sea, what Eurus' blast
   Intends and whence the clouds' unfailing water;   30

Whether there comes a day to undermine high heaven,
   Why the radiant bow drinks rainwater,
Or why Perrhaebian Pindus' summit trembled
   And the sun's orb mourned with black-clad horses,
Why Boötes is slow to turn his ox-wagon,   35
   Why the Pleiads dance so close in fiery cluster,
Or why the deep sea does not go beyond its bounds
   And the full year goes into four seasons;

Are there Gods' judgements in the Underworld and sinners'
      torments,   39
   The wheel, the boulder, the thirst in the pool,   42
Phineus' starvation or the Furies of Alcmaeon,   41
   If black snakes rage on Tisíphonë's head,   40
If the infernal cave is guarded by three-throated   43
   Cerberus and nine acres are too few for Títyos,
Or have fictitious tales come down to wretched mankind   45
   And can there be no fear beyond the pyre?

For me life's outcome shall be this, but you to whom
   Wars are more welcome, bring Crassus' standards home.

6

Lygdamus as go-between

Lygdamus, tell me the truth—what you noticed about our girl,
    As you hope to be free of the mistress's yoke.
You're no deceiver, are you, puffing me up with empty joy,
    Reporting what you think I want to hear?
Every go-between ought to be on the level   5
    And a slave have greater credence because of his fear.
Now tell me what you remember, from the very first.
    Begin. I'll prick up my ears and drink it in.

So you saw her weeping? Her hair dishevelled?
    In a flood of tears?   10
You saw no mirror on the made bed, Lygdamus?
    No jewels adorned her snow-white hands?
In fact a mourner's dress was draped on those soft arms
    And her vanity box lay locked at the foot of the bed?
The house was sad, and sadly the servants plied their tasks   15
    Around her, and she herself was spinning,
And pressed the wool to her moist eyes to dry them
    And plaintively recalled my angry message?

'Is this the reward he promised me in your hearing, Lygdamus?
    To break faith, even with a slave as witness, is punishable,   20
How can he desert poor me when I have done nothing?
    And keep in his house the sort I refuse to name?
Is he glad that I'm pining away, alone in an empty bed?
    He can dance on my dead body, Lygdamus, if he likes.
That slut has beaten me by drugs, not character.   25
    He's pulled by the strings of her magic wheel.
Drawn to her by a monster—a bloated natterjack,
    The assorted bones of shrivelled snakes,
A screech-owl's feathers found among ruined graves,
    And a woollen headband stolen from a corpse.   30
If, Lygdamus, my dreams sing truly, I declare
    That punishment, late but full, shall be at my feet,

And over an empty bed shall dusty webs be spun
    And during their love-nights Venus be fast asleep.'

If these were the girl's heart-felt complaints to you,   35
    Hurry back, Lygdamus, the way you came
And carry my message to her with many tears:
    'There's anger in my love but no deceit.
I too am laid above the selfsame fire—in torment.'
    I'll swear I've been continent twelve days now,   40
And if this great war ends for me in happy accord,
    For my part, Lygdamus, you shall be free.

7

An elegy for Paetus, drowned at sea

It's true then, Money—you cause a life of trouble.
    For you we take the early road to death.
You supply human vices with cruel nourishment.
    From your stock spring the seeds of discontent.

It was you sank Paetus three and four times in mad sea   5
    As he spread his sails for Pharos' harbour.
Pursuing you, poor man, he lost life's prime,
    And floats as fresh bait for far fishes.
Nor can his mother pay due tribute of pious earth
    Nor bury him among the graves of kindred.   10
But seabirds hover now above your bones;
    Your tomb is now the whole Carpathian.

Unlucky Aquilo, dread of ravished Orithyia,
    What great prize did you win from *him*?
Or what joy, Neptune, do you find in a broken keel?   15
    That hull's human freight was blameless.

Paetus, why count your age? Why mouth 'Mother dear'
    As you float? The breakers have no Gods.
For your cables, tied to the rocks in a storm at night,
    All fell away as the rope frayed.   20

It was the shore that witnessed Agamemnon's sorrow, marked
  By the punishment of Athamantiad Argynnus—
On this youth's loss Atrides would not launch the fleet,
  For which delay Iphigenia was slain.

Return the body to land. He paid the deep his life.   25
  Cheap sand, give Paetus involuntary burial.
And whenever a sailor passes Paetus' tomb let him say
  '*You* make even the brave afraid.'

Go, build curved ships and knit together means of doom.
  That death comes aimed by human hands.   30
Dry land was too little. To the fates we added sea.
  Our skill increased bad luck's approaches.
Should anchor hold you when your Household Gods could not?
  What his deserts who finds his own land too little?
The winds decide your every venture. There's no ship   35
  Grows old and even ports break faith.
Nature made level sea to ambush greed.
  Success can hardly once be yours.

The rocks of Caphåreus broke up a triumphant fleet
  When Greece was wrecked in the salt deep.   40
One by one Ulysses wept the loss of shipmates;
  His well-known wiles were useless against the sea.

But had he been content to plough with father's oxen
  And words of mine had weighed with him,
He'd live as guest of his own sweet Penates, poor   45
  But on land, with only wealth to weep for.

Our Paetus could not bear to hear the howling gale
  Or hurt his soft hands on rough ropes,
But in a bower of Orician terebinth or citrus
  Would rest his head on iridescent down.   50
Did waves, while he still lived, remove his nails by the roots
  And his poor gaping mouth gulp hateful water?
Did wicked night see this man clinging to a plank?
  Did so many ills combine to kill Paetus?

Yet weeping and lamenting he made this last appeal   55
   As the black brine closed his dying lips:
'Gods of the Aegean who rule the calm, you winds
   And every wave weighing down my head,
Why rob me of the wretched years of my first bloom?
   I brought long hands to your foam.   60
Alas, I shall be flung on the halcyons' sharp rocks.
   The Blue God aims his trident at me.
At least let the tide cast me up on Italy's coast.
   Enough if my remains can reach my mother.'

As he spoke a wave with swirling eddy dragged him under.   65
   Those words, that day, were Paetus' last.
O hundred deep-sea girls of father Nereus,
   And you, Thetis, drawn by maternal grief
You should have put your arms beneath his weary chin.
   Your hands would not have found him heavy.   70

But as for you, cruel Aquilo, you'll never see sails of mine.
   Give me an unadventurous death at my mistress' door.

8

Violence a sign of love

Sweet for me was the fight by yesterday's lamplight
   And all the manic abuse you voiced
When, mad with wine, you overturned the table and flung
   Full wine-cups at me in your fury.
Come on then, don't be afraid, attack my hair   5
   And scratch my face with those beautiful nails.
Bring fire and threaten to burn my eyes out.
   Rip my tunic, strip my chest bare.
Naturally I diagnose true passion; no girl
   Not deeply in love is so upset.   10

The woman whose frenzied tongue hurls insults
   Is grovelling at great Venus' feet—
Or if she surrounds him with crowds of guards

Or follows down the street like a stricken Maenad,
Or if mad dreams keep scaring her timid self   15
    Or some girl's picture makes her wretched.
I am a sure interpreter of this mental anguish
    And have often seen these signs of true love.
No faith is true that can't be moved to quarrel.
    I wish my enemy a placid girl-friend.   20

But let my peers see tooth-marks on my neck;
    Let bruises show that I've been with my mistress.
In love I want to suffer or hear suffering,
    To see my own tears or else yours,
When you send back hidden meanings with your eyebrows   25
    Or with your fingers secret signals.
I hate the sleep that sighing never punctuates,
    Want always to grow pale at female rage.

Paris found passion sweeter when he could bring joy
    To Helen after welcome struggle.   30
While Dánaäns were winning and fierce Hector resisting
    He waged his greatest wars in Helen's lap.
Against you or for you against rivals I'll be always
    Fighting. Where you're concerned I want no peace.
Be glad there's none so lovely. You would suffer   35
    If any were. Now you've just cause for pride.

But as for you who laid a trap for our love,
    Be father-in-lawed for life, with mother at home.
If now you're ever given the chance to steal a night,
    She has done it to spite *me*, not to please *you*.   40

9

Praise of Maecenas and a tactful refusal

Maecenas, knight of Etruscan royal blood,
    Keen not to rise above your rank,
Why launch me on a sea of writing so immense?
    Large sails do not suit my raft.

It's wrong to load your head with a weight you can't carry 5
    And then to give in, overburdened and bent-kneed.
Not everything is equally right for everyone
    And more than one palm can be won from the same summit.

Lysippus' glory is casting lifelike statuary;
    Calamis appeals to me with well-wrought horses. 10
Apelles demands first prize for his picture of Venus;
    Parrhasius claims a place for small-scale art.
Mentor's mould more frequently is given a theme,
    But Mys entwines acanthus' miniature path.
Phidias' Jove is decked in imaged ivory, 15
    While his own city's marble sells Praxiteles.
There's those the palm of Elis' four-horse chariot suits;
    There's those destined for glory by swift feet.
One man's born for peace, one right for military service;
    Everyone follows his natural bent. 20

But it's your rule of life that I accept, Maecenas,
    And must prevail by quoting your example.
When you might in Roman office move imperial axes
    And legal rulings in mid-Forum,
Or march among the aggressive lances of the Medes 25
    And hang up trophies to adorn your home,
And Caesar's power would further your success, and all
    The time wealth come your way so easily,
You hold back, humbly restrict yourself to modest shadow
    And choose to reef your swelling sails. 30
Believe me, this decision matches you with great
    Camillus; you too will live on men's lips,
And take your stand at Caesar's side in history.
    True loyalty will be Maecenas' trophies.

I do not cleave the ocean swell in a sailing-ship 35
    But am safely occupied on a little river.
I'll not mourn Cadmus' city's fall on paternal ashes
    Nor seven combats equally disastrous
Nor tell of Scaean Gates and Troy, Apollo's city,
    And how the Dánaän fleet returned in the tenth spring 40
When the victorious Wooden Horse of Pallas' making

Flattened Neptune's walls with a Grecian plough.
Enough if I can please along with Callimachus' verse
    And sing in your metre, poet of Cos.
May these my writings fire the hearts of boys and girls,   45
    May they call me God and bring me worship.

But lead the way and I'll sing Jove's arms and Coeus threatening
    Heaven and Eurýmedon on Phlegréan heights.
I'll tackle the lofty Palatine grazed by Roman bulls
    And the walls that Remus' murder strengthened   50
And the pair of princes reared on a woodland udder.
    My wit will grow to do your bidding.
I'll also track triumphal cars from either shore,
    The Parthian darts shot back in crafty flight,
Pelùsium's fortress undermined by Roman steel,   55
    And Antony's hands intent on his own doom.

As backer, though, of early manhood choose loose reins
    And signal your approval of my racing wheels:
You grant me that much praise, Maecenas, and thanks to you
    I too shall rate as one of your coterie.   60

10

Cynthia's birthday

I wondered why Camenae called on me so early,
    Standing by my bed in blushing sunlight.
They signalled that it was my girl's birthday
    And clapped their hands three times for luck.

May the day go without a cloud, winds halt in air,   5
    And threatening wave sink softly on dry land.
In today's light let me see no one sorrowing;
    Let even Niobe's stone cease weeping.
Let halcyon voices rest, laments forgotten,
    Nor Itys' mother mourn his death.   10

And you, my dear one, born with happy omens, rise
    And duly pray as the Gods demand.

But first with pure water dash away sleep
   And with deft fingers do your sleek hair.
Then put on the dress you wore when first you caught
     Propertius' 15
   Eyes, and do not leave your head ungarlanded;
And pray that the power of your beauty never fails
   And that you rule my head for ever.

Then when you've offered incense on the flower-crowned altar
   And favouring flame has lit up all the house, 20
Take account of table, let night run on among the wine-cups,
   And a myrrhine jar salve the nostrils with saffron oil.
Let dancing through the night tire out the strident pipe
   And your salacious wit have free play;
Let sweet conviviality banish ungrateful sleep, 25
   Deafening the air of the nearby public road.
Cast lots and let the fall of the dice inform us whom
   The Boy God whips with heavy wings.

When the time is up after many measures of wine
   And ministering Venus ordains nocturnal worship, 30
We'll solemnize the anniversary in our sanctum
   And so round off the journey of your birthday.

11

The power of women over men

   Why be surprised that a woman manages my life,
      Leading my manhood captive as her slave,
   And frame a shameful charge of cowardice against me
      Because I can't snap the yoke and break my chains?
   The sailor better forecasts the movement of the winds, 5
      The soldier has learnt from wounds to be afraid.
   I too in past youth used your boastful language;
      Let my present plight teach *you* to fear.

   A Colchian girl yoked fiery bulls with adamant,
      Sowed fights in armour-bearing ground, 10

And closed the guardian serpent's savage jaws
  So golden wool could go to Aeson's house.
Proud Amazon Penthesilea once dared from horseback
  Attack the Dánaän fleet with arrows,
And when the golden helmet had exposed her brow   15
  Conquered the conqueror with her beauty.
Omphale advanced to such renown for beauty
  (The Lydian girl who dipped in Gyges' lake)
That he who had raised his Pillars in a world at peace
  Spun her soft wool with horny hand.   20
Semiramis built the Persian city of Babylon,
  Rearing a massive work with walls of brick
On which two chariots could be sent to pass each other
  Without their sides being grazed by touching axles,
And she led Euphrates through the citadel she founded   25
  And bade the Bactrians bow down to her rule.
For why should I drag heroes and why Gods into court?
  Jove disgraces himself and his own house.

What of her who lately brought scandal on our arms,
  A woman even laid by her own slaves?   30
As price of her foul marriage she demanded that Rome's walls
  And Senators should pass into her power.
Delinquent Alexandria, land most attached to guile,
  And Memphis, to our cost so often blood-stained,
Where sand denuded Pompey of three Triumphs,   35
  That stigma Rome will bear for ever!
Better for you to have died on the Phlegréan plain
  Or bowed the neck to your father-in-law.
The harlot queen forsooth of incestuous Canopus,
  Sole stigma branded on us by Philip's blood,   40
Even dared oppose our Jove with her yelping Anubis,
  Force Tiber to endure the threats of Nile,
Repulse the Roman trumpet with her jangling sistrum,
  Chase beaked Liburnians with punt-poled barges,
Tent the Tarpeian rock with vile mosquito nets   45
  And hold court next to Marius' arms and statues!
What was the use of breaking Tarquin's axes
  (Whose proud life marks him with like name)
If now we had to endure a woman? Sing *Triumph*, Rome,

You're safe, and pray 'Long live Augustus!' 50
You fled, though, to the wandering streams of frightened Nile;
    Your hands accepted Romulus' fetters.
I saw your forearms bitten by the sacred snakes
    And your limbs channelling sleep's hidden progress.
'With this great citizen, Rome, you need not have feared me', 55
    So spoke even the tongue much wine had buried.

The lofty city on seven hills that rules the world
    In terror feared the threats of a female Mars. 58
But Gods were founders of these walls and Gods protect them; 65
    While Caesar lives Rome hardly need fear Jove. 66
Where now are Scipio's navies, where Camillus' standards 67
    Or, Bosporus, those lately won by Pompey's hand? 68
Spoils of Hannibal, monuments of conquered Syphax, 59
    Pyrrhus' glory broken at our feet? 60
Curtius raised a monument by the chasm he filled; 61
    Decius on galloping steed cut short the battle. 62
A lane attests the broken bridge of Cocles; 63
    There's one to whom a raven gave his surname. 64
Apollo of Leucas will call to mind those routed ranks; 69
    One day destroyed so great an armament. 70
But, sailor, whether bound for port or leaving it,
    On all the Ionian main remember Caesar.

12

A modern Ulysses and Penelope

Oh Postumus, how could you leave Galla in tears
    And follow Augustus' eagles as a soldier?
What price the glory of a Parthian plundered
    If your Galla begged you not to do it?
If only all you money-grubbers could die together 5
    And those who prefer the army to a faithful wife!
Yet you, the madman, clad in soldier's cloak, will drink,
    When weary, Araxes' water from your helmet,
While she will pine away at every empty rumour
    For fear this courage of yours turn sour for you, 10

And Median arrows revel in your murder
    Or a trooper in chain-mail on an armoured horse,
And your pitiful remains be brought back in an urn;
    For so return the fallen from that front.

Thrice, four times blest in your chaste Galla, Postumus,   15
    Your ways deserved a different wife.
What will a girl not do, relieved of fear's restraint,
    When Rome is there to teach her self-indulgence?
But don't you worry. Gifts will not win Galla
    And she'll forget your callousness.   20
For on whatever day the Fates send you back safe
    Faithful Galla will hang upon your neck.

Postumus—a second Ulysses with a model wife!
    So many long set-backs did *him* no harm.
Ten years of war, Ciconian Mt. Ísmara, Calpe,   25
    Then Polyphemus' eye burnt out,
Circe's deceit, the lotus and addictive herbs,
    Scylla and Charybdis (her waters riven alternately),
Lampétië's oxen mooing on Ithacan skewers
    (Lampetie fed them for her father Phoebus),   30
His flight from the bower of Aeaea's weeping girl,
    His swimming all those winter nights and days,
His entering the dark home of the silent ghosts,
    The approach with deaf oarsmen to the Sirens' pool,
His former bow's revival for the suitors' death   35
    And so the ending of his wandering—
In happiness, for his wife stayed true to him at home.
    But Aelia Galla's faith defeats Penelope's.

13

Luxury is destroying Rome

You ask why greedy girls charge so much for their nights
    And wealth drained dry by Venus bemoans its losses?
The cause of such disasters is clear beyond a doubt:
    The road to luxury is too wide-open.

The Indian ant exports her gold from hollow mines   5
    And from the Red Sea comes the Shell of Eryx,
And Cadmus' Tyre provides molluscan dyes
    And the Arab shepherd fragrant cinnamon.
These weapons even storm secluded virtue
    And girls fastidious as Penelope.   10
The matron promenades wearing a spendthrift's fortune,
    Parading dishonour's spoil before our eyes.
There's no restraint in asking, no restraint in giving,
    Or, if there is, cash cancels it at once.

Lucky their unique funeral law for Eastern husbands   15
    Whom red Aurora's horses darken.
For when the last torch is thrown on the death-bearing couch
    A faithful throng of wives with hair unbound stands by
And holds a fatal competition—to follow, live, their consort.
    They are ashamed if not allowed to die.   20
They burn victorious, bare their bosoms to the flame
    And kiss their husbands with charred lips.
But our kind of bride is faithless. Here among our girls
    There's no faithful Evadne or true Penelope.

Lucky of old the country youth, living in peace,   25
    Whose wealth was tree and harvest,
Their contribution quinces shaken from the bough
    And punnets full of purple blackberries,
Or hand-picked violets or payment of mixed lilies
    Translucent through their wicker baskets,   30
And bringing grapes wrapped up in their own leaves
    Or a speckled bird with iridescent plumage.

In caves and dells in those days girls gave stolen kisses
    Bought by these favours to their woodland men.
Only a fawn-skin used to cover lovers   35
    And grass grew deep on a natural couch,
And a leaning pine tree threw its lingering shade around.
    To glimpse a naked Goddess was not punishable.

Into the Arcadian shepherd's empty fold the ram,
    Horned leader, on his own led back the full-fed ewes.   40

Gods and Goddesses all, you who protect the fields,
   Your altars offered kindly words:
'Stranger who come in this glen of mine, you may hunt the hare
   And the wild fowl, if so be you look for them,
And call me, the God Pan, from the crags as your companion,   45
   Whether you seek the prize with fowling-rod or hound.'

But now the shrines are idle in forsaken groves;
   Religion conquered, all men worship gold.
Gold drives out honesty, justice is sold for gold,
   Law goes for gold, next, lawless, honour too.   50
Burnt-out portals prove the sacrilege of Brennus
   When he attacked the unshorn God's Pythian kingdom:
But from its bay-clad summit Mount Parnassus, shaken,
   Scattered dread snow upon the Gallic army.
Receiving gold the Thracian villain Polymestor   55
   Treated you, Polydorus, to a treacherous welcome.
That you too, Eriphyla, might wear gold on your arms
   Amphiaráüs vanished with his horses.

I'll speak out—would my country thought me a true prophet!:
   Proud Rome is rotten with her own prosperity.   60
I tell no lie but none believe. Nor was Cassandra
   Long ago believed about Troy's ruin.
She alone said that Paris plotted Phrygia's doom,
   That the Horse crept in with treason to her country.
Her ravings were momentous for country and for parent;   65
   Her futile tongue experienced God's truth.

14

The advantage of Spartan athletics

Sparta, we much admire the rules of your palaestra,
   But more its many female gymnastic attractions.
Naked girls and men wrestling together train
   Their bodies in games without dishonour,
When the ball deceives the arms in its swift flight   5
   And the hook clinks on the rolling hoop

And women covered in dust stand at the winning-post
   And suffer wounds in the cruel pancratium.
Now they gladly bind their arms with thongs for boxing,
   Now wheel the discus' weight in a circle before throwing.   10
They tread the ring on horseback, belt sword to snow-white thigh
   And protect girlish heads with hollow bronze,   12
And sometimes, with hair frost-powdered, follow their country's
      hounds   15
   Over Taýgetus' long ridges,   16
Like the belligerent throng of Amazons, bare-breasted,   13
   Who bathe in Thermódon's waters,   14
And like Pollux and Castor on Eurótas' sands   17
   (One soon to be prize boxer, the other horseman)
Between whom Helen with bare nipples took up arms
   They say, nor blushed before her brother Gods.   20

So Spartan law forbids the separation of lovers;
   In public each may be at his sweetheart's side.
There is no fear, no custody for enclosed girls,
   No punishment by strict husbands to be by-passed,
No go-between (you speak yourself of your own affairs),   25
   No tediously long rejection,
No Tyrian dresses to deceive the roving eye,
   No boring attention to perfumed hair.

But our girls move surrounded by a massive throng;
   There's not even room to insert a finger.   30
One has to guess at her looks and the fitting form of request.
   The lover gropes his way in the dark.
But had you copied the rules and contests of Laconia,
   I'd like you the better, Rome, for that attraction.

15

His faithfulness and the story of Dirce

So may I never know another lover's quarrel
   Or even face a sleepless night without you:
When the purple-hemmed gown's restraint was lifted from me
   And freedom granted to learn the way of love,

She who initiated my raw vigour, the accomplice   5
  Of those first nights, ah, won by no gifts, was Lycinna.
But for the last three years or very little less
  Our intercourse, I recall, has been a bare ten words.
Love for you has buried all else, nor after you
  Has any woman thrown sweet chains around my neck.   10

Dirce will witness, so enraged by the untrue charge
  That Nycteus' Antíope had lain with Lycus.
How many times the queen tore that girl's lovely hair
  And fastened cruel hands on her soft cheeks!
How many times burdened her slave with oppressive chores   15
  And ordered her to lay head on hard ground!
Often she let her live in filth and darkness,
  Often refused her hunger and thirst cheap water.

Jupiter, have you comfort nowhere for long-suffering
  Antiope? A hard chain galls her hands.   20
If God you are it shames you that your girl should slave.
  On whom but Jove can chained Antiope call?
Unaided though, exerting all her body's strength,
  She broke the royal handcuffs from both hands,
Then fled on frightened feet towards Cithaeron's heights.   25
  It was night, and hoarfrost made a wretched bed.

Often, scared by the fitful noise of Asópus' stream,
  She fancied her mistress feet were following.
She, their mother, found, when driven from her own farm,
  Amphíon soft and Zethus hard to her tears.   30
And as when level sea drops its mighty movements
  When Eurus ceases to contend with Notus,
The sound of the sand on the silent shore grows fainter,
  So the girl slipped, her knees gave way, and she fell.

Though late, devotion came: the sons realized their fault;   35
  You, the old man, trusty guardian of Jove's sons,
Restored their mother to the boys. The boys tied Dirce
  To the head of a wild bull to be dragged away.
Acknowledge Jove, Antíope. You triumph over Dirce
  Who is drawn to meet her death in many places.   40

Zethus' meadows are red with blood. Victorious
   Amphion sang the paean on Aracýnthus' crag.

So you should stop tormenting innocent Lycinna,
   Though woman's headlong anger knows no turning,
And let no scandal about *us* disturb your ears;   45
   Burnt on funeral firewood I'd still love only you.

16

The midnight summons

Midnight, and there has come a letter from my mistress
   Commanding my immediate presence at Tibur,
Where white hilltops display twin towers and the Anienan
   Nymph dives down to spacious pools.
What should I do? Trust myself to obstructive dark,   5
   Frightened of physical assault?
But if through fright I disobeyed her orders, tears
   Would be worse than any midnight foe for me.
Once I offended and was banished a whole year;
   She handles me with no light touch.   10

Besides, lovers are sacred. No one will harm them.
   They can stroll down the middle of Sciron's road.
Anyone in love can walk the Scythian wilds;
   There's no one barbarous enough to hurt him.
The moon attends his journey, stars reveal rough ground;   15
   Love himself leads, shaking a lighted torch.
Watch-dogs' fierce fury turns aside its gaping jaws;
   Such people find roads safe at any time.
What villain would be sprinkled with a lover's trickle of blood?
   Venus herself bears locked-out lovers company.   20

But even if certain doom were to follow my adventure
   I'd be quite prepared to pay that price.
She will bring me perfumes and adorn the tomb
   With garlands, sitting by my grave on guard.
May the Gods forbid that she lay *my* bones in crowded ground   25

Where the vulgar travel on the busy road.
Such lovers' tombs are desecrated after death.
Let lonely ground and trees in leaf protect me.
Or bury me under a small fenced heap of anonymous sand;
I'd not wish to be a name on the public highway.   30

17

Prayer to Bacchus to cure his love

Now, O Bacchus, we make obeisance at *your* altar.
Grant me calm thoughts, Father, and fair voyage.
You can still the gales of raging Venus;
Your wine can be a cure for care.
You can unite lovers and you can separate them.   5
Bacchus, wash away the fault from my heart.
For in the stars, as proof that you too are no novice,
There's Ariadne, carried to heaven by your lynxes.
This trouble that keeps old fires burning in my bones,
Only death will cure it—or your wine.   10
Always a sober night tortures lonely lovers;
Hope and fear torment their hearts as they toss and turn.

But if, O Bacchus, by your gift this heated brain
Can summon slumber to my bones,
I will sow vines myself and plant the hills with rows   15
Which I shall watch, so no wild beast can strip them.
Provided that my vats are swollen with purple must
And the new bunches stain the feet that tread them,
I'll live the rest of my life through you and your horns, Bacchus,
And be known as poet of your power.   20

I'll tell how Etna's bolt brought on your mother's labour,
Of Indian armies routed by Nyséan dances,
Of Lycurgus vainly raging against the new-found vine,
Of Pentheus' corpse dismembered by three gangs,
How Tuscan sailors in the shape of curving dolphins   25
Dived from a vine-wreathed ship into the sea,
And how for you sweet-smelling rivers flow through Dia

From which the Naxian throng drink your neat wine.

Your white neck shall be laden with trailing ivy-clusters
    And a Lydian bonnet circle your Bassaric hair. 30
From your smooth nape shall drip the fragrant olive oil
    And a flowing robe stroke your bare feet.
Dircéan Thebes shall thump the wanton tambourine
    And goatfoot Pans play on their hollow reeds.
Nearby with tower-crowned head Cybébe, the Great Goddess, 35
    Shall clash harsh cymbals for Idéan dances.

Before the temple door, as priest pouring libation
    Of wine from a gold crater in your worship,
These things, to be remembered by no humble buskin, I
    Shall report with Pindar's stormy inspiration: 40
Do you but free me from proud slavery
    And overpower this troubled head with sleep.

18

An elegy on the death of Marcellus

Where sea, enclosed by shadowy Avernus, plays
    With Baiae's steaming pools of warm water,
And where in sand there lies Troy's trumpeter Misenus
    And the highway built by Hercules' labour can be heard;
Here where cymbals clashed together for the Theban God 5
    When he sought out mortal cities with his favour—
But now, O Baiae hated for a great offence,
    What hostile God has halted by your water?—
Here overwhelmed he sank his face in Stygian waves
    And that fine spirit wanders on your lake. 10

What help to him were birth or virtue or the best
    Of mothers or his link with Caesar's hearth?
Or lately the awnings floating over a packed theatre,
    And everything his mother's hands achieved?
He died, and for poor him the twentieth year stood still; 15
    In such small compass Time closed so much good.

Go now, lift up your spirits and imagine Triumphs,
  Enjoy whole theatres standing to applaud,
Outdo Attalic tapestries and for your great Games
  Bejewel all—you throw it on the pyre.   20

To this, though, all must come, highest in rank and lowest;
  Evil the road but everyone must tread it.
One must win mercy from the Dog's three barking throats
  And board the grim Greybeard's public ferry.
The wary can surround himself with iron and bronze   25
  But Death will drag his head from its enclosure.
Good looks gave Nireus no exemption, nor strength Achilles,
  Nor wealth, born of Pactólus' water, Croesus.
This grief once devastated the ignorant Achaeans
  When Atrides' second love cost them so dear.   30

For you, though, Sailor who ferry mankind's faithful shades,
  They carry here the body emptied of its soul,
Which, like Sicily's conqueror Claudius and like
  Caesar, has left the paths of humans for the stars.

19

Women more lustful than men

You keep protesting to me about our lechery;
  Your sex, believe me, is more prone to that.
You, when you break the bridle of scorned modesty,
  Can't keep your mind's obsession within bounds.

Sooner could flames be quenched in burning cornfields,   5
  Rivers run backwards to their source,
Syrtes give sailors a calm haven, and wild Maléa
  Welcome them to a safe shore,
Than anyone could check you in mid-career
  And blunt the goad of your mad lust.   10

Witness that victim of a Cretan bull's disdain,
  Donning a wooden cow's false horns;

Witness Salmonis, ardent for Thessaly's Enipeus,
    Desiring total submission to a fluid God;
Myrrha too, that scandal, on fire for her ageing father,   15
    Entombed among the leaves of a new tree.

No need to cite Medea—that time when mother-love
    Placated rage by murdering her children;
Or Clytemnestra, thanks to whom all Pelops' house
    Stands shamed by adultery at Mycenae;   20
And you who sold yourself for Minos' looks, O Scylla,
    Shearing that purple lock—your father's kingdom.
Such, then, the dower a virgin pledged her enemy!
    Love opened your gates, Nisus, by deceit.
May *you* burn happier marriage-torches, unwed girls!   25
    Hanging from a Cretan ship she's dragged along,
But not without good cause Minos sits judge in Orcus:
    Though victor he was fair to the enemy.

20

A proposal

Do you suppose he still remembers how you look,
    The man you saw sail away from your bed?
How callous to trade-in one's girl for profit!
    Was all of Africa worth your tears?
You're foolish to presume on Gods and empty words;   5
    He's likely rubbing bosoms with another love.

You have compelling beauty, chaste Pallas' accomplishments,
    And you shine with a learned forebear's reflected fame.
How happy your home if only you had a faithful friend!
    I will be faithful. Run, girl, to my bed.   10
And you who drive your summer fires too far afield,
    Phoebus, cut short the course of lingering day.
First night for me is coming. Make time for first night!
    O linger longer, Moon, on our first bed!

But there are still terms to be fixed, conditions sealed,   15

A contract written for this new love of mine.
Love will himself tie up these pledges with his seal;
    Witness, the starry Goddess' plaited crown.
How many hours must needs be given to my discussions
    Before Venus provokes us to sweet war!   20
For when a union is not bound by a fixed agreement
    There's no avenging God for sleepless nights,
And lust soon breaks the bonds of those it has imposed on.
    For us, though, may first omens ensure faithfulness.

So then whoever breaks the altars pledged in contract,   25
    Profaning marriage rites with a new love,
His be all the sufferings love knows
    And he be target for shrill gossip,
And his mistress' window stay shut nightly to his tears;
    Let him ever love and ever lack love's fruit.   30

21

Travel is the only cure for love

I must away on the great journey to learned Athens
    To rid myself by travel of love's burden.
One's care for a girl grows by continual gazing;
    Love is its own chief nourishment.
I have tried every means of putting him to flight   5
    But after all the God still grips me.
She never admits me, or only once after many refusals,
    And if she comes, sleeps clothed on the bed's edge.
The only cure will be foreign travel. Then love
    Will go as far from mind as Cynthia from sight.   10

Oh come then, comrades, push the boat down to the sea
    And draw lots, pairing off, for your oar-stations,
And hoist sail to the masthead with good luck, already
    The breeze promises sailors a clear voyage.
Farewell, towers of Rome, and you, my friends, and you, 15
    My girl, however you treated me, farewell.
So I'm to sail now, the Adriatic's callow guest,

Forced now to pray to breaker-thundering Gods.
Then when my yacht has crossed the Ionian and lowered
    Tired sails in the calm water of Lechaeum,   20
For what remains make haste, my feet, to bear the burden
    Where Isthmian mainland separates two seas.
Next, when the shores of Piraeus' harbour welcome me,
    I'll mount the long arms of Theseus' Way.

There I'll begin to improve my mind in the training ground   25
    Of Plato or learned Epicurus' Garden.
Or I'll pursue the study of the tongue, Demosthenes' weapon,
    And the wit of smart Menander's books.
Or at any rate painted panels will catch my eyes
    And work in ivory or, better, bronze.   30
Either the lapse of years or the deep's long distances
    Will heal the wound in my silent breast,
Or I shall die, broken by Fate, not shameful love,
    And the day of my death shall do me honour.

22

To Tullus in praise of Italy

Has cool Cyzicus where Propontis' waters wash
    The isthmus pleased you, Tullus, all these years?
And Dindyméan Cybébe carved in holy vinewood
    And the road which carried Dis the abductor's steeds?
Though you may like the cities of Athamantid Helle   5
    Yet remember, Tullus, how I miss you.

Were you to see Atlas carrying the whole sky,
    And Medusa's head severed by Perseus' hand,
Géryon's stables, marks in the dust where Hercules
    And Antaeus wrestled, the dance of the Hesperides—   10
Were oarsmen of yours to sweep the Phasis and you to retrace
    The voyage of the vessel hewn on Pelion,
Where swam between rocks, following the Argóan dove,
    An untried pinetree, bent to the shape of a strange prow,
And though Ortygia should be seen, Caÿster's mouth,   15

And the stream that tempers seven channels,
The Roman land beats all the wonders of the world;
    Here Nature has placed them all from everywhere.

Fitter for war than friend of felony this land.
    Fame is not ashamed of Roman history.   20
For strong we stand through duty no less than by steel;
    In victory our anger stays its hand.
Here flows Tiburnian Anio, Clitumnus from Umbrian glen,
    And Aqua Marcia, lasting monument,
Alban and Nemorensian Lakes from neighbour streams,   25
    And the healthy spring that Pollux' charger drank.

But no cerastes slides along on scaly belly
    Nor do Italian waters rage with weird monsters.
Not here the clank of Andromeda's chains for her mother's fault
    Nor has Phoebus fled in horror at Ausonian feasts   30
Nor have distant fires burnt anyone to death
    As a mother planned her son's destruction.
No savage Bacchanals hunt Pentheus in his tree;
    No substitute doe frees the Dánaän fleet.
Juno has not had power to curve horns on a mistress   35
    Or disfigure beauty with bovine looks .

                    *   *   *   *   *

Sinis' arboreal crosses, and rocks inhospitable
    To Greeks, and tree-trunks curved to kill them.

This is your mother, Tullus, this your loveliest seat.
    Here you should strive for the honour your clan deserves.   40
Here's scope for civic eloquence, here's ample hope
    Of grandchildren and future wife's fit love.

23

Lost, the poet's writing tablets

Lost after all—my clever writing-tablets,
    And lost too all those well-turned phrases!

My frequent handling had long worn them down.
    No need of a seal to prove them mine.

They had learned, without me, to make my peace with girls 5
  And to speak, without me, the words that told.
No gold fittings made them valuable;
  They were just soiled wax on common boxwood.
Even so they always remained faithful to me
  And always earned good results. 10

Perhaps they carried some such message as this: 'I'm cross,
  You brute, that you were so late yesterday.
Have *you* found someone prettier? Are *you*
  The one spreading unkind lies about me?'
Or was it 'Come today. We'll relax together. 15
  Love will provide night-long entertainment,'—
And whatever a talkative girl who's willing and no fool
  Thinks up when making a date for secret love?

Oh dear, some miser is writing his accounts on them
  And shelving them with his callous ledgers. 20

Gold shall reward the finder who returns them to me.
  Who'd keep firewood when he could be rich?
Quick, boy, go and post up this notice on a pillar
  And give your master's address—the Esquiline.

24

Free from love at last

Woman, you're wrong to be so sure of your good looks;
  It's my eyes long since made you arrogant.
Such praises, Cynthia, my love accorded you
  That I'm ashamed my verses brought you fame.
I praised you as compounded of assorted beauty 5
  So that love thought you were what you were not;
Many's the time I likened your colour to rosy Dawn
  When in fact your cheeks were white with make-up—
A practice family friends could not dissuade me from
  Nor witchcraft wash away in the endless ocean. 10

I'll make this true confession, not forced by fire and steel
    And even by shipwreck in the Aegean sea.
Carried away I was roasting in Venus' cruel bronze,
    A prisoner, hands tied behind my back.
But look, my ship has entered harbour, garlanded;   15
    I've passed the Syrtes and dropped anchor.
Now, tired of the endless surge, I can at last think straight.
    That open wound of mine has knit and healed.
Good Sense, if you're a Goddess, I dedicate myself
    To your shrine. Jove was deaf to all my prayers.   20

25

Goodbye and fare ill

I've been a laughing-stock among the guests at banquets
    And everyone could chatter on about me.
I managed for five years to serve you faithfully;
    Gnawing your nails you'll often miss my faith.
Weeping can't move me. I've been caught by that performance.   5
    Cynthia, your tears are always calculated.
I too shall weep at parting, but outrage conquers grief.
    You do not let the yoke sit comfortably.

Farewell now to the doorstep that sheds tears at my words
    And the door I never smashed despite my anger.   10
But you—may age and the years you've hidden weigh you down
    And wrinkles come to spoil your beauty!
May your desire then be to root out the white hairs,
    While the mirror, alas, accuses you of wrinkles.
Excluded in your turn may you suffer pride's disdain,   15
    A crone complaining you're done by as you did!
These curses my prophetic page has sung for you;
    So learn to dread your beauty's aftermath!

BOOK IV

I

Poet and astrologer: a dialogue

PROPERTIS

'This panorama, stranger, now Imperial Rome,
  Till Phrygian Aeneas' time was hill and grass.
Where stands the Palatine, sacred to Naval Phoebus,
  Exiled Evander's cattle lay together.
These golden temples grew for Gods of terracotta;   5
  An artless hovel was no slur on them.
The Tarpeian Father used to thunder from bare rock
  And Tiber was an alien to our cattle.
Where yonder house of Remus rises up on steps
  One hearth was once the brothers' whole domain.   10
The Curia, now shining high for purple Senate,
  Held simple rustic fathers wearing hides.
A cow-horn called old-world Quirites to debate;
  Their Senate was often one hundred in a field.
No rippling awnings hung above a hollow theatre.   15
  And no stage reeked of ceremonial saffron.

No one then was keen to seek out foreign Gods
  When the awe-struck crowd hung on their fathers' ritual.
Straw bonfires celebrated Pales' annual feast
  And such lustrations as now a bob-tail horse renews.   20
Impoverished Vesta rejoiced in flower-crowned donkeys;
  Lean kine drew her humble sacred emblems.
Small crossroad shrines were purified by fatted pigs
  And piping shepherds found Gods' favour with sheeps' lights.
Hide-clad ploughmen brandished whips of hairy goatskin;   25
  Hence the lewd rites of Fabius Lupercus.

No uncouth soldier threatened in his gleaming armour;
  They fought their battles unprotected, with fired staves.

In wolfskin helmet Lycmon pitched the first Praetorium
    And most of Tatius' exploits concerned sheep.   30
Hence manly Titiës, Ramnes, and Solonian Luceres;
    Hence Romulus drove the four white horses.
Bovillae indeed was not a suburb when Rome was small,
    And Gabii, now nothing, a multitude.
And Alba stood, a power, born of the white sow's sign,   35
    When going from here to Fidenae was a long journey.
The Roman nursling has no inheritance but his name;
    No shame to have a she-wolf foster-mother.

Well was it, Troy, you exiled your Penates here.
    Ah, with what augury the Dardan ship set sail!   40
The omens were already good when the opening
    Of the Wooden Horse's womb brought her no harm
And when the anxious father clung to his son's neck
    And fire feared to burn those pious shoulders.
Then came the nerve of Decius and Brutus' axes,   45
    And Venus herself brought us Caesar's arms,
Carrying the victorious arms of Troy reborn.
    Happy the land that housed your Gods, Iulus!
If indeed the shaken Sibyl's Avernian tripod
    Told of fields to be purged by Aventine Remus,   50
Or if the songs of the Pergamene seer, too late fulfilled,
    Were true as touching long-lived Priam:
"Dánaäns, take back the Horse! You win in vain. The land
    Of Ilium shall live. Jove shall arm these ashes."

She-wolf of Mars, best of nurses for our Republic,   55
    What walls have grown up from your milk!
And now I seek to plan those walls in devoted verse:
    Alas that the sound in my mouth is weak!
But still whatever the stream that flows from my feeble breast
    All of it shall serve my birthplace.   60
Ennius can wreathe his sayings with a ragged garland,
    But give me, Bacchus, leaves from your own ivy,
That Umbria may swell with pride at our books,
    Umbria, birthplace of Rome's Callimachus!
Whoever sees her hilltops climbing from the valleys   65
    Should rate those ramparts by my genius.

Be gracious, Rome. For you the work proceeds. Grant happy
   Omens, citizens. Sing, bird, favouring the attempt.   68
I'll say "Troy, you shall fall and rise again as Rome";   87
   I'll sing of distant graves on land and sea.   88
I'll sing of rites and days and the ancient names of places.   69
   This is the goal towards which my steed must sweat.'   70

HOROS

'Unstable Propertius, why this ignorant rush to turn prophet?
   Your thread was not spun from a dexterous distaff.
Your cantillations will end in tears. Apollo's against them
   You'll rue the words you force from a reluctant lyre.

I bring you Truth, on True Authority, or I'm a seer   75
   Unable to operate his orrery.
I am Horos, whom Archýtas' scion, the Babylonian
   Orops, begat; my family descends from Conon.
The Gods will witness I am no disgrace to my relations
   And in my writings credibility takes first place.   80
But now they turn the Gods to profit and (Jove is fooled
   By gold) the repeated Signs of the Slanting Circle
And Jove's auspicious and Mars's predatory stars
   And Saturn's planet, dangerous to all alike,
What Pisces augurs and the valiant Sign of Leo   85
   And Capricornus, washed in the Western Sea.   86

I prophesied, when Arria brought forth twin sons   89
   (She destined them for the army against God's will),   90
They could not bring their javelins home to the Penates.
   Two graves now prove my credibility:
Lupercus the horseman, while shielding his wounded face,
   Alas, did not foresee his horse's fall beneath him;
Gallus in camp, while guarding the Standards in his care,   95
   Fell before the bloodstained beak of his own Eagle.
Ill-fated lads, two victims of their mother's greed!
   And so my words came true—against my will.
Then, when Lucína lengthened Cínara's labour-pains,
   Delaying the slow burden of her womb,   100
I said "Make sacrifice to Juno. Your prayer is heard."
   She gave birth and my almanacs won the palm.

Such things Jove's sandy Libyan cave can't straighten out
    Or a liver's lobe announcing divine secrets
Or any interpreter of raven's wings in flight   105
    Or a ghost materializing in magic water.
One must observe Heaven's path and the true bypass through
    The stars and seek one's proof from the Five Zones.

Let Calchas be a warning, for he launched from Aulis
    Ships well moored to God-fearing rocks.   110
He also plunged his knife in the neck of Agamemnon's
    Girl and gave the Atridae bloodstained sails.
The Dánaäns, though, did not return. Restrain your tears,
    Sacked Troy! Remember the Euboean coast!
At nightfall Nauplius displays avenging fires   115
    And Greece is flotsam, sunk with all her spoils.
Now seize and rape the prophetess, victorious Ajax,
    Whose robe Pallas forbade you to tear off!

So much for History. I turn now to your stars.
    Resign yourself to hearing tearful news.   120
Ancient Umbria bore you, to widely known Penates.
    Do I lie or is your homeland's border reached
Where misty Mevania drips on the low-lying plain
    And the Umbrian Lake grows warm in summer
And Assisi's climbing rampart rises on the hill,   125
    Rampart your genius makes wider known?
Too young for such gathering you gathered your father's bones
    And were yourself reduced to hard-up Lares.
Though many were the steers that ploughed your country estate
    The ruthless rod annexed your landed wealth.   130
Anon, when the golden locket left your callow neck
    And you donned freedom's toga before your mother's Gods,
Apollo then dictates you fragments of his song
    Forbidding you the mad Forum's verbal thunder.

Well, make up elegies. Tricky work! This is your field.   135
    Let crowds of others write with you as model.
You'll face campaigning under Venus' deceptive arms
    And make a useful target for her Cupids.
Whatever palms of victory your hardships gain

One girl will mock them and your grasp. 140
Though you shake off the hook imbedded in your chin
　　It's no good—the gaff's prong will spike you.
At her dictation you will see darkness and light
　　And shed a tear but when she orders it.
To seal her door and post a thousand guards won't help you; 145
　　A chink's enough if she's resolved to cheat.

And now, your ship can wrestle with mid-ocean's waves
　　Or you can walk defenceless into armed foes
Or earth can quake and open up a yawning chasm—
　　Only, beware the baleful back of the eight-legged Crab!' 150

2

The god Vertumnus explains himself

If you're surprised at my one body's many forms
　　Learn the ancestral signs of the God Vertumnus.
A Tuscan I, of Tuscans sprung, with no regrets
　　At leaving my Volsinian hearth in wartime.
I like the crowds here nor delight in ivory temples; 5
　　Enough that I can see the Roman Forum.
Once Tiberinus journeyed this way, and they say
　　The sound of oars was heard striking the shallows.
But after he conceded this much to his nurslings
　　I'm called Vertumnus from the river turned. 10
Or else as I pre-empt the turning year's first-fruits
　　They're thought to be Vertumnus' perquisite.
For me the first grapes *vari*egate in mottled clusters
　　And the corn-spikes *tum*esce with milky grain.
Here you can see sweet cherries, here autumnal plums, 15
　　And on a summer's day red mulberries.
The grafter here will pay vows with a wreath of fruit
　　When pear bears apples on reluctant stock.

You wrong me, lying Fame. My name has other warrant.
　　Believe a God's own words about himself. 20
My nature is conformable to every shape;

Turn me to which you please I'll still look good.
Clothe me in Coan silks, I'll make a graceful girl;
    But in a toga who'd say I'm no man?
Give me a scythe and bind my brow with plaited hay,   25
    You'll swear my hands have mown a meadow.
I once bore arms, and won praise, I recall, as soldier.
    Carrying a heavy basket I turned picker.
Sober in court, when I put on a garland
    You'll protest the wine has gone to my head.   30
Wind my head in a turban, I'll steal Iacchus' role,
    And Phoebus' if you'll just hand me a plectrum.
Load me with nets, I hunt; but taking up a reed
    I'm then the God who favours feathered-fowling.
Vertumnus also appears as charioteer, and rider   35
    Who lightly leaps from one horse to another.
In broad-brimmed hat with rod I'll catch fish, and I'll walk
    In flowing tunic as a dapper salesman.
I can be shepherd leaning on a crook, or else
    Bring roses in rush baskets through the dust.   40
Why should I add the thing for which I'm most renowned,
    That choicest garden gifts are in my keeping?
The dark-green cucumber and the pot-bellied gourd
    And cabbage tied with light rush are my badge.
And no flower opens in the meadow but, when placed   45
    Upon my forehead, droops down prettily.
So from the fact that singly I turn into all shapes
    My country's tongue has given me my name.

And you, Rome, also recompensed my Tuscan kindred,
    Whence today's *Vicus Tuscus* has its name,   50
What time the Lycomedian came with allied arms
    And crushed the Sabine arms of barbarous Tatius.
I saw ranks giving way myself and weapons dropped
    And the enemy turn tail in shameful flight.
But grant, O Sower of the Gods, the toga'd throng   55
    Of Romans pass before my feet for ever.

Six lines remain. You, Sir, who hasten to answer bail,
    I'll not delay you. This is my last lap.
A maple stump was I, rough-hewn by hasty sickle,

Pre-Numa a poor God in a grateful city. 60
But you, Mamurrius, the engraver of bronze figures,
May Oscan earth not crush your artist's hands,
For your skill cast me for such well-adapted uses.
The work is one, its privileges many.

3

Letter to a husband at the front

This briefing Arethusa sends to her Lycotas—
    If you can be mine when you're away so much.
But if a smear makes any passage hard to read
    It will have been my tears that blotted it.
Or if the uncertain shape of any letter beats you 5
    It means my right hand was half dead.

Bactra has lately seen you in the re-travelled East,
    Lately too the Seric foe on mail-clad steed,
The wintry Goths and Britain with her painted chariots
    And the dark Indian pounded by Eoan seas. 10
Is this your marriage pledge and the love-nights promised me
    When I deferred, naïvely, to your insistence?
The torch that headed for good luck my bride-procession
    Caught its black flame from a fallen pyre,
And I was sprinkled from a Stygian pool, a crooked 15
    Fillet bound my hair and the Marriage-God was absent.
On all Rome's gates my vows (alas, no help!) are hanging.
    This cloak's the fourth I've woven for your campaigns.

Death to the man who hacked palisades from harmless trees
    And shaped the wailing trumpet from harsh bone. 20
Worthier he than sidelong Ocnus to twist rope
    And feed a donkey's endless hunger.
Tell me, does the corslet chafe your tender arms?
    The heavy spear blister hands not meant for war?
Sooner such hurts than that some girl should leave tooth-marks 25
    Upon your neck to make me cry.
They say your face is gaunt and drawn; I only pray
    Your pallor comes from missing me.

For me when the Evening Star brings nights of bitterness
  I kiss some weapon of yours left lying here.   30
Then I complain that the clothes keep slipping off the bed
  And the birds that herald dawn are slow to sing.
On winter nights I work away at wartime stints
  And the best Tyrian fleece for your parade cloak.
I learn just where Araxes flows, your next objective,   35
  How many miles a Parthian horse can go unwatered,
And needs must learn by heart worlds painted on a board
  And the way in which a clever God arranged things,
Which lands are frost-bound and which pulverize in drought,
  What wind will best bear sail to Italy.   40
One sister sits with me, and my pale, worried nurse
  Pretends that wintry weather holds you up.

Lucky Hippolyta! Bare-breasted, under arms,
  With helmet barbarously shielding her soft hair!
If only the camp would open up to Roman girls!   45
  I'd be a faithful baggage on your campaign.
And Scythian alps would not delay me when the Father
  Binds deep waters to ice with bitter cold.
All love is great but greater when one's husband's there:
  Venus in person fans that flame to life.   50
What use to me now is purple shining from Punic stuffs
  Or aqueous crystal to grace my hands?

There's everywhere dumb silence, and on rare Kalends
  My closed house hardly opens to one girl.
I'm even grateful when my doggie Craugis whines;   55
  She alone claims your side of the bed.
I cover shrines in flowers, wreathe crossroads with verbena,
  And savin crackles on ancient altar-hearths.
Or if, perched on a nearby beam, the night-owl hoots
  Or grudging oil-lamp needs a touch of wine,   60
That day demands a sacrifice of this year's lambs,
  And servers, loins girt up, are keen for their fresh pickings.

Please do not overrate the glory of Bactra scaled
  Or finest linen looted from some perfumed chief,
When leaden shot is scattered by the whirling sling   65

And sly bows twang from horses in retreat.
But (so, when Parthia's fosterlings have been subdued,
  May the plain spear-shaft follow your triumphant steeds)
Preserve inviolate the covenant of my bed!
  On these terms only would I have you back;   70
And when I bring Porta Capena votive weapons
  I'll sign 'A girl's thanks for her husband's safety'.

4

The story of Tarpeia

Of the Tarpeian grove and of Tarpeia's shameful tomb
  I'll speak, and of old Jove's precinct captured.

There was a thriving wood, hid in an ivied glen,
  And many a tree murmured against a natural stream,
Silvanus' branchy home, where the sweet-sounding pipe   5
  Would bid sheep go from the heat to drink.
Tatius fences this spring with a maple palisade
  And rings his camp securely with an earthen rampart.

What then was Rome when the Curétan trumpeter
  Shook Jove's nearby rocks with long-drawn blare?   10
And where now legal rulings are given to subject lands
  Sabine javelins stood in the Roman Forum.
Hills were her wall. The present Curia was sheepfolds.
  The war horse drank from that spring.

From here Tarpeia drew spring-water for the Goddess,   15
  Earthenware pitcher pressing the crown of her head.
And could one death be enough for a wicked girl
  Prepared to betray your fire, Vesta?
She saw Tatius manoeuvring on the sandy plain
  And raising his bronze helmet adorned with yellow plumes. 20
She was stunned by the king's good looks and kingly weapons,
  And the pitcher slipped from her forgetful hands.

She often pretended the innocent moon gave bad omens
  And said she must dip her hair in running water.

She often brought silvery lilies for the gentle Nymphs   25
  Lest Romulus' spear should spoil Tatius' good looks.
And she returned with forearms scratched by prickly brambles
  While she climbed the misty Capitol at first smoke,
And seated she thus bewailed from the Tarpeian height
  The wound of hers that Jove would not forgive: 30

'Camp-fires and praetorium of Tatius' troop,
  And Sabine armour, lovely in my eyes,
O would that I sat a prisoner by your Household Gods
  If as prisoner I could see my Tatius' face!
Farewell, Roman hills and hill-established Rome   35
  And Vesta to be shamed by my offence.
The horse whose mane Tatius himself combs to the right,
  That horse shall transport my love to his camp.

No wonder Scylla savagely attacked her father's hair
  And her white loins were changed to savage hounds.   40
No wonder the horns of a monstrous brother were betrayed
  When the winding way was revealed by gathered thread.
What a great reproach I shall bring upon Ausonian girls,
  A traitress, chosen to tend the Virgin Hearth!
If any be surprised at Pallas' fire quenched   45
  Let him forgive. My tears have showered her altar.

Tomorrow, they say, there will be drinking throughout the city.
  You must capture the dewy spine of the thorn-grown ridge.
The path is all slippery and treacherous, for always
  Its deceptive course hides unheard waters.   50
O that I knew the Muse of magic's incantations!
  Then this tongue too could help my fair one.
The embroidered toga should be yours, not his who in motherless
  Disgrace was suckled by a horrid wolf's hard dug.

Thus let me be feared as a foreign queen in my country's court;   55
  Rome betrayed is no mean dowry for you.
Or else, lest the kidnapped Sabine women go unavenged,
  Kidnap *me* and restore the balance, like for like!
As bride I have power to separate the combatants;
  Reach a fair settlement, thanks to my robe.   60

Strike up, Hymenaeus. Trumpeter, cease your martial blare.
   Trust me, my marriage-bed will tame your weapons.

And now the fourth cow-horn sounds the coming of daylight
   And even the stars are falling, dropping into Ocean.
I'll try to sleep and hope to see you in my dreams.   65
   Come as a kindly shadow to my eyes.'

So saying she relaxed her arms in fitful sleep,
   Not knowing that new madness was her bedmate.
For Venus, fortunate protectress of Troy's ashes,
   Feeds her fault and hides more firebrands in her bones.   70
She runs amok, like Strymon's daughter by fast-flowing
   Thermódon, bosom bared by her torn tunic.

It was the city's feast-day—*Parília* the Fathers
   Called it—the birthday of Rome's walls,
The shepherds' annual festival, games in the city,   75
   When village food-trays drip with riches,
When, over spaced-out heaps of burning straw, the drunken
   Crowd leap, dirtying their feet.
Romulus ordered the sentries off duty and the camp
   Silent, trumpets discontinued.   80

Tarpeia, thinking this her time, meets the enemy,
   Strikes a bargain—a bargain to include herself.
The hill was hard to climb but unguarded for the feast;
   In a trice with a sword she forestalls the barking watchdogs.
Sleep was everywhere, but Jupiter alone   85
   Resolved to watch—for his revenge.
She had betrayed the trust of the gate and her prostrate country
   And she asks for the wedding-day of her choice.

But Tatius (though a foe, he paid no honour to crime)
   Said 'Wear the wedding-veil and mount my kingdom's bed!'   90
So saying he buried her beneath his comrades' piled up shields.
   This, Virgin, was fit dowry for your services.

The hill acquired its name 'Tarpeian' from the guide.
   O watcher, you have an unjust reward!

5

A bawd and her advice

May earth, Procuress, overgrow your grave with thorns
    And (what you would not wish) your ghost feel thirst,
Your soul not rest in the ashes, and avenging Cerberus
    Scare your vile bones with hungry howl.

Even able to lure austere Hippolytus to Venus   5
    And ever bird of direst omen to happy love,
She could have forced Penelope to discount rumours
    About her husband and marry lewd Antinous.
Magnets at her behest lose power to attract iron
    And birds become stepmothers to their chicks.   10
Indeed by using Colline herbs at her magic trench
    She'd wash a standing crop away by flood.
Bold to impose conditions on the moon bewitched
    And disguise herself as a nocturnal wolf,
That she might blind the watchful husband by her wiles   15
    Her nails gouged out crows' undeserving eyes.
She called in vampires for my blood and used against me
    Hippómanes, the seed of pregnant mares.

She plied her trade, alas, with specious words, just as
    Persistent water bores its way through rock: 20
'If you like the Dorozántes' Eóan golden shore
    And those proud shells beneath the Tyrian sea
And fancy Eurýpylus' woven work of Coan silk
    And antique figures cut from Attalic couches
Or merchandise imported from palmaceous Thebes   25
    And myrrhine goblets fired in Parthian kilns,
Then spurn good faith, hurl down the Gods, let falsehood
    win,
    And break the rules of ruinous chastity.

It even pays to invent a husband. Use excuses;
    Love's all the stronger for a night's delay.   30

Suppose he messes up your hair, anger is useful,
  For later when he buys a truce you'll squeeze him.
Then when you've sold him an embrace and promised Venus
  Pretend it's Isis' days of abstinence.
Let Iole harp on April, and Amycle keep   35
  Reminding you that the Ides of May are your birthday.
Suppose he sits in supplication, write at your desk—
  Anything. If this trick scares him then he's yours.
Make sure you have fresh tooth-marks on your neck, for him
  To think them given in a lovers' tiff.   40

And don't be impressed by Medea the follower's tirade
  (Of course she was despised, for daring to ask first)
But rather by smart Menander's pricey Thais, when
  As comedy tart she tricks the wily Geta.
Fit in with your man's moods. If he strikes up a song   45
  Go with him and add your tipsy voice to his.
The doorman must wake for givers; when the empty-handed knock
  Let him dream on, deaf, with the bolt shot to.
Don't turn down soldiers, though they're clumsy lovers,
  Nor sailors if their horny hands bring cash,   50
Or those from whose barbarian necks a label hung
  When with chalked feet they capered in mid-Forum.

Inspect their gold and not the hand that offers gold.
  Listening to verses what will you get but words?
Why choose, dear life, to step out with styled hair   55
  And move sheer curves in Coan costume?
When a man offers verse, not gifts of Coan costume,
  You must be deaf to his unsophisticated lyre.
In the blood's springtime while the years are wrinkle-free
  Use them, lest tomorrow nibble at your looks.   60
I've seen rose-gardens likely to beat sweet-smelling Paestum's
  Wither in a morning, cooked by the Sirocco.'
While thus Acanthis tried to change my girl-friend's mind
  The bones beneath my thin skin could be counted.

But oh, Queen Venus, accept for favour shown a ring-dove   65
  Whose throat's been cut before your altar-hearth.
I've seen a cough congesting in that scrawny neck

And bloodstained sputum oozing through those rotten teeth,
Yes, and her last foul breath on the parental drugget
    Shaking the crazy shed, its hearth stone-cold.   70
She will have left a stolen ribbon that held her wisps,
    A faded turban, stained and dusty,
And a bitch, to my distress too vigilant
    When my thumb should quietly have slid the bolt.

May the bawd's tomb be an ancient wine-jar with chipped neck 75
    And may a wild fig-tree's vigour burst it.
You lovers all, break up this grave with jagged stones
    And add, while stoning, miscellaneous curses.

6

A celebration of the victory at Actium

The bard is sacrificing: mouths must favour sacrifice
    And stricken heifer fall before my altar-hearth.
Let Roman wreath vie with Philetas' ivy-clusters
    And the urn serve Cyrenéan water.
Give me soft spikenard and the honours of sweet incense   5
    And let the ball of wool go thrice about the hearth.
Asperge me and let the ivory pipe at new-built altar
    Pour libation in the Phrygian mode.
Away with lies; let mischief breathe another air:
    Pure laurel smooths a new path for the bard.   10

Muse, we shall tell of Palatine Apollo's shrine.
    The theme, Calliope, deserves your blessing.
A song is shaped in Caesar's name. While Caesar
    Is sung pray, Jupiter, attend yourself.

There's a haven of Phoebus, running back to Athamanian
      shores,   15
    Whose bay hushes the loud Ionian Sea,
A gulf, the Iuléan keel's Actian monument,
    For sailors' prayers no laborious course.
Here the whole world joined battle. A mass of pinewood towered

On the flood but unequal omens blessed their oars.   20
One fleet, its Roman javelins shamefully controlled
  By female hand, was doomed by Teucrian Quirinus.
In the other was Augustus' ship, by Jove's favour full-sailed,
  And standards trained to conquer for their country.

Nereus at last had curved the lines into twin crescents   25
  And with reflected gleam of arms the water shimmered,
When Phoebus leaving Delos (held fast by his protection,
  For though once mobile it withstood the angry gales)
Posted himself on Augustus' poop, and sudden flame
  Flashed thrice zigzagging with slant torch.   30
He had not come with unbound hair about his neck
  Or peaceful music on his lyre of tortoiseshell
But with the face he showed Pelopéan Agamemnon,
  Emptying the Doric camp with greedy pyres,
Or such as when he loosed the crawling Python's twisted   35
  Coils that scared the unwarlike Goddesses.

'O saviour of the world', said he, 'from Alba Longa,
  Augustus, proven greater than Hectorian forebears,
Conquer at sea. Yours now the land. My bow serves you
  And all this load upon my shoulders favours.   40
Free Rome from fear, who now, trusting in your protection,
  Has placed her corporate prayers upon your prow.
Unless you guard her, in vain did Romulus, the augur
  Of her foundation, see Palatine birds go by.

Look, with their oars too near they venture. Shame that Latin   45
  Waves should suffer a queen's sails in your principate!
But though their fleet has oarage of a hundred wings
  Fear not—it glides through a reluctant sea.
And though their prows bear Centaurs threatening with rocks
  You'll find them hollow boards and painted terrors.   50
It is their cause that breaks or raises soldiers' strength;
  If that is unjust, shame throws down their weapons.
Now is the time. Commit your fleet. I, the time's planner,
  Will guide the Julian ships' beaks with laurelled hand.'

He spoke and spent his quiver's burden on his bow;   55
  Close second to the bow was Caesar's spear.

Rome wins by Phoebus' pledge. The female pays the price,
    Her shattered sceptre swept away on Ionian waves.
But Father Caesar marvels from the Idalian star:
    'I am a God. Here's proof of our blood.'   60
Triton escorts with music and all Sea-Goddesses
    Applauded, round about, Liberty's standards.
She makes for Nile, a fleeing skiff's dishonoured cargo;
    Hers only this—to die not on the appointed day.
Thank Heaven! A fine Triumph one woman would have made 65
    On streets where once Jugurtha was paraded!
In this way Actian Phoebus won his monument,
    For one aimed arrow of his could sink ten ships.

My war-song's over. Conquering Apollo now demands
    The lyre, unarmed for peaceful dances.   70
White-robed let banqueters now enter the soft grove
    And roses' flattery float about my neck
And wine be poured that's squeezed out of Falernian presses
    And saffron of Cilicia drench our hair.
Let the Muse excite the wit of poets toping   75
    (Bacchus, you inspire your brother Phoebus);
Let one relate the enslavement of Sygambrian fenmen,
    Another sing Cephéan Méroe and dusky realms,
Another tell of Parthian surrender in late treaty:
    'Returning Remus' standards, next he'll lose his own.   80
Or if Augustus partly spare Eoan quivers
    Those trophies are postponed for his own boys.
Crassus, rejoice, if you can feel in those black sands:
    Euphrates permits travel to your tomb.'

So with libation, so with song I'll spend the night   85
    Till daylight thrust its rays into my wine.

7

Cynthia's Ghost

A ghost is something. Death does *not* close all.
   A pale shade escapes, defeating the pyre.
For I have seen Cynthia leaning over my bed-head
   (Though lately buried by the busy road)
While sleep for me was hung up on love's funeral   5
   And I mourned my bed's cold kingdom.
She had the same hair as when borne to burial,
   The same eyes; but the dress she wore was charred
And the fire had eaten into that beryl on her finger
   And Lethe water had chafed her lips.   10
Anger and voice were those of the breathing woman
   As her brittle hands snapped their thumbs:

'Traitor, from whom no woman need expect good faith,
   Can you have fallen asleep so soon?
So soon forgotten stolen joys in the wakeful Subura?   15
   Those tricky nights and my worn windowsill
From which, time and again, I hung on a rope for you,
   Descending hand under hand to your embrace?
We often shared Venus at the crossroads breast to breast,
   Our cloaks warming the road,   20
Alas for that secret understanding whose specious words
   Deaf southern winds have blown away!

Yes, no one keened for me as my eyes closed. Had *you*
   Called me back I'd have gained an extra day.
No watchman rattled a split cane near me   25
   And the crock against my head hurt.
Besides, who saw you bowed in grief above my body
   Or in a black toga hot with tears?
If it bored you to go further you could at least have slowed
   The bearers' pace to the city gates.   30
Ingrate, why weren't you there to pray for wind for the pyre?
   Why were my flames not perfumed with nard?

Was it even too much trouble to strew cheap hyacinths
    And hallow my ashes from a broken wine-jar?

Put Lygdamus to torture! Hot irons for the home-bred slave!   35
    I knew, when I drank the poisoned wine that turned me pale.
Though artful Nomas hides away her secret juices
    The fiery potsherd will show whose hands are guilty.
Yesterday's prostitute parading for cheap nights
    Now sweeps by in a gold-embroidered gown,   40
But hands out heavier stints in unfair basket-loads
    To any girl who gabs about my beauty.
For taking garlands to my tomb old Petale
    Must suffer chaining to a filthy clog,
And Lalage is hung up by the hair and flogged   45
    For daring to ask favours in my name.
You sit by while Madame melts down my golden bust
    To gain a dowry from my cremation.

But I'll not nag, Propertius, much as you deserve it;
    In your books my reign was long.   50
I swear by the Fates' irrevocable chant
    (So may the Triple Dog not snarl at me)
I have kept faith. If I speak false may vipers
    Hiss in my grave and curl up on my bones.

For beyond the sullen flood two places are assigned   55
    And the whole crowd rows across on different courses.
One carries Clytemnestra's foulness and the Cretan
    Queen's who faked a monstrous wooden cow.
But see, the other group swept along in a flower-crowned boat
    To where blest airs caress Elysian roses,   60
Where numerous lutes and where Cybebe's brazen cymbals
    And Lydian plectra twang for turbaned dancers.
Andromeda and Hypermnestra, guileless wives,
    Tell of the well-known perils of their story.
The first complains her arms were bruised by her mother's
    chains   65
    And her hands did not deserve cold rocks.
Hypermnestra tells how her sisters dared an outrage
    And how her own heart quailed at it.

So with death's tears we strive to heal life's loves,
  Though *I* hide all your criminal bad faith.   70

But now, if you have feelings and are not fast bound
  By Chloris' potions, here are my requests.
See that my nurse Parthenia in frail old age lacks nothing;
  Towards you she could have been but was not greedy.
Don't let my darling Latris, named for usefulness,   75
  Hold out the mirror for a new mistress.
And all those verses you have made on my account,
  Please burn them. Cease your boasting about me.
Plant ivy on my grave and let abundant clusters
  Gently bind my bones with tangled tendrils   80
Where fruitful Anio descends on branchy fields
  And ivory, thanks to Hercules, never yellows.
Here on a column write me a fit epitaph but brief
  So travellers in haste from Rome may read it:
HERE IN TIBURTINE GROUND LIES GOLDEN
      CYNTHIA, BRINGING   85
GLORY TO YOUR BANKS, FATHER ANIO.

And pay good heed to dreams that come from the Gates of Duty;
  When dreams of duty come they carry weight.
At night we roam around. Night frees imprisoned shades
  And Cerberus too can range unchained.   90
At first light law demands return to Lethe Lake;
  We embark and Charon counts his freight.
Others may own you now. Soon I alone shall hold you.
  You'll be with me and bone on mingled bone I'll grind.'

Having thus dealt with me in bitter accusation   95
  The shade from my embrace faded away.

8

An evening party wrecked

Learn what scared the aquatic Esquiline last night
  When all who live near the New Fields came running,   2
When a sordid brawl was heard in an obscure *taverna*,   19
  If without me, not without stain on my good name.   20

An aged snake has long been guardian of Lanuvium;   3
    An hour's delay is specially well spent there
Where the sacred descent vanishes into a dark cavern,   5
    Where enters (virgins, beware of all such journeys!)
The hungry serpent's due when he demands his yearly
    Food, with coiling hisses from earth's depths.
The girls sent down upon this sacred errand blench
    At blindly trusting their hands to the snake's mouth.   10
He snatches up the morsels offered by the virgin;
    Even the basket in the virgin's hand trembles.
If they've been chaste they return to their parents' embrace
    And farmers shout 'The year will be fruitful!'

It was here my Cynthia drove her close-clipped ponies,   15
    Juno the excuse, the real reason Venus.
Appian Way, pray tell what a Triumphal ride you witnessed
    As her wheels raced along over your stones,   18
Herself a fine sight, seated, leaning over the yoke-pole,   21
    Daring to shake out the reins over rough places.
I'll not describe her smooth-faced toy-boy's silk-lined chaise
    And the dogs with fancy collars on their Molossian necks.
Later he'll have to sell his soul for filthy stodge   25
    When a shaming beard overcomes those hairless cheeks.

Because our bed was being wronged so often
    I meant to strike camp and change couch.
Next door to Aventine Diana there lives a Phyllis—
    When sober, rather dull; when drinking, quite delightful.   30
Another girl, named Teia, lives in Tarpeia's Grove—
    Pretty, but when drunk too much for one man.
By inviting these I planned to pass an easier night,
    Sampling once more the stolen joys of unknown Venus.

There was one small couch for three on a secluded lawn.   35
    You ask how we lay? I was between the two,
With Lygdamus to mix the wine, and the summer glassware
    And the Greek bouquet of Methymnéan.
Nile, yours the piper, yours the castanet-girl, Baetis,
    Neat without art, prepared to be pelted with roses,   40
And Magnus too, the dwarf with misshapen limbs,
    Waved stumpy hands in time to the hollow boxwood.

But though the lamps were filled their flames kept flickering
   And the table collapsed on its hinged legs.
Besides at dice when I tried for the lucky Venus throw   45
   Always the losing Dog jumped out.
I didn't hear the singing, I was blind to naked breasts,
   I was on my own alas at Lanuvium's gates;
When suddenly the front-door grated on its hinges
   And muffled noises came from the entrance-hall.   50
Next moment Cynthia flung the folding doors wide open,
   Her hair a mess, but lovely in her fury.
My fingers lost their grip and dropped the glass,
   And loosened by the wine my lips turned pale.
Her eyes flashed and she raged as only a woman can;   55
   The sight was frightful as a city's sack.
She dug her angry talons into Phyllis' face;
   Terrified Teia shouted 'Neighbours, fire!'
Uplifted lights disturbed the sleeping citizens
   And every alley rang with midnight madness.   60
The two girls, dresses torn and hair dishevelled, fled
   To the nearest tavern where the street was dark.

Pleased with her trophies Cynthia rushed back victorious
   And slashed my face with a back-handed slap
And stamped her mark on my neck, biting till it bled,   65
   And struck at my eyes, the chief offenders.
Then, when at last her arms were tired of hitting me,
   Lygdamus cowering behind the couch's head on the left
Was discovered and dragged out, begging my protection.
   Lygdamus, I couldn't help—like you, her prisoner.   70

But in the end with suppliant palms I sued for peace
   While she would hardly let me touch her feet
And said 'If you would have me pardon your offence
   You must accept the list of my conditions.
You shall not strut about dressed up in Pompey's Porch   75
   Or when they strew sand in the ribald Forum.
Take care you don't turn round and stare at the upper Theatre
   Or let an open litter sweat while you delay it.
Lygdamus most of all, the whole cause of my grievance—
   Sell him, double-fettering his feet.'   80

Such were her terms. I answered 'I accept the terms.'
  She laughed, exulting in the power I gave her.
Then, fumigating every place those girl intruders
  Had touched, she scoured the threshold with pure water
And ordered me to change my clothes again completely   85
  And touched my head three times with fire of sulphur.
Eventually when all the bed-clothes had been changed
  I answered and we laid down arms over the couch.

9

Hercules founds the Ara Maxima

What time Amphitryóniades had driven his steers,
  O Erythéa, from your steadings,
He came to the sheep-grazed Palatine, unconquered hill,
  And, weary himself, halted his weary cattle
Where the Velabrum flowed into a lake and where   5
  Boatmen vailed their sails on urban waters.
But, with untruthful Cacus host, they did not stay
  Uninjured: he polluted Jove with theft.

Cacus had settled there, the robber with dreaded cave,
  Whose utterance was split between three mouths.   10
To leave no evidence of bare-faced robbery
  He dragged the cattle tail-first to his cave.
But the God witnessed it. The cattle bellowed 'Thief'
  And rage broke down the thief's implacable door.
Cacus was felled, his three brows struck by Maenalian branch,   15
  And 'So then', said Alcides, 'go, you cattle,
Go, cattle of Hercules, last labour of my club,
  Cattle twice sought by me, my booty twice,
And with your lengthy lowing hallow the Cattle Fields;
  Your pasture will become Rome's famous Forum.'   20

He spoke, and with parched palate thirst tormented his mouth
  And the teeming earth had water to offer.
But, some way off, he heard the laughter of enclosed girls
  Where a sacred grove made a shady ring of trees,

A close of the Women's Goddess and a spring to be kept holy   25
    And rites revealed to no man with impunity.
Festoons of purple covered a secluded doorway
    And a crumbling cottage was lit by scented fire.
A long-leaved poplar decorated the shrine
    Whose dense shade hid singing birds.   30

Hither he rushed, the dust thick-strewn in his parched beard,
    And at the door flung out words that demeaned a God:
'O you who play in the grove's secret covert, please
    Open your hóspitable shrine to weary men.
Needing a spring I stray and around is the sound of water;   35
    Enough what cupped hands take up from a stream.
You have heard of one who bore the sky's vault on his back?
    I am he. The world I rescued calls me Alcídes.
Who has not heard of the brave deeds of Hercules' club?
    Of his arrows, never missing monstrous beasts?   40
And how the Stygian gloom lit up for one human?

                    *   *   *   *   *

Now this corner of the world receives me dragging out   65
    My fate. Tired as I am, this land hardly welcomes me.   66

But were you making sacrifice to spiteful Juno,   43
    Albeit a stepmother she would not refuse water.
And if my looks and shaggy lion-skin and hair   45
    Bleached by Libyan suns should frighten anyone,
I too, clad in Sidonian robe, have done a servant's
    Chores and a daily stint with Lydian distaff.
A soft breast-band confined my hairy chest;
    I was a proper girl, though heavy-handed.'   50

Alcídes thus, and thus the kindly priestess,
    Her white hair bound with scarlet thread:
'Spare your eyes, stranger, and withdraw from this dread grove.
    Withdraw at once and leave the threshold, safely escaping.
Forbidden to men, this altar which protects itself   55
    In a lonely cottage is hallowed by a fearsome law.
Prophet Tiresias paid dear for seeing Pallas
    Bathing her strong limbs, the Gorgon laid aside.
God grant you other springs. This water, set apart
    With hidden channel, flows for girls alone.'   60

Thus the old dame. He with his shoulder forced the sheltered
  Doorposts and the closed door gave way to angry thirst.
But after he had drained the stream and quenched his heat,
  With lips hardly dry he laid down this stern rule: 64
'The Ara Maxima, vowed for the finding of my herd,'   67
  Said he, 'the Greatest Altar made by these hands,
This must never be open to the worship of any girl,
  Lest Hercules' thirst be forever unavenged.'   70

Thus, because he had sanctified the world cleansed by his hands, 73
  Tatius' Cures stablished him as *Sancus*.
Hail, Father Sacrosanct, now favoured by harsh Juno,   71
  Sancus, vouchsafe a helpful presence in my book.

IO

Jupiter Feretrius and the spolia opima

I'll now proceed to explain why Jove is *Feretrian*
  And the three trophies captured from three leaders.
Great is the road I climb but glory gives me strength,
  Disdaining garlands picked from easy summits.

You, Romulus, set the example for this prime distinction,   5
  Returning laden with enemy spoil, the day
Caeninian Acro attacked the gates and you as victor
  With spear-point felled him on his fallen mount.
Hercúlean Acro, chieftain from Caenína's fort,
  Was once the terror of Rome's borders.   10
Daring to hope for spoil from Quirinus' shoulders
  He yielded it himself, and bloodstained too.
Romulus saw him aiming his spear before the hollow
  Towers and forestalled him with a vow fulfilled:
'Today this Acro, Jove, shall fall your sacrifice.'   15
  He vowed and the other fell as spoil to Jove.
Thus Rome's and valour's sire was wont to win the day,
  Who from bleak home put up with cold campaigning,
As horseman used to harness and also used to ploughing,
  His wolf-skin helm adorned with hairy plume,   20

His painted targe not flashing with inlaid pyropus,
    His supple baldric furnished by slain oxen.

Cossus comes next, with Veientine Tolumnius' slaughter
    In days when Veii's conquest was a labour;
No sound of war as yet beyond Tiber, furthest prize   25
    Nomentum and captured Cora's acres three.
Alas, historic Veii—you too were then a kingdom
    And in your Forum stood the golden chair.
But now within your walls the plodding shepherd's horn
    Echoes and men reap fields above your bones.   30
It chanced that the Veientine chief stood on the gate-tower
    And confident in his city offered parley,
But while the ram battered the wall with its bronze horn
    Where the long mantlet shielded work in progress,
'The brave', said Cossus, 'better meet in open field.'   35
    Forthwith both took their stand upon the plain.
The Gods helped Latian hands. Tolumnius' severed head
    Bathed Roman horses in its blood.

Next, Claudius fighting off the foe who had crossed the Rhine
    Brought back the Belgic shield of their huge leader   40
Virdómarus; he boasted descent from Rhine himself,
    Famed for hurling darts from forward chariot.
As in striped trousers he advanced to make his throw,
    The unhooked torque dropped down from his slit throat.

Now the three spoils are stored up in *Feretrius*' shrine   45
    Because by Heaven's favour chief with sword *felled* chief;
Or since the victors on their shoulders *ferried* these arms,
    Hence the proud altar is called *Feretrian* Jove's.

I I

The dead Cornelia speaks in her own defence

Cease, Paullus, to importúne my tomb with tears.
    The black door opens to no prayers.
When once the dead have entered infernal jurisdiction
    The roads are blocked by inexorable adamant.

The God of the dim palace may hear you pleading   5
   But the deaf river-bank will drink your tears.
Vows move the Gods above. When the Ferryman takes his fee
   A wan gate bars the burnt-out pyre.
So sang the mournful trumpets when the unfriendly torch
   Was put to my bier and made away with my person.   10
Marriage to Paullus, forebears' Triumphal chariots, and all
   The pledges of my good name—what help were they?
Cornelia's Fates were none the less unmerciful
   And I am a burden five fingers can collect.

Nights of the doomed, and you marshes, stagnant shallows,   15
   And whatever wave entangles my feet,
Here have I come before my time but still not guilty.
   May the Father here grant gentle justice to my shade.
Or if some Aeacus sits in judgement, urn in place,
   When my bones' turn for trial comes up may he discharge me. 20
Let the brothers sit with him, Minos' chair next his, and
   The Eumenides' stern throng in the hushed Forum.
Let Sisyphus rest from his boulder, Ixion's wheel be silent,
   Tantalus gulp down the deceptive water
And shameless Cerberus today attack no shades   25
   And his chain hang loose from the silent door-bar.
I speak in my own defence. If I lie may the Sisters' doom,
   The luckless water-jar, weigh down my shoulders.

If fame from ancestral trophies brought anyone distinction
   African kingdoms tell of my Numantine forebears;   30
A second throng makes mother's Libónes their equals;
   Both houses have their honours to support them.
Later, when my *praetexta* gave way to marriage torches
   And a different headband bound my swept-up hair,
I shared your bed, Paullus, only to leave it thus;   35
   On this stone let them read me married to one man.

I swear by the ashes of ancestors honoured by Rome
   Under whose titles Africa lies crushed,
And by him who when Perses aped his forebear Achilles' valour
   Shattered the house so proud of Achilles its forebear,   40
That I neither softened the Censor's ruling nor at any

Fault of mine have your hearths blushed.
Cornelia brought no disgrace on your great achievements
  But was even a model member of your great house.

Nor did my life-style change; it was blameless throughout,   45
  I lived respected, between both torches.
On me my birth imposed laws deriving from blood
  Nor could fear of judgement make one better.
Whatever urn may pass strict sentence upon me
  No woman need be ashamed of supporting me—   50
Not you whose rope moved dilatory Cybébe,
  Claudia, rare handmaid of the tower-crowned Goddess,
Nor she who, when impartial Vesta claimed her fire,
  Proved the hearth live with her white linen.

Nor did I injure you, sweet head, Scribonia mother.   55
  What but my fate would you wish changed in me?
A mother's tears, and Rome's lamentations are my praise,
  And my bones are defended by Caesar's grief.
He mourns the death of a fit sister for his own daughter,
  And we have seen his godhead shedding tears.   60
And yet I earned the fruitful honour of my dress
  Nor was I abducted from a barren home.
You, Lepidus, and you, Paullus, are my comfort after death;
  My eyes were closed in your embrace.
We also saw my brother double the curule chair;   65
  In the festive time of his consulate our sister died.
You, my daughter, born to mark your father's censorship,
  Make sure you copy me and hold to one husband.
You all must strengthen our breed with lineage. Gladly I'll sail
  On the skiff when I've so many to enlarge my destiny.   70
This is woman's final prize, the female Triumph—
  When children's fame brings praise to her deserving pyre.

Now I commit to you our common trust, the children,
  Whose care still breathes in me, branded on my ashes.
Their father, you must play a mother's part. Your neck   75
  Must bear the weight of all my own dear throng.
Kiss them when they cry, and add their mother's kisses.
  Henceforth the whole house is in your charge.

And if ever you grieve don't let them see, but when
  They come deceive their kisses with dry cheeks!   80
Be satisfied with weary nights spent missing me
  And frequent dreams in which you seem to see my face.
And when you speak in private to my portrait
  Make each remark believing I'll reply.

Yet if the door should change the marriage-bed opposite   85
  And a wary stepmother sit on my couch,
Approve, my children, and accept your father's partner;
  She will surrender, won by your behaviour.
Don't praise your mother too much. When compared with her
  The new wife will take offence at unguarded speech.   90
But if, remembering, he remains content with my shade
  And thinks so highly of my ashes,
Learn in good time to notice the coming of old age
  And leave no clearway for a widower's worries.
May the years removed from me be added to your own;   95
  So through my children may Paullus find a happy old age.
And all is well. As mother I never put on mourning;
  The whole group followed my funeral.

I rest my case. Rise, witnesses, and weep for me
  Till the grateful ground pays me life's reward.   100
Heaven too has opened to character. May my deserts
  Over honoured waters win my bones conveyance.

EXPLANATORY NOTES

BOOK I

1

See Introduction, p. xix.

4 One thinks of Love the Conqueror treading on the head of his victim and perhaps too of the love-poet with metrical feet tormenting his brain.

5–6 The Latin too is ambiguous here.

9–14 allude to a less well-known version of the story of the Arcadian huntress Atalanta (here called Iasis as the daughter of Iasius, a king of Argos). The Centaur Hylaeus tried to rape her; Milanion her long-suffering suitor must have been wounded in her defence.

Tullus, to whom in effect Propertius dedicates this book, was nephew of the Roman governor of Asia in 30–29 BC (see i. 6. 19).

Parthenius: a mountain in Arcadia.

18 Lit. 'Nor remembers to go known ways as in the past.'

24 *Colchian*: the Oxford Classical Text has *Cytaeines* 'the woman from Cytae' in Colchis, birthplace of Medea, witch *par excellence.*

27 *knife and cautery*: lit. 'iron and cruel fires', which would include the red-hot branding iron and instruments of torture.

38 Lit. 'Alas, with how great grief he'll recollect my words!'

2

2 The island of Cos was famous for its silks.

3 'Antioch on the Orontes was the chief port for the export of goods that came from the east by caravan' (Richardson).

15–16 Leucippus was Helen of Troy's uncle. The story of how the Dioscuri, Castor and Pollux, Helen's brothers, carried off Phoebe and Hilaira is told in Theocritus, *Idyll* 22.

17–18 Phoebus Apollo tried to rob Idas of his wife Marpessa, daughter of the river-god Evenus. Jupiter prevented him and gave Marpessa the choice; she chose Idas.

19–20 King Oenomaus of Elis promised his daughter Hippodamia to the suitor who could beat him in a chariot-race. Pelops, son of Tantalus, from Phrygia, won by bribing the king's groom to remove a linchpin from his chariot.

22 *Apelles*: a famous fourth-century BC painter from Cos.

26 *smart*: and (with Lyne) 'courted'.

28 *Calliope*: chief of the nine Muses.

Aonia: old name of Boeotia where was Mt. Helicon, sacred to the Muses.

30 Or 'And everything that Venus and Minerva approve'.

Minerva: see iii. 20. 7 note.

3

See Introduction, p. xxi.

1–2 Ariadne, daughter of Minos, king of Crete, enabled the Athenian hero Theseus to kill the Minotaur by giving him a ball of thread which he could unwind so as to find his way out of the Labyrinth at Knossos, built by Daedalus. Theseus made her his wife but deserted her on the island of Dia (see Catullus 64).

3–4 Cepheus, king of Ethiopia, was Andromeda's father. His wife Cassiopea claimed to be more beautiful than the Nereids and Neptune punished her arrogance by demanding the sacrifice of Andromeda to a sea-monster. She was rescued by Perseus, mounted on the winged horse Pegasus.

5–6 *Maenad*: lit. 'Edonian woman', the Edoni being a people of Thrace where the orgiastic worship of Dionysus originated.

on grassy Apidanus: for 'on the grassy banks of Apidanus', unless P. has forgotten that this is a Thessalian river.

20 Io was turned into a cow by Jupiter in a vain attempt to hide her from his wife Juno, who than set Argus with his hundred eyes to keep a watch on her.

26 *pocket*: in tunic or toga this was a hanging fold over the chest. Others render: 'Gifts often rolling from her sloping lap (*or* breast).'

34 Strictly 'Thus she spoke, digging . . . '

44 Lit. 'At frequent long delays in outside love'. For 'outside love' as love outside marriage see ii. 32. 31. Others render: 'Your frequent long absences with other women'.

46 Or 'That was the final worry for my tears.'

4

1 Bassus was also a friend of Ovid (see *Tristia* iv. 10. 47–8), who there refers to his fame as a poet of *iambi* or invective verse.

5–6 *Hermione*: daughter of Menelaus and Helen.

    Nycteus: son of Neptune.

    Antiope: mother by Jupiter of Amphion and Zethus.

13 *Well-bred complexion*: in Latin 'beauty' (*forma*) refers primarily to shape. 'Propertius only wants to say that Cynthia had the fair complexion associated with free birth (cf. ii. 3. 10)' (Shackleton Bailey).

14 Textual trouble here.

5

6 Thessaly was the birthplace of witchcraft according to Apuleius, *Metamorphoses* ii. 1.

8 Lit. 'She will not know how to be gentle in her anger with you.'

11–12 Lit. 'She will not leave you sleep any more, she will not leave you (*or* your) eyes. She is the only woman (*or* she above all) with her moods can tie up untamed men.'

30 *shoulder*: lit. 'bosom.'

31 Gallus is also addressed in i. 10, 13, and 20. He cannot have been the poet of that name, who was not of noble birth.

32 As though she were a goddess.

6

See Introduction, p. xxi.

2 For Tullus see i. 1. 9 note.

3 A legendary mountain range in the far north.

4 Memnon, son of Tithonus and Aurora (the Dawn), was king of Ethiopia.

5–6 Lit. 'But the words of a girl embracing me delay me, and her grave pleas with frequent changes of colour.' The translation assumes that there is play here with legal language.

15–18 Lit. 'So that Cynthia may revile me at the ship's launching and stigmatize my face with her mad hands, and say that kisses are owed to her (*or possibly* by her to) the wind being adverse and that nothing is more cruel than an unfaithful man.'

19 Lucius Volcacius Tullus was consul in 33 BC and proconsul of Asia 30–29. His nephew must have been going out as a special commissioner. The consular axes were carried by the lictors in their *fasces*, see iii. 4. 5 note.

20 'forgetful': or 'forgotten'.

23 *that Boy*: Cupid.—*a lover's*: lit. 'our'.

24 Or, reading *omnia* for *omina*, 'and everything known to my tears'.

31 The Ionian cities of Asia were famous for their luxury.

32 The Pactolus flowed through Sardis and had the reputation of being a gold-bearing river.

36 Or 'Know that I live under a cruel star.'

7

1 Ponticus, also a friend of Ovid, was writing an epic on the Seven against Thebes. King Oedipus' sons Eteocles and Polynices fought over the succession. Polynices assembled an army led by seven heroes and attacked Thebes, but in the ensuing battle the two brothers killed each other.

11 *I only*: the Latin is equally ambiguous.

12 *cultured*: the Latin is *docta* 'educated, learned'.

16 Text uncertain. Lit. 'But, ah, I would not wish our gods to will that.'

8 A

2 Illyria on the east of the Adriatic included parts of modern Yugoslavia and Albania.

8 Lit. 'Can *you*, Cynthia, bear the unaccustomed snows?'

10 The rising of the Pleiades (*Vergiliae* in Latin) marked the opening of the sailing season.

18–20 *Galatea*: a sea-nymph.

Ceraunians: mountains in N. W. Epirus.

Oricos: An Illyrian port (modern Ericho).

25 The Autaries and Hyllei were Illyrian tribes.

26 Lit. 'She will be (*periphrastic future*) mine.'

8 B

35–6 *Hippodamia*: see i. 2. 19 note.

Elis: a state in N. W. Peloponnese whose inhabitants ran the Olympic Games. It was famous for its horses.

38 *pocket*: also 'lap'; see i. 3. 26 note.

39 *mother of pearl*: lit. 'Indian shells'.

43 Lit. 'Now it is allowed me to touch the highest stars with the soles of my feet.'

9

5 The doves at the ancient oracle of Dodona in Chaonia provided prophetic omens.

10 Amphion's music is fabled to have moved the stones that built the walls of Thebes.

11 *Mimnermus*: a seventh-century BC Greek elegiac love-poet.

15 Lit. 'What if you hadn't easy access?'

20 Ixion tried to seduce Juno and was punished by being tied to an ever-revolving wheel in Tartarus.

23–4 Lit. 'Love never gives anyone easy wings without alternately laying a heavy hand on him.' A controversial couplet.

26 For Ponticus see i. 7. 1 note.

10

5 For Gallus see i. 5. 31 note.

19 This is what ancient philosophers did.

11

1 *Baiae*: a fashionable spa in the north of the Bay of Naples opposite Puteoli, in a volcanic area famous for its hot springs and reputedly site of the battle between the Giants and the Gods.

2 The shallow Lucrine Lake between Baiae and Misenum was separated from the sea by a strip of land said to have been cast up by Hercules.

3-4 In 37 BC Agrippa had connected Lake Avernus, behind the Lucrine Lake, with the sea, so as to form a deep-water harbour for the fleet.

Thesprotus' realm: explained by Hyginus, *Fabulae* 88, 'Thyestes, when his abominable crime became known, fled to king Thesprotus where Lake Avernus is said to be.'

8 'This involves a jump in thought, for he means of course "steal you from my embraces (so that I no longer have you for my inspiration)"' (Camps). Also an implied threat that he will cease to write poetry about her?

12 The legendary hero Teuthras was associated with Cumae, a coastal town near Baiae.

19 *writings*: lit. 'booklets'. Another veiled threat?

12

1-2 A much disputed couplet. Perhaps 'Why don't you (an anonymous addressee) stop falsely accusing me of idleness because we stay in Rome where my shame is known?'

3 *Hypanis*: probably the Ukrainian river Bug that flows into the Black Sea.

Eridanus: Greek name for the Po.

6 Or 'Nor does she whisper sweetly in my ear.'

10 The Caucasus, where Prometheus was chained after stealing fire from heaven.

20 *last*: lit. 'the end' (*finis*).

13

1 For Gallus see i. 5. 31 note.

7 *someone*: by using *quadam* P. suggests that he could name the person if he wished.

21-2 Lit. 'Not thus, mingled with Haemonian Enipeus, did the Taenarian god embrace Salmoneus' daughter with easy love.' Tyro, daughter of Salmoneus, loved the Thessalian river-god Enipeus; Neptune, who had a sanctuary at Taenarus (Cape Matapan) was in love with Tyro and impersonated Enipeus.

23–4 Hercules burnt himself to death on Mt. Oeta in Thessaly, was
      resurrected by Jupiter, made a god, and given Hebe, the goddess of
      youth, in marriage.

29–30 Leda, wife of Tyndareus king of Sparta, was seen bathing in the
      Eurotas by Jupiter, who assumed the form of a swan, arranged with
      Venus that she should pursue him as an eagle, and fled for apparent
      protection to Leda's arms. Leda's three daughters were Phoebe,
      Clytemnestra, and Helen.

14

2 Mentor was a famous fourth-century BC Greek silversmith.

5–6 Lit. 'And every grove (*or* all the grove) stretches its planted woods
    upward with trees as great as those that burden Caucasus.'

11 For Pactolus see i. 6. 32 note.

19 *onyx*: lit. 'Arabian', because according to Pliny the Romans originally
   thought that onyx was only found in Arabia.

20 *crimson*: lit. 'ostrine' from *ostrea*, 'oyster', referring to the murex, the
   shellfish that produced Tyrian purple.

   For Tullus see i. 1. 9 note.

24 *Alcinous*: the rich king of the Phaeacians in the *Odyssey*.

15

3 *grave danger*: presumably illness, which prevents him from visiting
   her.

4 Or 'But though I'm afraid, you're slow to visit me and unfeeling.'

9 Calypso, the sea-nymph, detained Ulysses (the Ithacan or the Dulichian)
   for seven years on her island of Ogygia, promising him immortality
   if he would stay with her.

17 Hypsipyle, queen of Lemnos, was loved by Jason when the Argonauts
   visited her island on their way to Colchis.

21 Evadne, wife of Capaneus, one of the Seven against Thebes (see i. 7.
   1 note), threw herself on his funeral pyre.

15 Alphesiboea married Alcmaeon, who was forced by an oracle to leave
   her. Her brothers killed him and she avenged his murder by killing
   them.

32   Or 'but never leave me'. Lit. 'not a stranger (*or* someone else's)
     though.'

16

2   The adjective 'Tarpeian' surely cannot refer to the Tarpeia of iv. 4,
     the Vestal Virgin who betrayed her country for love. But the word
     was used of the Capitoline hill, sacred centre of Roman religious
     observance, and site of the joint temple of Jupiter, Juno, and Minerva.

10   Lit. 'Though noble, condemned to obscene songs', which may possibly
     refer, not to graffiti, but to lovers' serenades in which the door is
     verbally attacked.

29   *Sicania*: poetical name for Sicily; it is not clear what stone is meant.

17

3   *Cassiope*: important harbour-town in the north-east of Corfu, port of
     call for those crossing the Adriatic to or from Brindisi.

18   *Tyndarids*: Castor and Pollux, sons of Tyndareus and protectors of
     sailors.

19   *There*: i.e. in Rome or Italy.

25   *Doris*: sea-goddess, wife of Nereus and mother of the Nereids.

18

2   *Zephyrus*: the west wind.

13   Both 'though you have hurt me' and 'though I have earned the right
     to hurt you'.

17   i.e. 'Have I not gone pale enough to prove I love you?'

27   The adjective 'sacred' (*diuini*) does not go well with the two that
     follow and is probably corrupt.

32   Lit. 'Nor lonely rocks be empty of your name'; so that the last line
     contains, like the Latin, two echoes of the first couplet.

19

1   *The Underworld*: lit. 'the gloomy Manes (spirits of the dead)'.

5   *the Boy*: see i. 6. 23; cf. i. 7. 15.

7   Protesilaus, grandson of Phylacus, was the first Greek hero to be killed at Troy, very shortly after his marriage to Laodamia (see Catullus 68. 73–87).

9   *disappointed*: also 'illusory'.

24   *faithful*: the Latin *certa* can also mean 'determined'.

25   Latin *inter nos* ('mutual' or 'each other') is omitted.

20

P.'s sources for the story here told in the Hellenistic manner are Theocritus, *Idyll* 13, and Apollonius Rhodius, *Argonautica* i. 1182–1272.

1   *For lasting love's sake*: i.e. 'because we have been friends for a long time' and also 'to keep your loved one'.

4   *Ascanius*: a Bithynian river, scene of the abduction of Hylas, Hercules' boy-friend.

    Minyae: the Argonauts, many of whom were grandsons of Minyas, a Thessalian king.

7–10 refer to holiday resorts—at Tibur (Tivoli) on the Anio and at Baiae, for which see i. 11. 1 note.

11–12 Nymphs and Dryads here refer to real-life girls. Ausonia is a poetical word for Italy.

17–18 *Pagasa*: coastal town in Thessaly.

    Argo: the first ocean-going ship.

    Phasis: river in Colchis (Georgia).

19   *Athamantis' waves*: the Hellespont, Helle being the daughter of Athamas. See ii. 26A. 5 note.

20   The rugged coast of Mysia on the sea of Marmora.

25–30 This episode is not in Theocritus or Apollonius and presumably derives from a painting of the winged sons of Boreas (Latin *Aquilo*) the north wind, molesting Hylas.

31   *Pandion*: king of Athens, grandfather of Orithyia the mother of the Boreads.

33   *Arganthus*: a mountain in Mysia.

Pege: this Greek word means 'spring'.

34   *Thynian*: Bithynia marched with Mysia.

45   The Dryads (or (32) Hamadryads), strictly wood-nymphs, here appear
     as water-nymphs. This rhetorical figure is called *catachresis*, cf.
     'Thynian Nymphs' (34) in Mysia.

49   *Alcides*: patronymic of Hercules, grandson of Alceus.

21

A difficult epigram whose dramatic date is 41 or 40 BC, when Mark
Antony's brother Lucius was being besieged in Perusia (Perugia) by the
young Octavian (Caesar). After a long siege the defenders were starved
into surrender and their leaders, except Lucius Antonius, killed. Here a
dying man addresses a fellow-soldier (a connection of his, according to line
4, and cf. 1 'kindred') and asks him to take the news of his death to his
sister—whose sister is not quite clear, though the parents in 5 are the
addressee's. The MSS in 6 offer 'Lest sister learn . . .' See Introduction,
p. xii.

5   *so may . . .*: conditional on the fulfilment of 6, cf. i. 18. 11–12.

22

See Introduction, p. xi.

Penates: the gods of the store-cupboard with their images in the atrium or
hall of a Roman house. They stand here for 'home'.

For Tullus see i. 1. 9 note.

3   A reference to the Perusine War of 41–40 BC, waged by Fulvia, Mark
    Antony's wife, and Lucius his brother against Octavian and ended by
    the capture of Perusia (see note on poem 21 above).

6–8 It is hard not to connect this with 21 by supposing that the kinsman
     is Gallus and that he was married to P.'s sister. He addresses the soil
     of Etruriá, on which his kinsman's bones lay unburied.

9–10 P.'s birthplace is described in more detail at iv. 1B. 120—6.

BOOK II

I

See Introduction, pp. x and xxii.

1 *You*: plural.

3 *Calliope*: see i. 2. 28 note.

5 *Cos*: see i. 2. 2 note.

14 Homer's *Iliad* comprises 24 books and over 16,000 lines.

17 *Maecenas*: Gaius Cilnius Maecenas, Roman knight, wealthy and luxurious descendant of Etruscan kings, was Octavian's close friend and adviser. An amateur author himself, he was a famous patron of literature; Virgil and Horace were his protégés. Clearly Propertius has now been admitted to his circle and by implication dedicates this book of elegies to him.

19–20 The war of the Titans, gigantic sons of Heaven and Earth, against the Gods is described in Hesiod, *Theogony* 629 ff. The Giants Otus and Ephialtes piled Mt. Ossa on Olympus and Pelion on Ossa to reach Heaven in the war of the Giants against the Gods (cf. *Odyssey* xi. 305 ff.). The two wars are often confused.

21–2 *Thebes*: see i. 7. 1 note.

Pergama: the citadel of Troy.

The Persian king Xerxes, invading Greece, cut a canal through the isthmus behind Mt. Athos in Chalcidice.

23 *Remus' first realm*: i.e. the early history of Rome, Remus standing for the metrically difficult Romulus, his twin brother and Rome's founder.

Carthage: a reference to Rome's three Punic Wars.

24 The Cimbri, a Germanic tribe from the modern Himmerland (North Jutland), invaded Italy and were defeated by Marius in 101 BC.

25 *Caesar*: Octavian (Augustus in 27 BC).

27 Mutina, besieged by Mark Antony, was relieved in 43 BC by Octavian with the help of the two consuls Hirtius and Pansa, who were both killed in the attack.

Philippi in Macedonia was the site of the battle in which Antony and Octavian defeated Brutus and Cassius in 42 BC.

28 A reference to Octavian's war against Sextus Pompey, who was defeated by Agrippa in 36 BC.

29 For the siege of Perusia see i. 21 note.

30   *Pharos*: an island off Alexandria containing the famous lighthouse of that name.

Ptolemy was one of Alexander's generals; his descendants ruled Egypt from 323 to 30 BC.

31–4 refer to Octavian's Triumph in 29 BC after his victory over Antony and Cleopatra at Actium in 31 BC and his conquest of Egypt in 30 BC. Representations of countries, rivers, etc., were carried on floats in Triumphal processions, which ascended the Capitol by the Sacred Way.

37–8 Achilles and Patroclus, Theseus and Pirithous (son of Ixion) were famous pairs of loyal friends. A couplet must have fallen out here, celebrating Octavian and Maecenas as model friends on earth.

39   We are back with the Giants again. They battled against the Gods on the plain of Phlegra in Thessaly (or near Cumae in Italy—see i. 11. 1 note).

40   *Callimachus*: 'Of Cyrene, third century BC, the greatest of the Greek elegists, whose Roman successor Propertius aspires to be (cf. iv. 1. 64) and whose aversion from the epic he shares (cf. iii. 1. 1 ff.)' (Camps). The couplet contains allusions to Callimachus' own poetry.

42   A reference to the descent of the Julian *gens* from Aeneas the Trojan, through his son Iulus.

51   Phaedra, Theseus' wife, fell in love with her stepson Hippolytus.

53   *Circe*: the divine sorceress of *Odyssey* X.

54   A reference to Medea (see i. 1. 24 note) and her attempt to rejuvenate Jason's father at Iolcus in Thessaly.

59   Machaon was surgeon to the Greek army at Troy. Philoctetes had been bitten by a snake on his way to Troy.

60   The Centaur Chiron, son of Philyra, cured Phoenix's blindness.

61–2 Asclepius brought Minos' son Androgeon back to life.

63–4 Telephus, king of Mysia, was wounded by Achilles' spear and cured by rust from the same spear. The Latin has *Haemonian spear*, Haemonia being poetical for Thessaly, and Achilles Thessalian.

65–6 Tantalus betrayed the Gods' trust and was punished in Tartarus by standing up to his neck in a pool of water with fruit above his head; his attempts to eat and drink were eternally frustrated.

67–8 The daughters of Danaus killed their husbands on the wedding night and were forever condemned to fill up a leaky water-tank in the Underworld.

69–70 *vulture*: lit. 'bird'. For Prometheus see i. 12. 10 note. A vulture fed daily on his entrails which grew again in the night.

76 *gig*: Latin *essedum*, a fast two-wheeled Celtic war-chariot used by the Romans for pleasure.

 engraved: or maybe 'decorated' with embossed metal-work.

2

1 *I spoke my mind*: taking the primary sense of *liber* here as at *Oxford Latin Dictionary* s.v. 11. Lit. 'I was free'.

5–10 Cf. Yeats, 'A Thought from Propertius'.

6 Juno was both sister and wife to Jupiter.

7 Dulichium was an island near Ithaca. Pallas Athena (the Latin Minerva) was protectress of the Ithacan Odysseus (Ulysses).

8 Athena's aegis, here thought to be her breast-plate, displayed the Gorgon's head. For the Gorgon see ii. 25. 13 note.

9–10 A reference to the fight between Lapiths and Centaurs at the wedding of the Lapith Pirithous, when the Centaurs tried to abduct the Lapith women.

11–12 *Boebeis*: a Thessalian lake. The myth is obscure.

13–14 refer to the Judgement of Paris, who in a beauty contest between the three Goddesses Juno, Venus, and Minerva awarded the prize to Venus.

16 The Sibyl of Cumae was offered eternal youth by Apollo if she would accept his love. She refused him and her punishment was an eternity of growing old.

3

11 *Maeotian*: of Lake Maeotis (the Sea of Azov).

16 Lit. 'I'm not a lover who flatters for no reason.'

17 *Iacchus*: cult title of Bacchus, here used by metonymy for wine.

18 For Ariadne see i. 3. 1–2 note.

19 *Aeolian*: Lesbian, because Aeolic was the dialect spoken in Lesbos, home of the lyric poets Sappho and Alcaeus.

20 *Aganippe*: the spring on Mt. Helicon sacred to the Muses.

21 *Corinna*: a Boeotian poetess contemporary with Pindar.

22 Textual trouble here.

24 Sneezing was a good omen, cf. Catullus 45.

32 Lit. 'After Helen this second beauty returns to earth.'

36 *Pergama*: see ii. 1. 21 note.

45–6 In this reading of a controversial couplet he prays that Cynthia may remain his only love.

47–54 revert to the theme of 1–8, the lover's resignation to love's inescapable servitude.

51–4 The seer Melampus, son of Amythaon, for love of Pero, Neleus' daughter, undertook to recover the cattle that Iphiclus had stolen from Neleus.

54 The tradition is that Melampus won Pero for his brother Bias.

4

This poem can be taken either as a piece of advice to an unknown friend or as a soliloquy in which the *you* is indefinite, like 'one'.

7 *no midnight sorceress*: lit. 'no nocturnal Cytaeis (= Medea)'.

8 *Perimede*: paired with Medea as a witch in Theocritus, *Idyll* 2. 16.

10 Lit. 'The road by which so many troubles come is blind.'

5

1 Or 'Is this true, Cynthia? That you gad around in Rome? | That your life's . . . ?'

6–7 *make you jealous*: or 'pull you to pieces'.

11 The sea round the island of Karpathos between Rhodes and Crete was proverbially stormy.

14–16 The poet addresses himself.

17 *Juno*: the Goddess of marriage and also the guardian spirit of every woman as the Genius was of every man.

21 and 23 look like a reference to Tibullus i. 10. 61–2, in which case 25–6 here will be a thinly veiled attack on Tibullus.

26 Ivy, sacred to Bacchus, garlanded dramatic, lyric, and elegiac poets.

28 Lit. 'Cynthia, powerful beauty; Cynthia, in words lightweight.'

See Introduction, p. xxii.

1 *Lais*: a famous courtesan of Corinth (old name Ephyra) at the end of the fifth century BC.

3 *Thais*: an Athenian courtesan after whom Menander named a comedy, was Alexander's mistress and later married Ptolemy I of Egypt.

4 *Erichthon*: strictly 'Erichthonius', an early king of Athens.

5–6 The Boeotian courtesan Phryne offered to pay for the rebuilding of Thebes after its destruction by Alexander.

17–18 See ii. 2. 9–10 note.

23 Alcestis died to save the life of her husband Admetus.—Penelope remained true to her husband Ulysses during his long absence in the Trojan war.

26 Or, reading *quidlibet*: 'If any bride can be anything she likes.'

35–6 Textual trouble. Camps recommends transposing to follow 26.

7

See Introduction, pp. xiii and xviii.

1–3 These lines are the only evidence for the law in question.

8 i.e. give up a real passion for a conventional marriage. A much disputed line.

16 Helen's brother Castor was famous for his horsemanship; see iii. 14. 17–18.

18 *Borysthenes*: the modern river Dnieper.

19 Lit. 'You alone please me, may I please only you.'

8

See Introduction, p. xxii.

13–14 Or 'So I've been over-bold, have I, you selfish woman, | After all these years of putting up with you and yours?'

21 *Haemon*: son of King Creon of Thebes, killed himself on discovering that his fiancée Antigone was dead. 'The point of comparison here is that Haemon killed himself for loss of his loved one' (Camps).

29–38 The story of Homer's *Iliad* in brief.

9

12   *Simois*: a river near Troy.

15–16 The poet here addresses Achilles, whose father was Peleus and mother the sea-goddess Thetis; Deidamia, daughter of Lycomedes, king of the island of Scyros, bore Achilles' son Neoptolemus.

26   *Styx*: a river of the Underworld.

31   *you*: plural here.

33   *Syrtes*: shifting sandbanks off the coast of Tunisia and Libya.

40   *you*: again plural.

49–52 In these difficult lines the rival is addressed.

   Theban princes: Oedipus' sons (see i. 7. 1 note) whose mother was Jocasta.

10

1   *Helicon*: the mountain of the Muses in Boeotia where they consecrated Hesiod as a didactic poet.

2   *Haemonian horse*: (see ii. 1. 63 note) stands for epic.

4   *my leader*: explained in line 15.

8   *As*: ambiguous. Could be 'when'. In Latin the perfect is sometimes used of the future.

9   *eyebrows raised*: lit. 'face uplifted'. Apparently to raise the eyebrows was a sign of seriousness among the Greeks and Romans.

12   *Pierides*: the Muses came from Pieria in Macedonia.

13   A difficult line, which must glance at the well-known practice of the Parthian cavalryman of shooting his arrows while retreating. Goold prefers 'No longer does the Euphrates allow Parthian horsemen to glance behind their backs.'

14   In 53 BC Marcus Licinius Crassus had been disastrously defeated by the Parthians at Carrhae.

15–16 The use of the name Augustus here dates this poem after 16 January 27 BC when Octavian took that name. The line is a grotesque exaggeration. Aelius Gallus, Prefect of Egypt, mounted an unsuccessful invasion of Arabia in 25 BC.

19   *line . . . lines*: lit. 'camp'.

25   *Ascra*: Hesiod's home; its fountain stands for poetry in epic hexameters.

Permessus: a stream at the foot of Mt. Helicon, standing for elegiac love poetry, a lower form than epic.

11

Usually taken as an independent epigram, but it would fit on to 10, explaining line 8 there, *scripta puella mea est* being picked up by *scribant de te alii*.

6 *clever*: the Latin is *docta* lit. 'taught', also 'educated, learned', cf. i. 7. 12 note.

12

3 *senselessly*: Latin *sine sensu*; surprising because it could mean 'without feeling'. It looks as though Propertius relies on context to rule out irrelevant meanings.

6 *from human hearts*: this fits with 15 *from my heart*, but it could mean 'in human hearts'.

10 *Cretan*: the so-called *epitheton ornans* or ornamental epithet, the Cretans being famous as archers. ·

from each shoulder: odd. Two quivers seem unlikely, also one in the middle of his back where it would be hard for him to get at the arrows. At iv. 6. 40 Apollo's arrows also hang from his 'shoulders' (plural).

18 *For goodness' sake*: lit. 'for shame'.

24 *in sandals*: not explicit in the Latin but hinted at perhaps by *soleant*, *solea* being a sandal (Camps).

13

1 *Achaemenid*: Persian, Achaemenes being the founder of a Persian dynasty.

Susa: capital of Persia.

3 *Muses so slender*: love poetry in elegiac couplets. Also implying that he follows Callimachus (see ii. 1. 40 note), who objected to 'fat', i.e. verbose, poetry.

4 *Ascra*: see ii. 10. 25 note. One might perhaps paraphrase 'And bade me write didactic love poetry'.

5–6 *Pierian*: see ii. 10. 12 note.

Ismarus: mountain in Thrace. The couplet alludes to the Thracian Orpheus.

8 *Linus*: another legendary poet.

15 Lit. 'And if maybe she turns kind ears towards peace.'

21–2 Lit. 'Let no couch then be spread for me with ivory head-rest | Nor my death be laid on Attalic cushion.' King Attalus (III?) of Pergamum is said to have invented a method of weaving cloth of gold.

25–6 Book II as it stands (34 poems comprising 2,316 lines) is by no means a *libellus*, or 'slim volume', and originally it was probably two books.

Persephone: Pluto's consort in the Underworld.

38 *the Phthian hero*: Achilles, at whose tomb the Trojan princess Polyxena was sacrificed; he was born at Phthia in Thessaly.

43 *the Sisters Three*: the Parcae or Fates.

46 *Nestor*: the eloquent Greek greybeard in the *Iliad* who lost his son Antilochus at Troy.

53 The young Adonis whom Venus loved was killed while hunting on Mt. Idalium in Cyprus.

14

1 *Atrides*: Agamemnon, son of Atreus and leader of the Greeks against Troy (= Dardania, because founded by Dardanus).

Laomedon: the king who built the walls of Troy.

4–5 *Dulichia*: poetical variant for Ithaca, Ulysses' native island. See ii. 2. 7 note.

5–6 A reference to the recognition scene in Sophocles' *Electra* where Orestes sends his sister Electra an urn supposedly containing his ashes, but reveals himself to her when he comes home in disguise to avenge the death of his father Agamemnon.

7–8 See i. 3. 1–2 note.

12 *puddle*: lit. 'pool', 'trough'.

16 Lit. 'Now medicine is given to my ashes.'

23 *Parthia*: see ii. 10. 14 note.

24 Lit. 'This will be booty, this kings, this chariot to me.' The reference is to a Roman Triumphal procession.

25 *Cythera's Queen*: Venus, because the island of Cythera (now Kíthira)

off Cape Malea was supposedly where she stepped ashore after her birth from the sea and was accordingly sacred to her.

29–32 If these lines are taken with 1–28 then we must suppose that Propertius is humorously undercutting their confident tone and disobeying his own recommendation in line 19. Many editors regard the two couplets as a separate fragment.

15

See Introduction, p. xiv.

1 *O dazzling night*!: lit. 'O night white *or* unclouded for me'.

15 *Endymion*: a shepherd boy on Mt. Latmos in Caria with whom the Moon-Goddess Diana fell in love and whom she visited in the dark times between the old moon and the new.

17–20 Contradicts ii. 5. 21–4.

38 Lit. 'even a year of life will be long' or perhaps 'they will be a long year of life'.

44 For Actium see ii. 1. 31–4 note.

45–6 A reference to the victories in the Roman Civil Wars of the first century BC that caused the death of so many Roman citizens.

53 *Walk so tall*: lit. 'breathe so big'.

16

1 After his year of office in Rome a Praetor normally served as governor of a province. For Illyricum (Illyria) and Ceraunian see i. 8A. 2 and 19 notes.

16 *ruined by*: could also be 'madly in love with'.

17 *Oceanus*: must be the Red Sea here, cf. i. 14. 12; for the Romans it included the Persian Gulf and the Arabian Sea.

27 This barbarian is typical of Propertius' *nouveaux riches* rivals. He started as a slave, forced to demonstrate his physical fitness in the slave-market.

29 Eriphyla was bribed to persuade her husband Amphiaraus to join the expedition of the Seven against Thebes, though he knew it meant his death. His sons avenged him by killing their mother.

30 *Creusa*: the bride Jason married when he deserted the Colchian princess Medea. Medea gave her a poisoned wedding present that killed her.

34 *Campus Martius*: ancient Rome's recreation ground.

37–40 A reference to Mark Antony, his love for Cleopatra, and his defeat at Actium in 31 BC by Caesar Octavian.

55 Sidon, like Tyre, was famous for its purple.

17

13–14 placed after 2 by Housman.

5 *Tantalus*: see ii. 1. 65–6 note.

7 *Sisyphus*: 'A king of Corinth, proverbial for his trickery; condemned in Hades for ever to roll uphill a stone that rolled back again' (*Oxford Latin Dictionary*).

18A

Camps, very reasonably, regards these four lines as the middle section of an elegy formed by 2. 17 and 18B, thus producing the pattern 18 lines + 4 + 18 and involving sudden changes of mood, a feature found in several elegies in this book.

2 'often' (*saepe*) is omitted.

18B

7 *Tithonus*: son of the Trojan king Laomedon and beloved by Aurora, goddess of the dawn. Offered one wish he chose immortality, forgetting to ask for eternal youth, and so grew ever older and more decrepit.

16 *Memnon*: son of Tithonus and Aurora, king of the Ethiopians, was killed in the Trojan war.

18C

26 *Belgic dye*: there was a dye called Batavian foam (*spuma Batava*) for turning the hair red.

28 *cheats*: could be 'cheated', producing a possible variant of the curse on the inventor, cf. ii. 6. 27–32; but that really demands the inclusion of 'first'.

35 *couch*: stands for 'love' here, and could also be the past participle 'chosen', meaning the poet.

19

10 She uses temple-visits as an excuse for assignations.

18 *Diana*: the Greek Artemis, goddess of the chase.

25 *Clitumnus*: an Umbrian river rising not far from Propertius' birthplace.

overlays: referring to the reflection of the woods in the water, but it could be 'shades'.

31 Or 'that your name will be on some persistent tongue', i.e. that you will have an importunate lover. The reading is uncertain here.

20

1 *Briseis*: see ii. 8. 35.

2 *Andromache*: Hector's widow whose son Astyanax was killed by Ulysses at the fall of Troy.

6 *Attic bird*: the nightingale, in Greek legend the Athenian princess Procne who murdered her own son Itys to punish her barbarous husband Tereus and thereafter ever mourned his death.

Cecrops: the first king of Attica.

7–8 Niobe boasted that she had more children than Latona, mother of Apollo and Diana, for which Apollo killed all her twelve children with his arrows. Niobe turned to stone on Mt. Sipylos in Lydia as she wept for them.

10 Danae was imprisoned by her father in a metal tower because an oracle foretold that her son would kill him. Jove fell in love with her and reached her through a window as a shower of gold, begetting a son Perseus who later unintentionally killed his grandfather; cf. ii. 32. 59–60.

20 *discipline*: lit. 'servitude'. The so-called *servitium amoris*, cf. i. 4. 4, 5. 19, 12. 18.

29 *Tragic Furies*: the Eumenides of Greek tragedy, avengers of guilt.

31 The giant Tityos tried to rape Latona and was punished in Hades by vultures who fed on his liver.

32 For Sisyphus see ii. 17. 7 note.

21

1 *Panthus*: this lover of Cynthia's only appears here. The Greek name is probably a pseudonym like Demophoon (ii. 22A), Lynceus (ii. 34), and Lycotas (iv. 3).

3 *Dodona*: see i. 9. 5 note.

11–12 See ii. 16. 30 note.

13 See i. 15. 9 note.

17 If the text is correct, the poet soliloquizes about Cynthia for one line, addressing her in the next one.

22A

2 *Demophoon*: in legend Theseus' son who deceived his lover Phyllis; probably a pseudonym, perhaps for the poet mentioned by Ovid in *Ex Ponto* iv. 16. 20 as famous for his telling of the story of Phyllis.

15–16 A reference to the eunuch priests of the Phrygian goddess Cybele.

19 The legendary Thracian bard Thamyras challenged the Muses to a competition and on losing was blinded by them.

25 Jupiter, impersonating Alcmena's husband Amphitryon, stopped the rotation of the Great and Little Bear round the pole so as to spend a longer night with Alcmena when he begot Hercules.

29–30 Cf. ii. 8. 29–38.   *spear*: lit. 'Thessalian weapons'.

31–2 Cf. ii. 20. 2.

42 Lit. 'An anxious mother rears twins more safely', because she can afford to lose one.

22B

Clearly these eight lines do not fit 22A. Camps in *Proceedings of the Cambridge Philological Society*, 37 (1991), 27–9, argues that they begin a new elegy including 23 and 24A and he would place 24A. 11–16 between

23. 20 and 21—an attractive solution to a controversial problem. The text of 48 and 50 is uncertain.

23

15 The Via Sacra or Sacred Way was a main street in Rome, lined with shops; cf. ii. 24. 14.

24A

1–10 These difficult lines will fit quite well on to ii. 23.

4 Or 'He should keep quiet about either love or decency.'

5 *comparable*: i.e. to the streetwalker's.

11–16 This fragment develops the theme of ii. 23. 8, gifts. It is reasonable to suppose that like 1–10 it belongs to 23, but something has dropped out between 10 and 11. For Camps's suggestion see note on 22B above.

24B

25–6 Among the labours of Hercules was the destruction of the Hydra of Lerna (a marsh near Argos) and the acquisition of the Golden Apples from the Garden of the Hesperides on the western edge of the world.

33 *Sibyl*: see ii. 2. 16 note.

34 *Alcides*: see i. 20. 49 note.

43 See i. 3. 1–2 note.

44 See ii. 22A. 2 note.

45 A reference to the story of the expedition of Jason and the Argonauts to fetch the Golden Fleece from Colchis. Cf. ii. 16. 30 note.

25

4 Calvus and Catullus were love-poets of the previous generation who celebrated respectively Quintilia and Lesbia.

10 For Tithonus see ii. 18B. 7 note, and for Nestor ii. 13. 46 note.

12 *Perillus*: the Athenian craftsman who made a brazen bull for Phalaris the tyrant of Agrigentum in which criminals could be roasted alive,

causing the bull to seem to bellow. Phalaris made Perillus the first victim of his invention.

13　*Gorgon*: alias Medusa, daughter of Phorcis, was a snake-haired monster whose gaze turned those who looked at her to stone. She was killed by Perseus, for whom see i. 3. 3–4 note and ii. 20. 10 note.

14　*Prometheus' vultures*: lit. 'Caucasian birds'. See ii. 1. 69 note.

26　A chariot-race normally had seven laps.

35　Or 'And yet if our days were graced by the girls of old'.

26A

5　*Helle*: 'daughter of Athamas, King of Thebes; she was persecuted by her cruel stepmother Ino and fled with her brother Phrixus, riding the magic golden ram, from which she fell while passing over the strait now called Hellespont after her. (It may be that Propertius here has in mind a painting of this famous scene from mythology.)' (Camps).

9　For Castor and Pollux see i. 17. 18 note.

10　'Ino, the persecutress of Phrixus and Helle, was attacked by her husband Athamas, whom Juno had driven mad, and in trying to escape him leapt into the sea; she was turned into a sea-goddess under the name *Leucothea* (here *Leucothoe*), in which role she had a benevolent character' (Camps).

13　*Glaucus*: a sea-god, son of Neptune.

15　*Nereids*: see i. 17. 25 note.

16　*Nesaea . . . Cymothoe*: names of Nereids in Homer, *Iliad* xviii. 40–1.

18　The seventh-century BC poet Arion from Lesbos was forced to walk the plank by sailors who had robbed him, but the music he played before doing so attracted a dolphin who carried him safely ashore. The story is told by Herodotus, i. 23–4.

26B

21–8 It is hard to see how these lines could fit on to ii. 26A. They are best regarded as starting a new poem.

29–58 are headed 26C by some editors. One must probably posit a lacuna before or after 29–30 to provide a balancing *seu*. But the lines develop the idea of devotion and faithfulness (27) and can be regarded as a continuation of 26B.

23 *Croesus*: the proverbially rich man, was king of Lydia in the sixth century BC.

 Cambyses: also sixth-century BC, king of Persia and a great conqueror.

24 *my*: lit. 'our'.

28 Lit. 'He who can give many presents can also take many loves.'

35–6 *Eurus*: east wind.   *Auster*: south wind.

37 *Ulysses*: Latin form of Greek Odysseus, the hero of Homer's *Odyssey* who took ten years to return home after the Trojan war.

38 The Greeks after their victory at Troy lost their fleet on the voyage home on the rocks of Caphareus, a promontory of Euboea.

39–40 'The reference is to the Symplegades or Clashing Rocks through which the Argo sailed after a dove had been sent experimentally to fly through them first; the story is told in Apollonius Rhodius ii. 324 ff. and 549 ff.' (Camps).

47 *Amymone*: daughter of Danaus who sent her out to find water in a drought.

48 *Lerna*: see ii. 24. 25 note.

51 *Orithyia*: daughter of Erechtheus king of Athens, was carried off by Boreas (Latin *Aquilo*), the north wind.

53–4 *Scylla*: sea-monster on the Italian side of the Straits of Messina who devoured any passing sailors she could get hold of.

 Charybdis: whirlpool on the Sicilian side of the Straits of Messina, personified as a female monster who alternately swallowed and ejected sea-water.

58 *me*: lit. 'us'.

27

3 The Phoenicians as a sea-faring people studied the stars, but the invention of astrology is usually ascribed to the Babylonians.

12 *Boreas*: ii. 26. 51 note.

13 *Stygian*: ii. 9. 26 note.

28A

33 *Juno*: ii. 5. 17 note.

4 The Dogstar, or Sirius, the brightest star in the sky, rising in July was supposed to bring on the hottest time of the year.

11 *Pelasgian*: = Argive. Argos was Juno's (Hera's) most ancient place of worship.

12 The goddess Pallas had grey eyes.

18 Io (i. 3. 20 note) was transformed into the Egyptian goddess Isis.

19 *Ino*: ii. 26. 10 note.

21 *Andromeda*: i. 3. 3–4 note.

23 *Callisto*: a nymph attendant on the virgin goddess Diana, was loved by Jupiter but turned into a bear by Diana as a punishment. Jupiter placed Callisto and her son in the heavens as Great and Little Bear.

27 *Semele*: mother by Jupiter of the god Bacchus, asked to see Jupiter in the full power of his divinity and was destroyed by his lightning.

29 *Maeonian*: = Lydian, but Homer was known as Maeonides and the adjective probably stands for 'Homeric' here.

28B

On the same subject as 28A and forms a pair with it; cf. i. 8A and 8B. The magical attempt to cure Cynthia is over and the outlook is bad, but suddenly Dis and Persephone relent and she recovers.

47 *Persephone*: ii. 13. 26 note. Her husband is Dis or Pluto.

51–4 These are the 'Maeonian heroines' of line 29 above.

60–2 Cynthia had vowed for her recovery dances to Diana and ten nights of abstinence to Isis (ii. 28A. 17–18 note and 33A. 1–2).

29A

These little boys are in origin the Hellenistic Erotes (Amores, or Amorini) and co-exist with Amor himself (line 18). They are Cupid's *fugitiuarii*, responsible for recovering his runaway slaves.

29B

Clearly not part of 29A, which is addressed to Cynthia, whereas this is addressed to the reader. But some take it as a sequel, despite the apparent contradiction between lines 1 and 42.

26 *crimson*: cf. i. 14. 20 note.

27　*Vesta*: goddess of the hearth.

32　*yours*: plural.

37–8 Lit. 'Look how there rises in all my body no breath known when adultery is committed.'

30A

2　*Tanais*: the river Don, in Sarmatia.

3–4 *Pegasus . . . Perseus*: see i. 3. 3–4 note.

12　Lit. 'If only he sees that prayers are present to help.'

30B

Looks like a separate elegy from 30A, despite the connexion of travel in lines 1–2, 14, and 19–20.

14　Lit. 'Only let us . . . wear away the road proposed.' In the Latin there is a connexion between *conuiuia*, 'parties', and *uita*, 'life'.

17–18 *Meander*: see ii. 34. 35–6.　　The reed pipe was invented by Pallas Athene, but when she saw her reflection as she played it, she thought it made her look ugly and threw it away.

19–22 A crux. With the reading given, Propertius refuses to serve as a soldier in the East and risk fighting Romans who had been captured by the Parthians at Carrhae (see ii. 10. 14 note) or their sons, who were now serving in the Parthian army. Alternatively he refuses to write epic on the subject of *Argonautica* or *Seven against Thebes*.

19　*Phrygian waves*: Hellespont and Propontis.

20　*Hyrcanian sea*: the Caspian.

22　*Lares*: Roman gods of the hearth and home.

27　*the Sisters Nine*: the Muses ('nine' is an addition to the Latin).

29　*burnt by Semele*: see ii. 28. 27 note; an intentional paradox.

　　Io: see i. 3. 20 note.

30　He became an eagle and carried off the Trojan prince, Ganymede as his cupbearer.

31　*the Winged One*: Cupid.

33　*those Maidens*: the Muses.

35　*Oeagrus*: father of Orpheus by this anonymous Muse, about whose identity there was learned dispute, Calliope being the favourite.

36   *Bistonian*: poetical for Thracian.

39   *the holy ivy*: see ii. 5. 26 note.

31

1–2 *Phoebus' . . . Portico*: Octavian had originally vowed a temple to
     Apollo after the naval defeat of Sextus Pompey in 36 BC, but he did
     not actually dedicate it on the Palatine till 28 BC after his defeat of
     Antony and Cleopatra at Actium in 31 BC. The temple complex
     contained a library and more than one portico. It is not clear whether
     this portico was dedicated at the same time as the temple, but
     the description of the temple here (9–16) suggests that it was
     contemporaneous.

3   *Punic pillars*: of African marble.

4   Danaus and Aegyptus, grandsons of Io, had respectively fifty daughters
     and fifty sons. Danaus fled to Argos with his daughters but was
     pursued by his fifty nephews who wanted to marry them. Danaus
     ordered his daughters to kill their husbands on the wedding night,
     which they did (all except one) and were punished in Hades by having
     for ever to fill a leaking amphora with water.

7   *Myron*: Athenian sculptor of the fifth century BC, famous for his
     animal statues.

10   *Ortygia*: Delos.

12   *Libyan ivory*: lit. 'Libyan tooth'.

13   A Gallic army under Brennus tried to sack Apollo's sanctuary at
     Delphi in 278 BC but were routed by the Delphians, aided by an
     earthquake and a storm with thunder and lightning, during which
     rocks from Mt. Parnassus fell upon the invaders.

14   *daughter of Tantalus*: Niobe, see ii. 20. 7 note.

16   *Pythian*: cult title of Apollo at Delphi, of which the old name was
     Pytho, after the monstrous snake living there which Apollo killed.

32

3   *Praeneste*: a town some 20 miles south-east of Rome with a famous
     temple of Fortune where people went to have lots drawn to answer
     their questions.

4   *Telegonus's walls*: Tusculum, a town about 14 miles south-east of

Rome, supposedly founded by Telegonus, the son of Ulysses by Circe of the island of Aeaea.

5 *Tibur*: modern Tivoli, some 18 miles ENE of Rome, with a famous temple of Hercules.

6 *Lanuvium*: a town some 18 miles south of Rome with a famous temple of Juno, on the Via Appia which went via Capua to Brundisium. See also iv. 8. 3 ff.

7 *here*: lit. 'in this place', i.e. Rome.

10 *Nemi*: the sacred grove of Diana (= Trivia, i.e. of the crossroads) at Aricia on the Appian Way south of Rome before Lanuvium.

1–2 Placed after 10, where they make better sense, by Camps.

11 *Pompey's Porch*: 'A rectangular court surrounded by colonnades, adjoining the theatre of Pompey in the Campus Martius' (Butler and Barber).

12 *Attalid tapestries*: see ii. 13. 22 note.

14 *Maron*: son of the wine-god Bacchus or of his attendant Silenus, perhaps sleeping with his head on a wineskin from which water pours.

16 *Triton*: this sea-divinity is usually depicted as blowing a conch, and presumably that is what spouts water here.

28 Phoebus the sun-god sees everything.

31 *Tyndaris*: Helen of Troy, daughter of Tyndareus.

33 An allusion to the story told in *Odyssey* viii. 267 ff.

35 The goddess seems to have been the Nymph Oenone on Mt. Ida in the Troad, referred to in the Latin of 39 as a Naiad.

37–8 *Hamadryads*: see i. 20. 45 note.

Sileni: elderly Satyrs.

Father of the Dance: presumably Bacchus.

44 *unfashionably*: or perhaps 'immorally'.

45 *Lesbia*: the mistress of Catullus.

47 Titus Tatius was a legendary Sabine king who fought Romulus and later shared with him the kingship of Rome. His name was proverbial for archaic simplicity.

52 *Saturn's reign*: the Golden Age. Saturn was Jupiter's father.

53 *Deucalion*: the Greek Noah, son of Prometheus. He and his wife Pyrrha survived the great flood in which Zeus drowned a sinful world.

58 *Minos' wife*: Pasiphae.

59 *Danae*: see ii. 20. 10 note.

33A

1–2 For Isis (= Io, daughter of Inachus) and her worship see also ii. 28A.
17–18 and 28B. 61–2. She wandered the world as a cow until on
reaching Egypt she became a goddess.

4 *Ausonian*: see i. 20. 12 note.

8 Lit. 'to enter many ways'.

18 The point of this line is obscure.

22 *When free*: or simply *Freed*.

33B

Like 33A in being about the lover's frustration and also in being 22 lines
long. It could be made a continuation of 33A if one supposed that the poet
had been reciting 33A. 1–20 to Cynthia at a drinking-party to celebrate the
end of the ten nights of abstinence.

24 *Icarus' oxen*: the Great Bear (*Ursa Major*) was also known as 'The
Seven Ploughing Oxen' (*Septentriones*). Icarus, or Icarius, was an Attic
farmer who entertained Dionysus and in return was given the vine and
the secret of wine-making. He shared his wine with some locals who
then murdered him in the belief that he had poisoned them. But
Dionysus set him among the stars as Bootes (the Ploughman) to drive
the Seven Ploughing Oxen. The Alexandrian poet Eratosthenes had
told the story in his *Erigone* (the name of Icarus' daughter).

29 *Cecropian*: see ii. 20. 6 note.

31 *Eurytion*: 'the Centaur who laid hands on the bride at the wedding
of Pirithous and Hippodamia, thus provoking the legendary fight
between the Centaurs and the Lapiths' (Camps). cf. ii. 2. 9–10.

32 'Ulysses intoxicated the Cyclops Polyphemus with wine of exceptional
strength and fragrance which had been given to him by Maron, priest
of Apollo at Ismarus in Thrace' (Camps).

35 *Lyaeus*: the Loosener, a title of Dionysus.

39 *Falernian*: a highly regarded Italian wine from Campania.

34

7 *an adulterer*: Paris, who abducted Helen.

8 *the Colchian . . . a strange man*: Medea and Jason.

9   *Lynceus*: this Greek name is presumably a pseudonym for a poet-friend of Propertius.

     my charge: also 'my love'.

27–28 Lynceus has studied ethics and cosmology and written both tragedy (41) and didactic poetry (51–4).

29   *Aratus*: of Soli in Cilicia (third century BC) was famous for his didactic poem *Phaenomena*, in which he versified a prose treatise on astronomy by Eudoxus of Cnidos.

31   *Philetas*: of Cos, tutor to Ptolemy Philadelphus (third century BC), was an important scholar-poet, called here 'long-memoried' presumably because of his interest in and use of earlier Greek literature. The Latin has *Philitas*, the less familiar form.

32   *Callimachus*: of Cyrene, the famous Alexandrian scholar-poet, flourished under Ptolemy Philadelphus. His poem *Aitia*, 'Origins', in four books began with an account of a dream; he was an enemy of bombast.

33   *Achelous*: this river-god fought with Hercules over Deianira and lost.

37–40 Allusions to episodes in the story of the Seven against Thebes.

41   i.e. 'Cease writing tragedies in the style of Aeschylus.' He was famous for his long, compound words. The cothurnus was the high boot or buskin worn by tragic actors.

42–4 i.e. 'Begin to write love elegy'.

45   Antimachus of Colophon and Homer here are examples of epic poets who fell in love, the first with his mistress Lyde, the second supposedly with Penelope, the heroine of his *Odyssey*.

46   *right*: i.e. 'proper', 'well-built'; cf. ii. 18. 25.

52   'Propertius is thinking not of eclipses . . . but of the monthly occultations of the moon' (Shackleton Bailey, *Classical Quarterly*, 43 (1949), 26).

59   Or 'on yesterday's garlands'.

61   'There was a temple of Apollo at Actium, overlooking the scene of Octavian's naval victory over Antony and Cleopatra' (Camps). Virgil describes the victory in *Aeneid* viii.

63–4 *arms . . . Lavinian shore*: an allusion to the opening of the *Aeneid*.

67–76 Propertius addresses Virgil and picks out themes from the love poetry of his *Eclogues*, though in fact the river Galaesus (near Tarentum) is never mentioned there.

77–80 Here Propertius turns to Virgil's *Georgics*, called by Virgil 'an Ascrean song' because they are in the tradition of Hesiod's *Works and Days*; see ii. 10. 25 note.

79 *tortoiseshell*: traditionally formed the sounding board of the lyre.

80 *the Cynthian*: Apollo, believed to have been born on Mt. Cynthus on the island of Delos.

81 *this*: i.e. love poetry.

83–4 A reference to *Eclogue* 9. 35–6 where Lycidas says: 'As yet I cannot rival Varius or Cinna | But gabble like a goose among articulate swans.' But the precise meaning is obscure. Perhaps Propertius thinks of Virgil as the Swan, and the Goose is the Latin poet Anser whose name means 'goose'.

85 Varro of Atax (born 82 BC) translated the *Argonautica* of Apollonius Rhodius and wrote love poetry to his mistress Leucadia, presumably a pseudonym like Lesbia.

    made perfect: also 'completed'.

87 The traditional dates for Catullus are 84–54 BC.

89–90 Catullus' friend Gaius Licinius Calvus, orator and poet, was born in 82 BC. Catullus' poem 95 refers to his elegy on the death of Quintilia.

91–2 Gaius Cornelius Gallus (69–26 BC), first Prefect of Egypt, was also the first Latin love elegist. Lycoris was his pseudonym for the actress Cytheris.

BOOK III

I

1–2 For Callimachus and Philetas see notes on ii. 34. 31–2. Propertius appeals to them as the two pre-eminent Greek elegists to accept him as a poet in their tradition. Philetas' 'sacrifices' (Latin *sacra*, cf. iv. 6. 1) are his poems. Groves and grottoes are associated with the Muses.

3–4 Continuing the religious metaphor Propertius claims to be the first Latin poet to write verse modelled on theirs; the 'mysteries' (*orgia* in the Latin) refer to the Italian content of his work, and the 'dances' to its Greek metrical form.

5 *both*: Latin *pariter* 'together, equally, at the same time'. Roughly 'In what poetic school did you together learn to write poetry with extreme economy of words?'

6 *On what foot entering?*: either 'What metre did you start with?' or, assuming it was the elegiac couplet, 'At what foot in the couplet did you start composing?'

What water drinking?: i.e. 'Whose work inspired you?' Cf. iii. 3. 5. In the whole of this passage Propertius alludes to words and ideas that Callimachus employs to describe his poetic ideal.

7 i.e. anyone who writes epic verse.

9 *the Muse*: here used of Propertius' verse introduces a description of his metaphorical Triumph as a conquering poet.

11 A triumphing general's children rode with him in the chariot.

13–14 The metaphor changes from Triumph to chariot-race; there's no room for overtaking on this racecourse.

15–16 A reference to epic poetry in the tradition of the *Annales* of Ennius, for whom see iii. 3. 6 note.

Bactra: a province of the Parthian empire, roughly the modern Balkh.

17–18 *the Sisters' mount*: Helicon (ii. 10. 1 note).

19–20 *Pegasids*: the Muses as Nymphs of Hippocrene, the spring on Mt. Helicon opened up by the hoof of Pegasus, the winged horse.

heavy wreath: the epic poet's.

25–30 Names and topics from Homer's *Iliad* and the Epic Cycle.

32 *Oeta's God*: Hercules, who was deified after his self-immolation on a pyre on Mt. Oeta in Thessaly. He captured Troy after being defrauded by Laomedon of his reward for killing a sea-monster. The second time it was his magic bow and arrows in the possession of Philoctetes that took Priam's city.

37 *the Lycian God*: Apollo, so called by Callimachus when he received the god's commission. Apollo had a famous temple at Patara in Lycia.

2

5–6 A reference to Amphion's music building the walls of Thebes, cf. i. 9. 10.

Cithaeron: a mountain range south of Thebes.

7–8 Theocritus in *Idyll* 11 records the serenade of the Cyclops Polyphemus to the sea-nymph Galatea.

11 *Taenarian columns*: of black marble from Taenaron (Cape Matapan) in the Peloponnese.

13 The fruit-trees of Alcinous, king of the Phaeacians, are described in *Odyssey* vii. 114 ff.

14 *Marcian water*: the famous *aqua Marcia*, brought into Rome by an

aqueduct completed by Quintus Marcius Rex in 140 BC, was highly prized for its purity.

16 *Calliope*: see i. 2. 28 note.

20 The temple of Olympian Zeus in Elis contained his famous statue by Phidias, like the Pyramids one of the Seven Wonders of the World.

21 *Mausoleum*: the tomb of the Carian king Mausolus built by his widow in the fourth century BC, another of the Seven Wonders.

3

1 *Helicon*: see ii. 10. 1 note.

2 *Bellerophon's horse*: Pegasus, see iii. 1. 19–20 note.

4 *Alba*: Alba Longa in Latium where the descendants of Aeneas ruled.

for my powers: Latin *neruis meis*, lit. 'for my sinews', at the same time suggesting, perhaps, 'for my lyre-strings'.

6 *Ennius*: Quintus Ennius (239–169 BC), the father of Latin poetry, wrote in many genres but was most famous for his epic *Annales* in eighteen books, recording the course of Roman history.

7–12 list themes from Ennius' *Annals*: the fight between the three Latin brothers Curiatii and the three Roman brothers Horatii (7), the naval Triumph of Aemilius Regillus after his victory over Antiochus the Great off Myonnesus in Ionia in 190 BC (8), the successful delaying tactics of Fabius Cunctator in the Second Punic War (9), Rome's defeat at Cannae in that war in 216 BC (9–10), Juno placated and Hannibal's failure to capture Rome (10–11), and the geese raising the alarm and saving the Capitol from the Gauls in 387 BC (12).

13 *the Castalian tree*: in fact the Castalian spring is on Mt. Parnassus, like Helicon a seat of the Muses.

15 *stream*: referring to 'the great spring' of line 5.

19 *tables*: Latin *scamnum*, lit. 'footstool' or 'step' for getting on to the high Roman couch.

24 *Most . . . in mid-ocean*: or 'The greatest turmoil's in mid-ocean.'

29 *orgia*: 'sacred things' (cf. iii. 1. 4), referring here to the tambourines or other musical instruments (cf. Catullus 63. 9).

Silenus: see ii. 32. 14 and 38 notes.

30 *Tegean*: Tegea was in Arcadia, Pan's home country.

32 *Gorgonean pool*: Hippocrene (cf. iii. 1. 19–20 note) because Pegasus sprang from the blood of the Gorgon Medusa.

33 The nine Muses.

37–8 *face*: shows that the name Calliopea (the Muse Calliope—cf. i. 2. 28) is here thought of as deriving from Greek *kalos* 'beautiful' and *ops* 'face'.

39 *swans*: associated with Venus.

42 *Aonian*: see i. 2. 28 note.

43–4 refer to Marius' defeat of the Teutoni in 102 BC and the Cimbri in 101; cf. ii. 1. 24.

45–6 The Suebi (Swabians), a German tribe, and their chief Ariovistus, were defeated by Julius Caesar in 58 BC; see his *Gallic War* i. 53.

47 *an alien*: also 'another's'.

48 *signs*: hints too at the military meaning of *signa*, 'standards, eagles'.

escapes: another military term, 'routs'.

52 *Philetas*: see ii. 34. 31 note and iii. 1. 1.

4

See Introduction, p. xiii.

1 The probable date lies between the end of 25 BC when Augustus returned from Spain and 20 BC when the Parthian question was settled by diplomacy.

3 *his men*: lit. 'men'.

4 *his*: lit. 'thy', addressing Caesar.

5 *Ausonian rods*: the *fasces* or bundles of rods carried by the Roman lictors attendant on praetors and consuls as symbols of their authority.

9 *Crassus' defeat*: see ii. 10. 14 note.

11 Vesta's fire in her small round temple in the Roman Forum was kept alight by the Vestal Virgins. The safety of the city depended on their never letting it go out.

16 *under their armour*: it may have been piled up above them on the Triumphal float on which they were displayed.

17 Cf. ii. 10. 13 note. The Parthians wore trousers.

19–20 Augustus counted as Venus' descendant because the *gens Iulia* to which he belonged claimed descent from Iulus, son of Aeneas who was the son of Venus and the Trojan Anchises.

22 *the Sacred Way*: see ii. 1. 31–4 note.

5

1 *venerate*: with a glance at Venus (genitive *Veneris*).

6 Corinth was famous for its bronzes. The particular alloy used was said to have been discovered accidentally by the fusion of gold, silver, and bronze when the city was burnt down by Mummius in 146 BC.

7 There was a tradition that the Titan Prometheus (see i. 12. 10 note) shaped the first man and woman out of clay.

8 The heart was generally regarded as the seat of the intelligence.

10 *emotions*: or maybe 'thoughts'; Latin *animus*.

13 *Acheron*: a river of the Underworld.

16 *Jugurtha*: the Numidian king brought to Rome as a prisoner by Marius in 104 BC.

17 *Irus*: the Ithacan beggar in Homer's *Odyssey*.

19 *Helicon*: see ii. 10. 1 note.

21 *Lyaeus*: paradoxical after 'fetter'; see ii. 33. 35 note. The reference is partly to the garland worn by drinkers at symposia, partly to drink fuddling thought.

29 *Eurus*: see ii. 26. 35 note.

32 'The rainbow was supposed to draw up water, which then came down again as rain' (Camps).

33 The Perrhaebians lived in northern Thessaly on the slopes of the Pindus mountain range.

35 *Bootes*: see ii. 33B. 24 note.

42 *the wheel*: the Lapith king Ixion was tied in the Underworld to a perpetually revolving wheel as a punishment for trying to rape Juno. For the other two punishments see notes on ii. 17. 7 and ii. 1. 66.

41 *Phineus*: king of Bithynia, blinded his children on the false accusation of their stepmother and was thereafter plagued by the Harpies, winged monsters who robbed him of his food.

   Alcmaeon: son of Amphiaraus (see ii. 16. 29 note), killed his mother Eriphyle and was punished by the Furies.

40 *Tisiphone*: 'Avenger of Bloodshed', one of the three Furies.

44 *Cerberus*: the three-headed hound guarding the entrance to the Underworld.

   Tityos: see ii. 20. 31 note.

48 *Crassus*: see ii. 10. 14 note.

6

1 *Lygdamus*: the name is Greek and in this dramatic monologue belongs
   to a slave who appears to be Cynthia's and who acts as go-between.

25 *drugs*: lit. 'herbs'.

30 *from a corpse*: lit. 'from a bier'. The line contains an unsolved crux.

7

4 *stock*: the Latin *caput*, lit. 'head', can be used of 'capital' as well as
   of a rooted tree-trunk.

5 *Paetus*: this poem provides our only information about him.

6 *Pharos' harbour*: Alexandria, see ii. 1. 30 note.

11–12 The poet here addresses Paetus; for the sudden switch cf. iii. 11.
   36–37 note.

   Carpathian: see ii. 5. 11 note.

13 See ii. 26. 51 note.

21–4 An allusion to a little known story from Phanocles' *Erotes* (third
   century BC). Argynnus, grandson of Athamas of Thebes, was loved by
   Agamemnon but drowned in the river Cephisus. Agamemnon in
   mourning presumably refused to give orders for the Greek fleet to sail
   from Aulis in Boeotia to Troy, after which the fleet was becalmed.
   Fair winds could only be bought by the sacrifice of Agamemnon's
   daughter Iphigenia.

25 *Return*: the Latin plural imperative must refer to Aquilo and Neptune
   above.

29 *Go build*: addressing those concerned.

33 The addressee is no longer Paetus, as line 38 shows, but any seafaring
   merchant.

39 *The rocks of Caphareus*: in southern Euboea, where Nauplius lit a
   beacon to lure the Greek fleet returning from Troy to destruction, in
   order to avenge his son Palamedes whom Ulysses had treacherously
   put to death.

41–2 A reference to Homer's *Odyssey*.

43–6 Could refer to Ulysses, but the Latin *uiueret* (45) is more naturally
   'he would live' than 'he would have lived' and the first fits Paetus
   better.

49 *Orician terebinth*: turpentine wood from Oricos (see i. 8A. 20 note).

57 *the calm*: lit. 'level seas', Latin *aequora*.

60 *long hands*: the implication is obscure; as a sign of beauty (cf. ii. 2. 5) the phrase may be relevant here and provide a pathetic touch.

62 *Blue God*: Neptune.

67 *Nereus*: see i. 17. 25 note.

68 *drawn*: if the reading is correct must mean 'drawn to the scene'.

8

1 The rhyme here represents disyllabic rhyme at caesura and line-ending in the Latin.

12 An alternative punctuation is full stop here and comma at 16.

17 *interpreter*: Latin *haruspex*, a diviner who inspected and interpreted the entrails of sacrificial victims.

25–6 Probably Cynthia is signalling not to Propertius but to another man. This would make Propertius weep or else he would make Cynthia weep for it.

29–32 embroider on themes from the *Iliad*.

35–40 This passage allows one to infer that Cynthia's fury (1–4) is because she suspects Propertius of being unfaithful, a suspicion fostered by his rival (37). Propertius assures her by implication that she is so beautiful that he cannot leave her for another.

35 *You would suffer*: i.e. 'because you would be jealous and also because I should leave you and have no qualms about attacking you physically if you were unfaithful.'

9

See Introduction, p. xiii.

1 *Maecenas*: see ii. 1. 17 note.

8 A crux. Lit. 'Nor is one palm brought from the same summit.' This 'summit' is the Muses' mountain. For the idea cf. iv. 10. 4.

9–16 A list of eight famous Greek artists of the fifth and fourth centuries BC to support the point made in 7–8.

16 *sells*: 'commends' (Camps).

17 *Elis*: see i. 8. 36 note.

suits: lit. 'runs with'; the pun is hard to represent in English.

23–6 i.e. he could have gone in for a public career and been a praetor or a consul.

23 *move*: an attempt to find a verb that will work with 'axes' and 'rulings', thus representing the zeugma produced by the Latin *ponere*. For these 'axes' cf. i. 6. 19.

32 *Camillus*: Marcus Furius, the early Roman hero who routed the Gauls after their sack of Rome in 390 BC and who was known as a second Romulus.

33 *stand . . . history*: Camps.

37–8 A reference to the sack of Thebes, which Cadmus had founded, by the Epigoni, or sons, of the Seven against Thebes; see i. 7. 1 note. The Seven are referred to in 38.

39–42 allude to the Trojan War.

43–4 See iii. 1. 1 note.

47–8 See ii. 1. 39 note.

49–50 i.e. the story of Rome's foundation, Romulus' murder of his twin brother Remus, and how they were both suckled by a she-wolf.

53–6 Further epic topics from recent Roman history.

either shore: i.e. east and west.

55 *Pelusium*: a frontier fortress town near the eastern mouth of the Nile, captured by Mark Antony and later surrendered to Octavian.

56 A reference to Mark Antony's suicide.

57–8 i.e. 'but I'm still young and would prefer you to back me as a poet of love.'

10

1 *Camenae*: Latin equivalent of the Greek Muses.

8 *Niobe*: see ii. 20. 7–8 note.

9 *halcyon*: Alcyone mourned the death of her husband by drowning and in pity the gods turned her into a bird, commonly thought to be the kingfisher.

10 *Itys' mother*: see ii. 20. 6 note.

11 *omens*: lit. 'wings'.

22 *myrrhine*: see iv. 5. 26 note.

26 Lit. 'Let the public air of the nearby road be filled with noise.'

28 *Boy God*: Cupid. Or, reading *grauius* for *grauibus*, 'which of us two the Boy hits harder with his wings'.

11

See Introduction, p. xii.

9 *Colchian girl*: Medea, who by her magic helped Jason to perform the tasks described in 9–11 in order to win the Golden Fleece.

12 *Aeson*: Jason's father.

13 *Penthesilea*: this Amazon queen fought on the Trojan side and was killed by Achilles, who fell in love with her when he lifted her visor.

17–20 Hercules fell in love with the Lydian queen Omphale, who forced him to wear drag and spin for her.   His Pillars are the Rocks of Gibraltar and Ceuta, set up after his last labour to signify that the world was now at peace.

21 *Semiramis*: the Assyrian queen reputed to have founded Babylon.

26 *Bactrians*: see iii. 1. 16 note.

27 *For why* . . . : one would expect 'But why . . . '. One can get nearer to that by taking *nam quid* as *quidnam* 'Why, pray . . . '

28 Either because of his susceptibility to female charms or because his temple in Babylon provided the god with a new concubine every night.

29–32 The reference is to Cleopatra, cf. 39–40. She married Mark Antony in 37 BC.

35 Pompey had triumphed over the supporters of Marius, over Sertorius, and over Mithridates; he fled to Egypt after his defeat by Julius Caesar at Pharsalus in 48 BC and was murdered on landing by one of his own freedmen.

36 Lit. 'No day will remove this stigma from you, Rome', the vocative despite the change of address in the next couplet, cf. 50–1.

37 *Phlegrean plain*: the volcanic area along the north coast of the Bay of Naples. Pompey was seriously ill at Naples in 50 BC.

38 Pompey had married Caesar's daughter Julia in 59 BC.

39 *Canopus*: a town on the western mouth of the Nile renowned for its luxury and immorality.

40 The Ptolemaic dynasty to which Cleopatra belonged claimed blood relationship with Philip of Macedon, Alexander's father.

41 *Anubis*: a jackal-headed Egyptian god.

43   *sistrum*: 'A metal rattle used in the worship of Isis' (*Oxford Latin Dictionary*).

44   *Liburnians*: fast warships armed with beaks for ramming.

45   *Tarpeian rock*: see i. 16. 2 note.

46   *Marius*: Gaius Marius the great Roman general, see iii. 3. 43–4 and 5. 16 notes.

47   Tarquinius Superbus, the last king of Rome, was driven out by Lucius Junius Brutus in 510 BC.

50   Octavian was given the name Augustus in January 27 BC.

53   *I saw*: in Octavian's triumphal procession of 29 BC an effigy of Cleopatra was displayed, lying on a couch with the asp biting her arm.

58   This line is omitted in our best witness and is probably spurious. Goold prints a supplement provided by Sandbach: 'Stands not to be destroyed by human hand'; they omit 'But' in 65.

67   *Scipio's navies*: probably the fleet with which the elder Scipio Africanus invaded Africa in the Second Punic War.

    Camillus: see iii. 9. 32 note.

68   *lately won*: in the war against Mithridates.

59–60 *Syphax*: a Numidian king defeated by the Romans in 203 BC who died in custody at Rome.

    Pyrrhus: king of Epirus invaded Italy but withdrew after a drawn battle in 275 BC.

61   *Curtius*: on horseback leapt fully armed into a chasm that appeared in the Forum, the soothsayers having assured him that his self-sacrifice would preserve the Roman state.

62   *Decius*: a Roman commander who offered himself as a sacrifice to the gods of the underworld to gain victory for his men. He charged the enemy single-handed and was killed.

63   *Cocles*: the Horatius who 'kept the bridge' over the Tiber against the Etruscans.

64   Marcus Valerius Corvus defeated a giant Gaul in single combat in 349 BC with the help of a raven who flapped about in front of the Gaul and gave Valerius his cognomen.

69   Apollo had a temple on the promontory of Leucas, overlooking the Bay of Actium, scene of Octavian's victory over Antony and Cleopatra in 31 BC.

12

1   Nothing is known for certain about the Postumus to whom this poem is addressed or about his wife Galla.

8   *Araxes*: an Armenian river.

11 *Median*: probably referring to Parthians here.

25–36 Topics taken from Ulysses' account of his adventures in Books IX–XII of Homer's *Odyssey*.

25 *Mt. Ismara*: in southern Thrace.

    Calpe: modern Gibraltar.

26 The Cyclops had one eye, which Propertius here refers to as *genae* 'cheeks'.

27 *Circe's deceit*: she turned Ulysses' comrades into swine.

    addictive herbs: explaining the lotus, drug of the lotus-eaters, which caused a blissful idleness and total forgetfulness of home and family.

28 *Scylla and Charybdis*: see ii. 26. 53–4 note.

29–30 Ulysses' men killed and ate the sacred cattle of the Sun-god.

31 It was Circe who lived on the island of Aeaea according to Homer, but Pomponius Mela and Hyginus assert that Calypso lived there and she must be the one meant here.

33 Ulysses descended into the Underworld to consult the soothsayer Tiresias.

34 He had himself bound hand and foot to the mast so that he could hear the Sirens' song without being carried away by it, and he blocked the ears of his crew with wax to prevent their hearing it.

35 In the archery competition that ends the *Odyssey* Ulysses is the only one capable of bending his great bow.

13

5   Herodotus and Pliny the Elder report that in India ants mine gold.

6   *Shell of Eryx*: = 'Venus' shell' because of her famous temple on Mt. Eryx in Sicily. Clearly 'pearl' or 'mother of pearl' is meant, though the phrase is unparalleled.

8   Tyrian murex was reckoned to be the finest.   Cadmus was son of Agenor, king of Tyre.

10 *Penelope*: Latin *Icariotis* 'daughter of Icarus'.

13 *giving*: on the man's part giving money, on the woman's her favours, as line 14 makes clear.

15 ff. refer to the ancient Hindu practice of suttee, the self-immolation of widows on their husband's funeral pyre.

24 *Evadne*: wife of Capaneus, one of the Seven against Thebes, who threw herself on his funeral pyre.

28 The word 'giving' is omitted before 'punnets'.

35 Text uncertain.

38 Actaeon and Tiresias both happened to see Diana bathing and were punished, Actaeon being killed and eaten by his own hounds, and Tiresias blinded.

39 The Arcadians claimed that their country was more ancient than the moon; it was the pastoral land *par excellence* and the home of Pan.

43–6 translate an epigram from the Greek Anthology (ix. 337) by Leonidas of Tarentum (third century BC).

in this glen of mine: Camps. Goold, 'along my path'.

51 *Brennus*: see ii. 31. 13 note.

52 *the unshorn God*: Apollo.

55–6 Polydorus, Priam's youngest son, during the Trojan War was sent to Thrace for safety's sake and put in the care of king Polymestor, who broke his solemn oath and murdered the boy for the gold he brought with him.

57–8 See ii. 16. 29 note. Amphiaraus was swallowed up by a chasm that Jove's thunderbolt opened in front of his chariot.

61 *Cassandra*: lit. 'the Ilian Maenad'. Priam's daughter, she was given the gift of true prophecy by Apollo but fated never to be believed.

63 *plotted . . . doom*: because his elopement with Helen was the root cause of the fall of Troy.

64 *the Horse*: the famous Wooden Horse, filled with armed men, which the Greeks treacherously persuaded the Trojans to admit into their city.

14

1 *palaestra*: the Greek word for 'wrestling school'. Or ' . . . we admire the many rules . . . '

8 *pancratium*: a Greek contest combining boxing and wrestling.

16 *Taygetus*: a mountain range in Laconia, overlooking Sparta.

14 *Thermodon*: a river in Cappadocia, home of the Amazons.

17 *Eurotas*: the river on which Sparta stands.

20 *brother Gods*: at Homer, *Odyssey* xi. 304, Castor and Pollux, the Tyndarids (see i. 17. 18 note) are said to have honour 'equally with Gods'. Castor was the horseman, Pollux the boxer.

32 Camps's translation.

15

3 *purple-hemmed gown*: the *toga praetexta* worn by free-born Roman boys until they assumed the *toga uirilis* usually between 15 and 18.

11 *Dirce*: her story bears witness to what happens to women who believe false accusations. She was the wife of Lycus, ruler of Thebes, and suspected her husband of consorting with his divorced wife Antiope, who had in fact been made pregnant by Jupiter and gave birth to the twins Amphion and Zethus, whom she was forced to hand over to a shepherd to bring up. Meanwhile she became Dirce's slave. Eventually she managed to escape and was recognized at last by the twins now grown up. They punished Dirce and Lycus.

25 *Cithaeron*: see iii. 2. 5–6 note.

27 *Asopus*: a river of Boeotia rising on Cithaeron.

32 *Eurus . . . Notus*: east and south winds.

42 *Aracynthus*: a mountain between Attica and Boeotia. Lit. 'on your crag, Aracynthus'.

45 *us*: or 'me'.

16

1 Lit. 'there has come for me a letter of our mistress.'

2 *Tibur*: see ii. 32. 5 note.

3–4 refer to the river Anio and the famous waterfalls at Tivoli.

12 *Sciron*: waylaid travellers and after robbing them forced them to wash his feet and as they did so kicked them over a cliff into the sea. Theseus disposed of him.

13 The Scythians were nomadic tribesmen living between the Carpathian mountains and the river Don.

17 *jaws*: lit. 'bites'.

29 Lit. 'Or let me be buried as a small fenced heap . . . '

17

2 *fair voyage*: lit. 'favouring sails'.

7–8 Bacchus, driving his lynx-drawn chariot, rescued Ariadne after her desertion by Theseus (see i. 3. 1–2 note) and married her, setting her wedding coronet in the sky as the constellation Corona.

16–18 An alternative punctuation is comma at the end of 16 and full-stop at the end of 18.

19 Bacchus is sometimes depicted with bull's or goat's horns, symbolic of his primitive power. He also 'gives men horns' as inspiring them with strength.

21–8 A list of the best known stories about Bacchus.

21 See ii. 28. 27 note.

22 *Nysean*: Nysa was a mythical place in India where Bacchus was brought up and from where he began his victorious journey westwards.

23 *Lycurgus*: king of Thrace, drove Bacchus out of his country, for which Bacchus sent him mad.

24 *Pentheus*: king of Thebes, resisted Bacchus and was torn to bits by three bands of Maenads led by his mother Agave and her two sisters. The story is told in Euripides' *Bacchae*.

25–6 From the Homeric Hymn to *Dionysus*. The sailors, not recognizing Bacchus' divinity, plotted to sell him as a slave, whereat their ship suddenly sprouted vines and they were turned into dolphins.

27–8 *Dia*: the earlier name for Naxos, the island on which Theseus abandoned Ariadne.

30 *Bassaric*: Bassareus was a cult name of Bacchus, after the fox-skins worn by his Thracian Bacchanals. Maybe his Lydian bonnet was made of fox-skin.

33 For Dirce see iii. 15. 11 note. There was a spring named after her near Thebes.

34 Pan is pluralized here, cf. Venuses, Cupids, and Sileni in Catullus.

35–6 Cybebe, or Cybele, the Great Mother, came from Mt. Ida in Phrygia, and her worship, like that of Bacchus, was orgiastic.

39 *buskin*: see ii. 34. 41 note.

40 Lit. 'with spirit such as thunders from Pindaric mouth'. He promises to write dithyrambs.

18

1–4 See i. 11. 1–4 notes.

3 *Misenus*: Hector's trumpeter during the Trojan War. He emigrated with Aeneas but was drowned off the coast of Campania and buried at Misenum, which was named after him.

5 *the Theban God*: Bacchus.

9 *he*: Marcus Claudius Marcellus, son of Augustus' sister Octavia; born in 42 BC he died at Baiae in the second half of 23 BC when he was aedile. Virgil too mourns his death in *Aeneid* VI.

12 Lit. 'or his embracing Caesar's hearth'. He married Augustus' daughter Julia in 25 BC.

13–14 refer to the magnificent shows put on during his aedileship. Octavia must have helped him financially or during his illness managed things on his behalf.

19 *Attalic tapestries*: see ii. 13. 22 note.

23 *the Dog*: Cerberus, cf. iii. 5. 44.

24 *the grim Greybeard*: Charon, see 31 below.

27 'Nireus who came as handsomest man to Troy | Of the other Greeks after Peleus' noble son (=Achilles), | But he was feeble and few folk followed him' (*Iliad* ii. 673–5).

28 *Pactolus*: see i. 6. 32 note.

29–30 if in place here seem to be saying: 'Grief such as we feel for the death of Marcellus afflicted the Greeks at Troy when for no apparent reason they were ravaged by plague, and it turned out that the plague was a punishment for Agamemnon's rape of Chryseis, the daughter of Apollo's priest.' Agamemnon's first love would then be Argynnus, for whom see iii. 7. 21–4 note.

31 *Sailor*: Charon.

32 *here*: Marcellus' body was carried from Baiae to Rome for a state funeral.

33 *Claudius*: Marcus Claudius Marcellus, ancestor of the present Marcellus, conquered Syracuse in the Second Punic War (211 BC).

34 A comet appeared in the summer of 44 BC during the funeral games celebrated for Julius Caesar and was thought to be his soul going up to heaven.

19

1   *our*: or 'my', see iii. 16. 1 note.

7   *Syrtes*: see ii. 9. 33 note.

8   *Malea*: easternmost of the three southern promontories of the Peloponnese.

11 *that victim*: Pasiphae, wife of king Minos of Crete, who fell in love with a bull; he spurned her advances until Daedalus fixed her up inside a wooden cow.

13 *Salmonis*: Tyro, daughter of Salmoneus; see i. 13. 21–2 note.

15–16 Myrrha fell in love with her father Cinyras, tricked him into intercourse, and was turned into a myrrh tree while giving birth to Adonis.

17–18 Or 'Why need I tell of Medea's passion, when it appeased the mother's anger by the slaying of her children?' (Goold). To punish Jason when he married Creusa (see ii. 16. 30 note) Medea killed her two boys.

19 *Clytemnestra*: Agamemnon's wife, who committed adultery with Aegisthus and murdered Agamemnon, grandson of Pelops, on his return from the Trojan War.

21 *Scylla*: daughter of Nisus, king of Megara, fell in love with Minos while he was besieging the city, and betrayed it to him by cutting off her father's purple lock of hair on which its safety depended. Minos punished her treachery by dragging her behind his ship until she drowned (or according to another account was changed into a bird).

27 Or punctuate 'But not without good cause!' In either case the poem ends with a man who was not a slave to lust and who saw to it that Nisus was avenged.

20

4   The Roman province of Africa extended from Cyrenaica to eastern Algeria.

7   *Pallas*: Minerva (cf. i. 2. 30), the Roman equivalent of Pallas Athena, was patron goddess of women's work and also goddess of wisdom, learning, and the arts.

8   *forebear*: lit. 'grandfather'. Apuleius, *Apologia* 10, states that Cynthia's real name was Hostia, and those who believe that Cynthia is addressed in this poem claim that her distinguished grandfather was the epic

poet Hostius (second century BC); a sub-group emend Hostia to Roscia
and make her grandfather the famous actor Quintus Roscius Gallus,
called 'learned' by Horace in *Epistles* ii. 1. 82. But is this poem
addressed to Cynthia? Its position in the book and lines 13–16 suggest
that it is not.

10   *to my bed*: Latin *in meos toros*; the plural is not metrically necessary
and contrasts with 14 *in primo toro*. There may be a double meaning
as the plural can be used to mean 'muscles'.

18   *the starry Goddess*: Ariadne, see iii. 17. 7–8 note.

21   *union*: Goold; lit. 'couch'.

22   If there is no contract there has been no oath and therefore no god
invoked to punish the breaking of it.

sleepless nights: when the lover is deserted.

24   *first omens*: auspices duly taken before the reading and signing of the
contract, as though this were a real marriage.

21

20   *Lechaeum*: the port of Corinth on the Corinthian Gulf.

22   He would walk across from Lechaeum to Corinth's eastern port of
Cenchreae.

24   *Theseus' Way*: the Long Walls connecting Piraeus with Athens.

25–6 Plato established his school in a gymnasium with a running-track near
Athens called the Academy after the hero Academus. Epicurus had
bought a house in Athens with a large garden, which became the
headquarters of his school.

27   *Demosthenes*: the fourth-century BC Attic orator who opposed Philip
of Macedon.

28   *Menander*: the late fourth-century BC writer of New Comedy.

29   *painted panels*: pictures were painted on boards, not canvas.

33   Lit. 'Or if I die ‹I shall die› by Fate, not broken by shameful love . . .'

22

1   *Cyzicus*: an important commercial centre on an island off the south
coast of the Propontis (Sea of Marmora), the modern peninsula of
Artaki.

2 *Tullus*: the dedicatee of Book I, see i. 1. 9 note, i. 6 and 22.

3 Dindymon was a mountain on the island of Cyzicus sacred to Cybele, for whom see iii. 17. 35 note.

4 Propertius here follows the tradition that places the rape of Proserpine by Dis (= Pluto, god of the Underworld) in Cyzicus, not on the plain of Enna in Sicily.

5 *Athamantid Helle*: see ii. 26. 5 note.

7 *Atlas*: the Titan in the Atlas Mountains fabled to support the sky on his shoulders.

8 For Medusa and Perseus see ii. 25, 13 note.

9–10 *Geryon*: a giant in the far west whom Hercules killed and whose cattle he captured.

Antaeus: a Libyan giant, killed by Hercules in a wrestling match.

Hesperides: Nymphs who guarded the legendary golden apples that Hercules had to bring back from the far west.

11–14 refer to the voyage of the Argonauts to Colchis in Argo, the first ocean-going ship, to fetch the Golden Fleece. See further ii. 26. 39–40 note.

15 *Ortygia*: either Delos (see ii. 31. 10) or more probably Ephesus, of which it was an old name.

Cayster: a river flowing into the sea near Ephesus, famous for its swans.

16 refers to the Nile and its delta.

22 Camps's version.

23 *Anio*: see iii. 16. 3–4 note.

Clitumnus: see ii. 19. 25 note.

24 *Aqua Marcia*: see iii. 2. 14 note.

25 These two lakes, Lago Albano and Lago di Nemi, are in the Alban hills.

26 The Nymph Juturna's pool in the Roman Forum where the Heavenly Twins Castor and Pollux are supposed to have watered their horses after the battle of Lake Regillus, in which they helped the Romans beat the Latins in 496 BC.

27 *cerastes*: the North African horned viper.

29 *Andromeda*: see i. 3. 3–4 note.

30 *Ausonian*: see i. 20. 12 note.　　The reference is to Atreus who killed his brother Thyestes' children and served them up to him at a banquet. The sun recoiled in horror and left the world in darkness. Thyestes had committed adultery with Atreus' wife.

31–2 Meleager's life depended on the non-burning of a log in the possession of his mother Althaea, but when he killed her brothers she threw it on the fire and he died.

33 *Pentheus*: see iii. 17. 24 note. He tried to hide in a tree while spying on the female Bacchanals at their worship.

34–5 In one version of the story of the sacrifice of Iphigenia (see iii. 7. 24 note) the goddess Diana miraculously substituted a deer for her and set her up as her priestess at a temple in the Tauric Chersonese (= the Crimea).

35–6 A reference to Io, for whom see i. 3. 20 note; here it is Juno who turns her into a cow.

37–8 There is clearly a lacuna before this couplet.

Sinis: a brigand who lay in wait for travellers on the way to Corinth. He would bend down two pine-trees and attach his victim to them so that when the trees sprang back he was torn apart. Line 38 would fit this story but in 37 he seems also to be accused of crucifying people on trees and of hurling them down from rocks in the manner of Sciron (see iii. 16. 12 note).

40 *the honour*: public office.

23

8 Camps's version.

14 *me*: or 'us'.

17 Or 'And whatever non-foolish things a talkative girl who's willing . . .'

18 *for secret love*: Camps. Lit. ' for charming tricks'.

24 *Esquiline*: one of Rome's Seven Hills, on the eastern side of the city. The poet is well enough known for this general address to find him.

24

5 'Often' (*saepe*) omitted.

6 Or possibly 'That love might think . . . '

9–12 A crux, of which no solution so far offered is entirely satisfactory. Goold prints a text which he translates thus: 'The infatuation that neither family friends could rid me of or witches of Thessaly wash away in ocean, this I have effected myself, not brought thereto by the knife or cautery, but (I will tell the truth) after being shipwrecked in a very Aegean sea of passion.' Camps favours the following version: 'My sickness (i.e. the compulsion to praise Cynthia in terms which flouted reality) was one which my family's friends could not rid me of, nor Thessaly's witches purge away with all the waters of the sea —about you I could not be got to confess the truth by cutting or burning or even shipwreck in the (stormy) Aegean.'

9 Cf. i. 1. 25.

10 *witchcraft*: lit. 'Thessalian witch'. Cf. i. 1. 19–24.

11 Cf. i. 1. 27.

12 Cf. i. 1. 29.

13 *cruel bronze*: cf. Phalaris' bronze bull (ii. 25. 12 note).

16 *Syrtes*: see ii. 9. 33 note.

18 'And now' omitted.

25

This final elegy can be regarded as the second half of 24.

6 Lit. 'You always weep from ambush'.

9 Cf. i. 16. 13.

17 Or 'These are the deadly curses my page has sung for you.'

18 *aftermath*: lit. 'outcome'.

BOOK IV

1

1 Lit. 'All this that you see, stranger, where greatest Rome is . . . ' The poet as guide addresses an anonymous visitor, who turns out to be the astrologer Horus.

2 *Aeneas*: see iii. 4. 19–20 note.

3 See ii. 31. 1–2 note.

4 *Evander*: an exiled king of Arcadia who with his family and followers established himself on the future site of Rome, called by him Pallanteum after his ancestor Pallas and later known as the Palatine.

7 *Tarpeian Father*: Jupiter, because the Capitoline on which he later had

his famous temple was also known as the Tarpeian Mount (see iv. 4. 93).

8   *alien*: because the Tiber was an Etruscan river. The text may be faulty, though.

9   *Remus*: see ii. 1. 23 note. The reference is to the temple of Quirinus, Romulus' divine name, on the Quirinal Hill.

11 *Curia*: the Roman senate-house.   Senators wore the purple-bordered *toga praetexta*.

13 *Quirites*: the old name for Roman citizens, later coming to mean Roman civilians as opposed to soldiers.

14 *one hundred*: under Augustus the number was six hundred.

15–16 Awnings were spread over the open-air theatre to provide shade, and saffron water was sprayed around.

19 *Pales' . . . feast*: the Parilia, a shepherds' festival (Pales was goddess of flocks) celebrated on 21 April, the date of Rome's foundation.

20 On 15 October a horse was sacrificed to Mars; its tail was cut off and the blood preserved for later use in a ceremony of purification.

21 *Vesta*: her festival was on 9 June. See ii. 29. 27 and iii. 4. 11 notes.

26 At the Lupercalia on 15 February the Luperci or priests of Faunus (the Roman Pan) ran naked round the Palatine striking with thongs of goat-skin any woman they met, to make her fertile.

27 Lit. 'gleamed in threatening arms'.

29 *Lycmon*: the Etruscan general who helped Romulus fight Titus Tatius and his Sabines.

    Praetorium: the commander's tent in a Roman camp.

30 Or 'and Tatius' wealth lay largely in his flocks' (Goold).

31 The three original Roman tribes, supposedly named after Tatius, Romulus, and Lucumo.

    Solonian: Lucomo reportedly came from Solonium in Etruria.

32 i.e. 'This was the world in which Romulus won his Triumphs.' The *triumphator*'s chariot was drawn by white horses.

33–6 A list of Latin towns near Rome.

33 Text uncertain.

35 Alba Longa (see iii. 3. 4 note) was named after the large white sow that Aeneas found after landing in Latium, a sign that this was the land promised him.

37–8 'This must refer figuratively to the Roman people . . . Rome has risen "from nothing" to her present greatness . . . But in their literal sense the words apply unmistakably to Romulus, first suckled by a she-wolf and then brought up as the supposed child of a landless shepherd' (Camps).

39–44 refer to Aeneas' rescue of his household gods and his father Anchises after the fall of Troy (Ilium), and to his voyage to Italy.

39 *Penates*: see i. 22. 1 note.

40 *Dardan*: Trojan, from Dardanus Troy's founder.

41–2 When the Greek heroes emerged from the Wooden Horse in the centre of Troy, the ship in which Aeneas and his followers were to escape had not been noticed, nor had it been after the sack of Troy.

45 *Decius*: see iii. 11. 62 note.

Brutus: one of Rome's first pair of consuls after the ejection of Tarquinius Superbus: see iii. 11. 47. The consular axes were carried by the lictors in their *fasces*, see iii. 4. 5 note.

46–7 Venus brought Aeneas to Italy, and the Julian *gens* to which Caesar belonged claimed descent from Aeneas' son Iulus.

49–50 The Sibyl of Cumae (near Lake Avernus) prophesied to Aeneas the expiatory death of Remus, killed by his brother Romulus for desecrating the walls of Rome by jumping over them in mockery while they were building. Remus is called Aventine because he took his station on that hill to observe omens for the founding of Rome.

51 *Pergamene seer*: Cassandra (see iii. 13. 61 note). There is a reference here and in what follows to the *Alexandra* of Lycophron (third-century BC Greek poet) in which Cassandra's prophecies are reported to king Priam by her jailer.

53 *Danaans*: like Argives a Homeric name for the Greeks.

61 *Ennius*: see iii. 3. 6 note.

62 *ivy*: see ii. 5. 26 note.

64 In claiming to be the Roman Callimachus Propertius goes further than he does at iii. 1 where he names Callimachus and Philetas as his models. He can make the specific claim here because of his intention, expressed in 69–70, to write the Roman equivalent of Callimachus' *Aitia* (see ii. 1. 40 and ii. 34. 32 notes). See Introduction, p. xv.

87–8 Placed after 68 by the Dutch scholar Marcilius in 1604; he is followed by Camps. The couplet is clearly out of place in the MS tradition, but there is no agreement about the best position for it.

76 Lit. 'not knowing how to move the signs on the brazen sphere', i.e. his planetarium.

77–8 *Horos*: Propertius uses the grander Greek form instead of the Latin

Horus. In origin it is the name of an Egyptian god, son of the goddess Isis.

Archytas: of Tarentum, a famous Pythagorean mathematician (fourth-century BC).

Babylonian Orops: or Horops, not otherwise known, but suggesting 'horoscope' and presumably an imaginary astrologer, cf. ii. 27. 3 note. His descent from Archytas suggests a spoof genealogy for Horos.

Conon: of Samos, a third-century BC astronomer and mathematician who discovered the constellation *Coma Berenices* (cf. Catullus 66).

81–2 *Jove . . . by gold*: text uncertain.

Signs: of the Zodiac on the Ecliptic that the sun appears to go round each year.

87–8 Transferred to follow 68.

89–102 Arria, Lupercus, Gallus, and Cinara are genuine names of (to us) otherwise unknown people.

91   *Penates*: cf. 39.

99   *Lucina*: goddess of childbirth, usually identified with Juno.

102   *almanacs*: lit. 'books'.

103   The famous temple and oracle of Jupiter Ammon stood in the oasis of Siwa in the Sahara.

103–6 refer to divination by inspection of entrails (extispicy), by observation of the flight of birds (augury), and by visions seen in a bowl of water (hydromancy).

107–8 *the true bypass*: the Ecliptic (cf. 82).

Five Zones: in the geocentric cosmology of antiquity these belts in the spherical heaven correspond to the earth's torrid zone and its two frigid and temperate zones.

109   *Calchas*: the Greek seer who revealed that Agamemnon must sacrifice his daughter to secure a fair wind for the Greek fleet from Aulis to Troy.

110   *God-fearing rocks*: the fleet was becalmed because Agamemnon had killed a stag sacred to Diana.

112   Or, reading *Atrides*, 'and Atreus' son spread bloodstained sails.' Atreus' sons were Agamemnon and Menelaus.

114–16 Nauplius, king of Euboea, wrecked the Greek fleet on its return from Troy in revenge for the treacherous murder of his son Palamedes by Ulysses.

117–18 *Ajax*: Latin *Oïliades*, 'son of Oïleus', to distinguish him from the better known Ajax, son of Telamon. At the sack of Troy he raped Cassandra in the temple of Pallas Athena. The goddess drowned him on his way home.

121 *Penates*: cf. 39.

123–4 *Mevania*: modern Bevagna on the Clitumno in the plain below Assisi.

Umbrian lake: now drained.

126 *climbing rampart*: the adjective goes with Assisi in the Latin but has been transferred to avoid ambiguity.

128 *Lares*: see ii. 30. 22 note.

130 *rod*: the Roman surveyor's ten-foot measuring pole. The confiscation will have been after the Perusine War of 41–40 BC; see i. 22. 3 note.

131 *locket*: the *bulla*, containing an amulet, worn round the neck of free-born Roman children.

132 *freedom's toga*: the *toga virilis*, see iii. 15. 3 note.

134 *verbal thunder*: legal and political oratory.

140 *and your grasp*: added to represent the double meaning in 'palms'.

142 The Latin metaphor from fishing is obscure.

150 i.e. 'the only thing you need fear is the sign of the Crab.' The point is lost on us.

2

4 Volsinii (Bolsena) in Etruria (Tuscany) was sacked by the Romans in 264 BC and Vertumnus' temple in Rome was probably built then. Or he may be referring to the occasion mentioned in lines 51–4.

7–8 The Velabrum through which the Vicus Tuscus ran (50) had originally been a shallow lake formed by the Tiber (see iv. 9. 5–6).

9 *this much*: i.e. 'this much ground'.

his nurslings: the Romans.

10 The etymology cannot be reproduced in English: *vert* (stem of *vertere* 'turn') + *amnis* 'river'.

11 *turning year*: similarly *vert* + *annus* 'year'.

13–14 This couplet seems to hint at yet another possible etymology, *var* + *tum*.

15 *Here*: i.e. 'offered at my shrine'.

19–20 This final etymology is explained in 47–8 (*vert + in omne* 'into everything') and illustrated in the intervening lines.

23 *Coan*: see i. 2. 2 note.

31 *Iacchus*: cult title of Bacchus.

32 i.e. Apollo's role as *citharoedus* or lyre-player.

34 *the God*: Faunus/Pan.

51–2 A reference to the help given the Romans by Lycmon and his followers, named Lycomedians, against the Sabines; see iv. 1. 29 note.

55 *Sower of the Gods*: must be Jupiter, though it would fit one etymology of Saturn.

57 *six lines*: not including the present couplet. The last three couplets are in the form of an inscription.

60 *grateful*: not only 'thankful' but 'pleasant' too.

61 *Mamurrius*: a legendary metal-worker in the time of Numa (715–673 BC).

62 The Oscans were an ancient Italic people of Campania.

64 Or 'One is my statue, not one the honour it receives' (Goold).

3

1 'The Greek names are romantic pseudonyms for a young Roman and his bride' (Goold). Richardson is against this: 'Both names must be fictitious, but it is unlikely they are pseudonyms, for there could be no reason here for disguise.'

7 *Bactra*: capital of the Parthian province of that name, cf. 63 below.

8 *Seric*: Chinese.

15 The Roman bride was sprinkled with lustral water before leaving her parents' home.

17 *vows*: written prayers posted up in public, promising thank-offerings on the safe return of the person in question, cf. 71 below.

18 *cloak*: Latin *lacerna*, a military cloak fastened at the shoulder.

19 *palisades*: every legionary soldier carried a wooden stake to form a palisade on the top of the rampart round a Roman camp.

21 The wretched Ocnus had a spendthrift wife who wasted all his earnings. As if this was not punishment enough he was also condemned in Hades to plait eternally a rope of straw which a donkey ate as he made it. He appeared in a famous picture of the underworld by Polygnotus (fifth century BC) at Delphi.

sidelong: 'he is *obliquus* because he sits sideways at his work and never sees what the ass is doing' (Butler and Barber).

35 *Araxes*: see iii. 12. 8 note.

37 Her map was on wood, not canvas.

42 *pretends*: lit. 'swears falsely'.

43 *Hippolyta*: the Amazon queen who married Theseus.

47 *the Father*: Jupiter, the sky-god.

48 Text uncertain.

49 *there*: Latin *aperto*, 'open'. Others, 'openly recognized'.

52 *aqueous*: rock-crystal was believed to be formed of congealed water.

53–4 Or with Goold: 'at most, performing a familiar rite on occasional Kalends, a solitary girl unlocks the shrine of the Household Gods.' It was the custom to make offerings to these gods on the first day of every month.

55 *Craugis*: a Greek name—'Yappy'.

57 *verbena*: this Latin word refers to leafy shoots from various shrubs used for religious purposes, not to our verbena.

58 *savin*: Latin *herba Sabina*, a species of juniper.

60 Apparently when a lamp was burning low one revived it with a drop of wine.

62 *servers*: Latin *popae*; they killed the victims at sacrifices and were given a share of the meat. They were proverbially fat.

66 The Parthians were famous for this, cf. ii. 10. 13 note.

68 *plain spear-shaft*: a spear without a point, awarded for bravery.

71 *Porta Capena*: the Roman gate on the Appian Way by which one would return from the East.

4

1 See i. 16. 2 note.

5 *Silvanus*: god of the woods.

7 *Tatius*: Titus Tatius, the Sabine commander, is making war against Romulus.   It is not clear how Tarpeia can draw water (15) if the spring is fenced off. Camps therefore emends: 'Over against this Tatius fences with a maple palisade . . . '

9 *Curetan*: Sabine, Cures being the Sabine capital.

13 *Curia*: the Roman Senate-house.

15 *the Goddess*: Vesta, see iii. 4. 11 note.

20 Or with the MS reading *arma*: 'raising blazoned arms above ‹his horse's› yellow mane.'

23–5 These were her excuses for going out to get a glimpse of Tatius.

27 *first smoke*: could be early morning or evening. But the camp-fires of 31 would surely be lit in the evening, and Tarpeia sits and meditates until the coming of daylight in 63.

31 *praetorium*: see iv. 1. 29 note.

36 Or 'Vesta before whom my wickedness should be ashamed'.

37 In Virgil, *Georgics* iii. 86, it is one of the points of a good stallion that his mane falls to the right.

38 'The horse that takes Tatius back to his camp will bear her heart with him, henceforth on the Sabine side' (Camps).

39–40 The Scylla of iii. 19. 21 and of ii. 26. 53 are here identified.

41–2 See i. 3. 1–2 note.

43 *Ausonian*: see i. 20. 12 note.

45 *Pallas' fire*: because Pallas Athena's (Minerva's) image, the Palladium, rescued from Troy, was kept in Vesta's temple.

51–2 She has Medea in mind, whose knowledge of magic helped Jason.

53–4 refer to Romulus who as king of Rome wore the *toga picta* which was later worn by triumphing generals.

55 *Thus*: 'i.e. by your becoming king of Rome' (Camps).   The text of this line is uncertain.

57–8 Tatius attacked the Romans to punish them for carrying off the Sabine women.

60 The robe (*palla*) is here worn by the bride and symbolizes her marriage.

61 *Hymenaeus*: the god of marriage.

63 The night (sunset to sunrise) was divided into four equal watches.

64 *falling*: possibly a pun, for Tarpeia has fallen, cf. [Tibullus] iii. 16. 2.

69 *protectress of Troy's ashes*: because she protected Aeneas when he brought the sacred fire from Troy on his long journey to Italy.   The MSS all give *Vesta* for *Venus*, but it seems incredible that Vesta should be the subject of 70, whereas a copyist might easily have altered Venus to Vesta because he misunderstood 69.

71 *Strymon*: a river marking the boundary between Macedonia and Thrace. The reference is to a Thracian Bacchante.

72 *Thermodon*: a river of Pontus usually associated with Amazons rather than Bacchantes.

73 Cf. iv. 1. 19 note.

82 Or 'a bargain—herself to accompany the bargainers'.

90 refers to her being covered by the shields of 91 and to their piling up.

94 i.e. she did not deserve to have the hill named after her. But there is also the hint that her punishment was unjust, her fault being love's.

5

1 *thorns*: a play on the bawd's name Acanthis (63) = 'thorny'.

3–4 According to ancient belief the spirit is in the ashes (including the bones) of the dead person, cf. ii. 13. 31–2 and 57–8.

Cerberus: see iii. 5. 44 note.

5 *Hippolytus*: son of Theseus and the Amazon Hippolyta, proverbial for his chastity; cf. ii. 1. 51 note.

8 *Antinous*: chief of the suitors of Penelope in Homer's *Odyssey*.

11 *Colline*: Vestals who broke their vow of chastity were buried alive near Rome's Colline gate. Herbs grown there would be magically potent.

18 *Hippomanes*: 'horse-madness', a secretion from mares on heat, believed to be an aphrodisiac.

19–20 Text uncertain.

21 *Eoan*: eastern. The Dorozantes' golden shore is otherwise unknown but no doubt suggestive of wealth and high fashion.

22 *shells*: of the murex that produced the best purple dye.

23 *Eurypylus*: commander of the Coan contingent of the Greek fleet in the Trojan War (*Iliad* ii. 677).

Coan silk: lit. 'Coan Minerva' (i. 2. 2 note).

24 refers to antique cloth of gold, cf. ii. 32. 12.

25 *palmaceous Thebes*: Egyptian as opposed to Boeotian Thebes. The adjective is suitably grandiose.

26 *myrrhine*: of *murra*, a mineral found in Parthia, which was probably fluorspar or perhaps a variety of agate.

34 The worship of Isis demanded periods of abstinence, ten nights according to ii. 33. 2.

35 *Iole . . . Amycle*: Greek maidservants.   April was Venus' month when lovers' mistresses would expect presents.

37 *sits*: suppliants adopted a special sitting posture.

at your desk: lit. 'when your chair has been brought in'.

41 Medea, having followed Jason from Colchis, spoke violently against him when at Corinth he proposed to desert her and marry Creusa, cf. ii. 24. 45–6.

43 'Menander's *Thais* is not extant, but a line of it . . . was famous enough to be quoted by St Paul (1 Cor. 15: 33)' (Goold).

Geta: the clever slave of Comedy.

51–2 Slaves on sale from abroad had their feet coated with chalk as a distinguishing mark. In the slave-market they would have to mark time at the double to show their physical fitness.

55–6 Acanthis scornfully quotes i. 2. 1–2.

58 *unsophisticated*: or 'penniless', reading *sine aere* for *sine arte*.

64 *my*: or 'her' referring to Acanthis.   Textual trouble.

69 *drugget*: Latin *tegetes*, 'rush matting.'

71 Or, reading MSS *exsequiae*, 'For funeral pomp there will have been . . .'

6

See Introduction, p. xv.

1 The poet-priest's sacrifice is the present poem, cf. iii. 1.1.

mouths must favour: by keeping quiet and thus avoiding words of ill omen.

3 *wreath*: Latin *serta*, an emendation of Scaliger's for *cera*, 'wax', of all the MSS, which would refer to the poet's wax writing-tablets and maybe also to a wax taper.

Philetas: see ii. 34. 31 note.

4 *Cyrenean*: Callimachean, see ii. 34. 32 note.

water: symbolic of stylistic purity. Callimachus and his followers were called 'water-drinkers' as opposed to Epic 'wine-drinkers'.

8 *Phrygian*: lit. 'Mygdonian', a poetic equivalent.   Plato (*Republic* iii. 398E) regards the Dorian and Phrygian musical modes as the only manly ones, inspiring courage, endurance, and self-restraint.   The MSS give 'from Mygdonian jars.'

10   *pure laurel*: for sprinkling lustral water.

11   See ii. 31. 1–2 note.

12   *Calliope*: see i. 2. 28 note.

13   *Caesar*: Augustus.

15   Here begins his description of the naval victory of Actium in 31 BC when Augustus (then Octavian) defeated Antony and Cleopatra for mastery of the Roman world.

 Athamanian: Athamania was a district in Epirus. The reference here is to the Ambracian Gulf.

17   i.e. it keeps alive the memory of the victory won by the adopted son of Julius Caesar, who claimed descent from Aeneas' son Iulus, see ii. 1. 42 note.

21   *javelins*: Latin *pila*, the long Roman throwing-spear.

22   *Quirinus*: the divine title of Romulus, who is called 'Teucrian (= Trojan)' here because of his descent from Iulus via his mother Ilia.

25   *Nereus*: a sea-god, father of the Nereids.

27   *Delos*: the island where Apollo was born. Callimachus (*Hymn* 4) describes how Delos was a floating island until after the birth.

33–4 A reference to *Iliad* I and the plague sent on the Greeks because Agamemnon refused to return the captive girl Briseis to her father, the priest of Apollo.

35–6 Apollo killed Python, the monstrous snake that frightened the Muses, when he took up residence in Delphi.

37   *Alba Longa*: see iii. 3. 4 note.

38   *Hectorian*: for 'Trojan' because Hector was the greatest Trojan warrior.

43–4 Ennius in his *Annales* had told how Romulus and Remus, on Palatine and Aventine respectively, watched for flights of birds in order to learn which of them the gods willed to found Rome.

47   *a hundred wings*: i.e. a hundred oars to each ship.

59   *Idalian star*: either the planet Venus or the comet that appeared at Julius Caesar's funeral.

63   *she*: continued refusal to honour Cleopatra by mentioning her name.

66   *Jugurtha*: see iii. 5. 16 note.

67   *his monument*: the temple of Palatine Apollo, see line 11.

73   *Falernian*: see ii. 33. 39 note.

77   The Sygambri, a German tribe north of Cologne, after invading Gaul and defeating Marcus Lollius had withdrawn and given hostages in

16 BC. Also in that year was inaugurated a four-yearly festival in honour of Augustus' principate, and it is likely that this aetiological poem was composed for that occasion.

78 *Meroe*: a town in Ethiopia; Cepheus, father of Andromeda, was a legendary Ethiopian king. In 22 BC the Roman Prefect of Egypt defeated an Ethiopian invasion.

79–80 In 20 BC the Parthians returned the standards they had captured from Crassus in 53 BC (see ii. 10. 14 note).

79 *surrender*: closer, 'admission of defeat'.

80–4 In inverted commas as an imaginary effusion of the poet of line 79.

80 *Returning*: lit. 'Though he returns'.

Remus: see ii. 1. 23 note.

81 *Eoan*: eastern. The Parthians were famous as archers.

82 *his own boys*: Augustus' grandsons Gaius and Lucius Caesar, sons of Agrippa and Julia, were adopted by him in 17 BC.

7

4 Lit. 'by the noise of the road's edge (*or* end)'.

5 Or, with Goold, 'when after my love's interment sleep hovered over me.' It seems unclear from the Latin whether he was asleep or awake; line 14 gives the answer.

8 Or, with Goold, 'her dress was charred at the side.'

10 *Lethe*: the river of forgetfulness in the underworld.

15 *Subura*: ancient Rome's Soho.

25 *rattled*: to scare away witches and evil spirits from the corpse as it lay on the bier before the funeral.

26 A broken tile supported her head.

29–30 Lit. 'If it bored you to proceed beyond the gates you could have ordered my bier to go there more slowly.'

30 Burials were forbidden within the city boundary.

33 *cheap*: lit. 'that cost nothing'.

34 *hallow*: by pouring wine on them.

35 *Lygdamus*: the slave of iii. 6. 1.

36 Or 'that poisoned yellow wine'.

37 *Nomas*: perhaps a Numidian slave.

39–48 The anonymous mistress here described is presumably the Chloris of line 72 and Cynthia's successor.

39 Lit. 'She who was lately on show for cheap nights as a public woman'.

44 *clog*: a heavy block of wood to which slaves had one foot shackled as a punishment.

43 *Petale*: a Greek servant, 'Petal'.

45 *Lalage*: another servant, whose Greek name means 'Prattler'.

by the hair: lit. 'by the twisted hair.'

52 *Triple Dog*: Cerberus, see iii. 5. 44 note.

53 *vipers*: taking *uipera* as collective singular.

57 The text is uncertain here, though its general meaning is clear enough.

Clytemnestra: see iii. 19. 19 note.

the Cretan Queen: Pasiphae, see iii. 19. 11 note.

60 Elysium was the Greek and Roman equivalent of the Christian Heaven.

61 *Cybebe*: see iii. 17. 35 note.

62 Cf. Milton, *L'Allegro* 136, 'Lap me in soft *Lydian* Aires.'

turbaned: or 'bonneted', cf. iii. 17. 30.

63 *Andromeda*: see i. 3. 3–4 note.

Hypermnestra: the one of Danaus' fifty daughters who refused to murder her husband on their wedding night; see ii. 31. 4 note.

69 'we strive to heal': or, reading *sancimus* with Goold, 'we confirm'.

73 *Parthenia*: = 'Virginal'.

75 *Latris*: = 'Maidservant'.

81–2 *Anio*: see iii. 16. 3–4 note; after the falls the river flowed through orchard land. The air at Tibur, where there was a famous temple of Hercules (cf. ii. 32. 5 note), was believed to preserve the whiteness of ivory.

87–8 Homer and Virgil (*Odyssey* xix 562 ff. and *Aeneid* vi 894 ff.) say that true dreams come through gates of horn and false through gates of ivory.

86 *Father Anio*: lit. 'Anienus'. 'The spirit of the Anio would be called *Anienus*, as the spirit of the Tiber was called *Tiberinus*' (Camps).

90 *Cerberus*: see above, 52 note.

91 *Lethe*: see above, 10 note.

92 *Charon*: lit. 'the sailor'.

8

1   *aquatic*: the Esquiline, where Propertius lived (iii. 23. 24), had many
    fountains and was crossed by three aqueducts.

2   *New Fields*: Maecenas had converted a former cemetery there into a
    park; see Horace, *Satires* i. 8. 14–16.

19–20 This couplet, obviously misplaced in the MSS, fits fairly well here.

3   *Lanuvium*: see ii. 32. 6. note.

16 *Juno*: the temple of Juno Sospita at Lanuvium.

17 The Appian Way ran from Rome to Capua.

22 i.e. not slowing down to avoid danger or discomfort.

24 Molossian dogs, a famous breed in antiquity, were named after a
    people in Epirus, on whose coins a dog's head appears.

25–6 *stodge*: Latin *sagina*, used of gladiator's food. The implication is that
    this young rake, having run through all his money and lost his
    pubescent charm, will be forced to turn gladiator to make a living.

29 There was an ancient temple of Diana on the Aventine.

31 *Teia*: she must have come from Teos on the coast of Ionia, the
    birthplace of the poet Anacreon.

    Tarpeia's Grove: see iv. 4. 1. The Latin has the plural 'Groves', but
    this may well be the so-called 'poetic' plural, found in this poem at
    e.g. 12 'basket' and 23 'chaise'.

37 *Lygdamus*: see iii. 6. 1 and iv. 7. 35.

38 Wine from Methymna in Lesbos was clearly rather special.

39 The piper (male) was from Egypt, the dancing-girl from Spain, Baetis
    (a conjecture for *Phyllis* of the MSS) being the modern Guadalquivir.

40 Or, reading *et* for *haec*, 'And there were roses in their artless grace
    for strewing.'

42 The pipe would be made of boxwood.

44 Lit. 'And the table fell back flat on its own feet.'

45 *dice*: lit. 'knucklebones' (*tali*). 'Four *tali* were used, marked on four
    sides only with I, III, IV, VI. The lowest throw was I, I, I, I (known as
    canis . . .); the highest I, III, IV, VI (known as *Venus*)' (Butler and
    Barber).

58 *fire*: lit. 'water'.

69 *begging my protection*: lit. 'appealing to my Genius (= Guardian
    Spirit)'.

75 *Pompey's Porch*: lit. 'Pompey's shade', see ii. 32. 11 note. Ovid (*Ars Amatoria* i. 67) recommends it as a good place to pick up a girl.

76 Gladiatorial shows were sometimes given in the Forum.

77 At the Theatre the sexes were segregated, the women sitting in the upper rows.

78 *sweat*: if this reading is correct we must imagine the litter-bearers sweating in the hot sunshine while Propertius chats up its female occupant.

85 *clothes*: to be honest this is not a fair translation of Latin *lacernas*, which (*a*) has to be taken as a poetic plural and (*b*) is in fact a cloak with a hood and would not be worn indoors. The alternative is *lucernas*, 'And ordered all the oil-lamps to be changed again', but what is the point? In either case 'again' has to be pleonastic, as in ii. 18. 12 'returned again'.

88 Another controversial line.

   I answered: 'i.e. he functioned normally again, in regard to sex' (Camps).

   arms: metaphorical as at i. 3. 16 and iii. 20. 20.

9

See Introduction, p. XVI.

1 *Amphitryoniades*: Hercules, sired by Jupiter on Alcmena in the likeness of her husband Amphitryon. This resounding patronymic first appears in Latin at Catullus 68. 112 as the second half of a pentameter; so Propertius makes it the first half of a hexameter.

2 *Erythea*: a legendary island outside the straits of Gibraltar inhabited by the giant Geryon, whose cattle it was Hercules' tenth labour to steal. Here personified, cf. Britannia.

3 *sheep-grazed*: an allusion to supposed etymologies of Palatium from *balare*, 'to baa', or *palare*, 'to wander'.

6 *vailed*: lowered. Latin *uelificabat*, 'made sail', giving the etymology of Velabrum (cf. iv. 2. 7–8 note).

7 *Cacus*: the ogre whose story is told in *Aeneid* VIII, Livy I, and Ovid, *Fasti* I.

15 *Maenalian branch*: Hercules' famous club. Maenalus is a mountain range in Arcadia.

16 *Alcides*: see i. 20. 49 note.   Strictly: Thus spoke Alcides 'Go . . . '

19 *Cattle Fields*: Latin *arua Bouaria*.

20 The Forum Boarium, Rome's cattle-market.

22 Hercules could have drunk from Velabrum or Tiber but he was tempted by the sound of female voices. This is more pointed than the reading of most editors: 'had no water to offer.'

25 *Women's Goddess*: the Bona Dea, whose temple was on the Aventine, which was also the site of Cacus' cave.

37 In one of his labours Hercules took over from Atlas for a while; see iii. 22. 7 note.

38 Possible allusion to Greek derivation of the name from *alké*, 'strength'.

41 Hercules' twelfth labour was to descend into Hades and bring back the monstrous watchdog Cerberus.

42 In the MSS the same as 66. Hence transposition of 65–6 here and lacuna.

43 Juno was Hercules' stepmother and persecuted him.

45 *lion-skin*: the skin of the Nemean lion, a monster sent to Nemea in Argos by Juno to destroy Hercules.

46 Hercules went through Libya in his quest for the golden apples of the Hesperides and also when he killed the giant Antaeus (see iii. 22. 10 note).

47–50 allude to Hercules' year of slavery to Omphale, the Lydian queen, who dressed him in her clothes while she tried on his lion-skin.

53 *Spare your eyes*: i.e. do not look at what is forbidden and risk being punished by blindness.

57 Tiresias lost his sight on this occasion but was compensated by the gift of prophecy.

58 *Gorgon*: see ii. 2. 8 note.

67 *Ara Maxima*: in the Forum Boarium (see 20 note).

70 Or, with *externi* for *aeternum*, 'lest alien Hercules' thirst be unavenged.'

72 *Tatius*: see ii. 32. 47 note.

    Cures: the ancient Sabine capital.

    Sancus: cult title of a Sabine god not elsewhere identified with Hercules.

10

1 The temple of Feretrian Jupiter was on the Capitol.

2 refers to the *spolia opima* or 'spoils of honour': 'the arms taken by a Roman general, in full command of his army, from the body of an

enemy leader whom he has killed in single combat. They were reckoned by the Romans to have been won three times: by Romulus from Acron, king of the Caeninenses, in the hostilities that followed the Rape of the Sabines; by Aulus Cornelius Cossus, according to Livy in 437 BC, when he killed Tolumnius the Etruscan king; and by M. Claudius Marcellus who killed the Gaul Viridomarus in 222 BC . . . A claim was made for the *spolia opima* in 29 BC by M. Licinius Crassus, proconsul of Macedonia, who had defeated the Bastarnae in battle and killed their chieftain Deldo. His claim was disallowed by Octavian on the grounds that he was not the holder of full *imperium*' (*The Oxford Companion to Classical Literature*).

7 Caenina was an ancient Sabine town near Rome (modern Ciano).

11 *Quirinus*: see iv. 6. 22 note.

21 *pyropus*: an alloy of gold and bronze.

24 *Veii*: an ancient Etruscan city some 12 miles north of Rome.

25–6 This couplet is sometimes transposed between 22 and 23 on the ground that it is not true of the time of Cossus.

  Nomentum: north-east of Rome (modern Mentana).

  Cora: south-east of Rome.

28 *golden chair*: throne of an Etruscan king, taken over by the Romans as their curule chair for higher magistrates.

40 *Belgic*: the Belgae lived in northern Gaul.

42 *Famed for*: or reading *mobilis* for *nobilis*, 'Nimble at'.

43 Textual trouble here.

45–6 It appears that the etymology consists of root *fer-* plus *tri-* 'three'.

  felled: Latin *ferit*, 'smote'.

47 *ferried*: Latin *ferebant*, 'carried'.

II

1 *Paullus*: Lucius Aemilius Paullus Lepidus, suffect consul in 34 BC, censor 22 BC.

5 *The God*: Pluto.

7 *Ferryman*: Charon. His fare for the ferry over the Styx was a bronze coin placed in the mouth of the deceased.

8 Text uncertain; the conjecture *euersos*, 'overturned, collapsed' (because burnt out), replaces the MSS *herbosos*, 'grassy'. This invisible gate,

like the door of line 2, prevents communication between the dead and the living.

11 *forebears*: the Scipios.

12 *pledges*: her children, see 63ff.

13 *Cornelia*: she was the daughter of a Cornelius Scipio whose wife Scribonia later married Octavian and bore Octavian's daughter Julia.

18 *the Father here*: Pluto.

19 *Aeacus*: son of Jupiter and the nymph Aegina, grandfather of Achilles and one of the judges of the dead. He draws lots from the urn to decide the order in which cases are to be tried.

21 *the brothers*: Minos and Rhadamanthus, sons of Jupiter and Europa.

22 *Eumenides*: 'the kindly ones', euphemistic title of the Furies, who punish evil-doers.

23 *Sisyphus*: see ii. 17. 7 note.

 Ixion: see iii. 5. 42 note.

24 *Tantalus*: see ii. 1. 65–6 note.

25 *Cerberus*: see iii. 5. 44 note.

27 *the Sisters*: the daughters of Danaus, for whom see ii. 31. 4 note.

30 Two Scipios earned the title of Africanus in the Punic wars, the younger also that of Numantinus after his conquest of Numantia in 132 BC, which ended the Celtiberian war in northern Spain.

31 Cornelia's brother, Lucius Scribonius Libo, was consul in 34 BC and father-in-law of Sextus Pompey.

33–4 Free-born Roman girls wore the *toga praetexta* (see iii. 15. 3 note) until marriage, when they put on the *stola*, a long dress, and altered their hair-style.

36 The fiction is that this elegy is carved on her tomb-stone.

38 See 30 note.

39–40 A crux. The text is very uncertain, but the reference is to Lucius Aemilius Paullus who defeated Perses (Perseus) of Macedon at Pydna in 168 BC. Perses claimed descent from Achilles.

41 Her husband was censor (see 1 note). Goold's version explains: she never 'caused the censor's law to be relaxed' by any misdemeanour on her part that he would be tempted to condone.

 I: lit. 'we'.

42 *your*: i.e. the ancestors'.

46 *both torches*: the marriage torches and the funeral torch that lit the pyre.

49   *whatever urn*: metonymy for 'whatever judge', the urn here being the
     receptacle into which Roman jurors cast their votes of acquittal or
     condemnation.

51–2 In 204 BC the ship carrying the primitive image of Cybele (see iii. 17.
     35 note) grounded in the Tiber. Quinta Claudia pulled it off single-
     handed, thereby proving her chastity. Cybele was often represented as
     wearing a turreted crown.

53–4 The Vestal Aemilia had left Vesta's sacred fire in the charge of a young
     Vestal who allowed it to go out. It blazed up again when Aemilia's
     robe touched it.

59   Cornelia and Augustus' daughter Julia were half-sisters, see note on
     13.

61   A married woman who produced three children was entitled to wear
     a special dress.

64   *my*: lit. 'our'.

65   Her brother Publius Cornelius Scipio was consul in 16 BC, which
     settles the date of this elegy. Presumably he had been praetor before
     that.

67   So the daughter was six, see 1 note.

70   *the skiff*: Charon's boat, see 7 note.

72   *children's fame*: Latin *libera fama*. This takes the adjective as standing
     for *liberorum*, a meaning it has nowhere else. Goold gives 'when
     candid opinion praises the full course of her married life'.

73   *to you*: she now turns to her husband Paullus.

85   The official marriage bed (*lectus genialis*) was placed in the atrium of
     the Roman house facing the front door.

99   *I rest my case*: cf. 27 'I speak in my own defence', as before one of
     the judges of the dead.

     Rise, witnesses: 'The allusion is to the custom of the courts, by which
     witnesses were called after the defence' (Paley). The witnesses are
     presumably family and ancestors.

100 i.e. 'Until the verdict on me is given', the ground being the under-
     world, which is 'grateful' for her good life.

101–2 i.e. 'Some people (e.g. Hercules) have been deified after death, but
     may I win a place on the underworld ferry to Elysium' (see iv. 7.
     59–60). Others, reading the emendation *auis* for MSS *aquis*, translate
     'conveyance to honoured forebears.'

APPENDIX
DIFFERENCES FROM BARBER'S
OXFORD CLASSICAL TEXT
(1987 REPRINT)

(Minor differences of spelling, capitalization, punctuation, etc. are not recorded).

BOOK I

2	13 *no obeli*
3	16 *no obeli*
4	14 dicere
5	8 sciet
6	24 omina
7	16 quod nolim nostros, heu, uoluisse deos
8	22 uera 25 Autaricis
9	4 quaeuis
11	5 adducere
12	9 num
13	24 ab Oetaeis . . . rogis 35 qui
15	15–16 *after* 22 21 elata
16	8 exclusi 38 irato dicere pota ioco
17	11 reposcere
18	9 crimina
19	17 *comma at line end*
20	50 fontibus
21	5 *omit* ut 6 me, soror . . . lacrimis
22	6 sed mihi

BOOK II

1	5 incedere uidi 45 uersamus
2	11 Mercurio aut qualis
3	22 carminaque illius 23 non 30 *and* 32 *interchanged*
4	15–16 *untransposed*

6   26 quoilibet   31 in tenebris   32 orgia   35–6 *after*
     26 *omitting exclamation mark*   41 deducet
7   1 Gauisa es . . ., Cynthia,   13 patriis
8   13 ergo ego tam
10   21 ut, caput   23 currum
12   18 bella
13   *single elegy*   1 armantur Susa   25 sat sit magna mihi si
15   37 interdum   48 proelia
16   27 excussis   29 amari   35 'at pudeat!' certe pudeat
17   13–14 *after* 2
18   21 quin ego deminuo curam?
19   31 metuam
21   17 quid restat?
22   11–12 *no square brackets*   44 et nullo   48 cum recipi
     quod non uenerit illa uetat   50 *no obeli*
23   1 indocti fugienda et semita   4 praemissa
24   4 aut pudor ingenuis aut reticendus amor
     13 interdum   49 consuesse
25   26 ante   31 uiro
26   8 teque   23 munera
27   1 Et uos   2 *and* 4 *query at line end*   8–9 *no lacuna*
     9 metuisque
28   28A = 1–34 *and* 28B = 35–62   26 *full stop at line end*
     51 *no obeli*   62 et mihi
29   10–11 *no lacuna*
30   11 at, iam si   19–22 *no square brackets*   19 num tamen
     immerito Phrygias   20 nolo maris   22 *query at line end*
31   5 *no obeli*
32   1–2 *after* 10   15 toto . . . orbe   25 cedere   34 *full
     stop at line end*   35 *no obeli*   36 *comma at line end*
33   6 *query at line end*   41–2 *after* 44
34   *single elegy*   18 possim   29 Aratei . . . lecti
     33 non rursus   38 tristia   39 *no obeli*
     53 restabimus undas   59 iuuat   93 quin uiuet

BOOK III

2   2 gaudeat ut   3 delinisse   16 nec
3   5 iam
4   3 uiris
5   2 sat mihi   6 misera   8 caute
     18 Parcae   39 reorum   40 *and* 42 *interchanged*

6	1 sensti 9 sicin eam 22–3 *query at line ends*
	28 exsuctis
7	21–4 *no square brackets* 22 Athamantiadae
	29 curuate 47 non tulit hic 49 sed 52–4 *query at line ends*
8	10 tam 13 seu 16 *full stop at line end* 26 tua
	27 quos 29 grata
9	36 tuta 55 claustraque
10	6 minax 13 at
11	5 uentorum . . . motus 49 cane 65–8 *after* 58
	59 *no obeli*
12	12 armato
13	39 Arcadii
14	15–16 *after* 12
15	3 releuatus 10–11 *no lacuna* 11 uano 27 uago
	33 sub
16	29 cumulus
17	2 pacato 3 flatus 12 toro 17 tumeant
	24 rapta 27 Diam 37 cratere antistes et
	38 *comma at line end*
18	1 alludit 8–9 *no lacuna* 9 hic 29–30 *no square brackets* 32 huc . . . portant *and comma at line end*
	33 quae Siculae ut uictor telluris Claudius utque
19	21–2 teque . . . | tondens purpuream . . . comam
	27–8 *untransposed*
20	13 da tempora nocti 17 constringet
	19–20 *untransposed*
21	28 munde (cf. iv. 5. 43)
22	2 qua 3 in uite 6 at *and full stop at line end*
23	16 parabit
24	10 *full stop at line end* 11 haec ego 12 *no parenthesis*

BOOK IV

1	4 concubuere 19 celebrata 36 hinc ubi
	38 pudet 57 iamque . . . conor 87–8 *after* 68
	93 eques 101 Iunoni 112 Atridis 125 Asisi
	142 suo
2	3 *omit* et 10–11 *no lacuna* 12 creditur
	28 corbis in 35 specie 37 sub petaso
3	10 tunsus . . . discolor 11 pactae tum mihi 34 in chlamydas uellera lecta tuas 51 nunc purpura 56 toro

4   13 Curia, saepta   20 aera   55 sic hospes *and semicolon*
     at line end   59 soluere nupta;   83 *no obeli; semicolon*
     at line end   93 Tarpeium

5   19–20 exercebat opus uerbis, heu blanda, perinde | saxosam atque
     forat sedula lympha uiam   55–6 *italics*   64 mihi sunt
     numeranda   65–6 *untransposed*   71 exuuiae

6   8 modis   28 ante   36 deae   45 en . . . Latinos
     74 perque   75 potis

7   34 *query at line end*   36 *full stop at line end*   37 ut
     Nomas arcanas   57 stuprum et stuprum altera Cressae
     69 sanamus   79 pone   80 mollis . . . alliget *and no full
     stop at line end*   82 *full stop at line end*

8   19–20 *after* 2   39 Baetis   41 Magnus
     45 secundam   78 sudet   84 ac   85 lacernas

9   22 non nullas   42 *lacuna and insert* 65–6 *after it*
     60 una   72 Sance   74 Sancum

10   23–4 *untransposed*   42 nobilis euectis   43 illi uirgatis
     iaculanti ante agmina bracis

11   8 euersos   21 , iuxta Minoia sella, et   39–40 et, Perses
     proaui simulat dum pectus Achilli, | qui tumidas proauo fregit
     Achille domos   53 uel cui, iusta suos cum   70 fata
     102 aquis

BRIEF BIBLIOGRAPHY

Editions and Commentaries

BARBER, E. A. (1960²). *Sexti Properti Carmina*, Oxford Classical Text.

BUTLER, H. E. (1912). *Propertius*, Loeb Classical Library, London.

—— and BARBER, E. A. (1933). *The Elegies of Propertius*, Oxford.

CAMPS, W. A. (1961–7). *Propertius, Elegies: Books I–IV*, 4 vols., Cambridge (Books II and III repr. with supplementary notes in 1985 by Bristol Classical Press).

ENK, P. J. (1946). *Sex. Propertii Elegiarum Liber I*, 2 vols., Leiden.

—— (1962). *Sex. Propertii Elegiarum Liber II*, 2 vols., Leiden.

GOOLD, G. P. (1990). *Propertius: Elegies*, Loeb Classical Library, London.

HODGE, R. I. V., and BUTTIMORE, R. A. (1977). *The Monobiblos of Propertius*, Cambridge.

LUCK, G. (1964). *Properz und Tibull*, Artemis Edition, Zurich.

PALEY, F. A. (1872²). *The Elegies of Propertius*, London.

POSTGATE, J. P. (1884²). *Select Elegies of Propertius*, London.

RICHARDSON, L. (1976). *Propertius: Elegies I–IV*, Norman, Oklahoma.

English Translations

BUTLER, H. E. (1912). See above; prose.

GOOLD, G. P. (1990). See above; prose.

HODGE, R. I. V. and BUTTIMORE, R. A. (1977). See above; verse.

MUSKER, R. (1972). *The Poems of Propertius*, London; verse.

PHILLIMORE, J. S. (1906). *Propertius*, Oxford; prose.

SHEPHERD, W. G. (1985). *Propertius: the Poems*, Penguin Classics; verse.

WATTS, A. E. (1966²). *The Poems of Propertius*, Penguin Classics; verse.

Studies

HUBBARD, M. (1974). *Propertius*, London.

LYNE, R. O. A. M. (1980). *The Latin Love Poets*, Oxford.

PAPANGHELIS, T. D. (1987). *Propertius: a Hellenistic Poet on Love and Death*, Cambridge.

SHACKLETON BAILEY, D. R. (1956). *Propertiana*, Cambridge.

SULLIVAN, J. P. (1964). *Ezra Pound and Sextus Propertius*, London.

—— (1976). *Propertius: a Critical Introduction*, Cambridge.

The Oxford World's Classics Website

www.worldsclassics.co.uk

- Information about new titles
- Explore the full range of Oxford World's Classics
- Links to other literary sites and the main OUP webpage
- Imaginative competitions, with bookish prizes
- Peruse the Oxford World's Classics Magazine
- Articles by editors
- Extracts from Introductions
- A forum for discussion and feedback on the series
- Special information for teachers and lecturers

www.worldsclassics.co.uk

American Literature

British and Irish Literature

Children's Literature

Classics and Ancient Literature

Colonial Literature

Eastern Literature

European Literature

History

Medieval Literature

Oxford English Drama

Poetry

Philosophy

Politics

Religion

The Oxford Shakespeare

A complete list of Oxford Paperbacks, including Oxford World's Classics, Oxford Shakespeare, Oxford Drama, and Oxford Paperback Reference, is available in the UK from the Academic Division Publicity Department, Oxford University Press, Great Clarendon Street, Oxford OX2 6DP.

In the USA, complete lists are available from the Paperbacks Marketing Manager, Oxford University Press, 198 Madison Avenue, New York, NY 10016.

Oxford Paperbacks are available from all good bookshops. In case of difficulty, customers in the UK can order direct from Oxford University Press Bookshop, Freepost, 116 High Street, Oxford OX1 4BR, enclosing full payment. Please add 10 per cent of published price for postage and packing.